PÉGUY
AND *LES CAHIERS DE LA QUINZAINE*

IN JANUARY 1914

I published under the title 'Quelques nouveaux maîtres' a set of essays of which the most important was about Charles Péguy.

In 1918, I took up these essays again, re-wrote them adding fresh material, made Charles Péguy the central figure, and published them in a book called 'Charles Péguy et les Cahiers de la Quinzaine.'

After more than twenty years I have turned to this book again, made more alterations and additions, and now publish what is to all intents and purposes a new book.

I am not disregarding the fact that the un-published work is still considerable and that the study of Charles Péguy is still at the research stage.

OCTOBER 1940

I

CHILDHOOD

'THERE IS NOTHING more mysterious than those dim periods of preparation which every man encounters on the threshold of life,' says Péguy in one of his last books, *l'Argent*. 'The whole stage is set before we are twelve years old.' This is true of his own experience. He made no effort to become accessible to outside influences, his life-long effort was to keep alive those first gleams of light, the assumptions and affections of childhood, or those from a distant past, rooted and transmuted in him in the shape of intuitions and instincts. His life-long effort was to remain, or become again, the child he had once been.

He belongs to the oldest midlands of old France, the very heart of our land. At a short distance from the Morvan hills, on the banks of the Allier river, the land rises in two gentle slopes to woods on the sky-line. On one of these slopes sprawls the village of Genetinnes. Moulins, the capital of the province, is nearby, its spires are visible. From Genetinnes-en-Bourbonnais came Charles Péguy's mother and grandmother, three-quarters of a century ago. We know nothing of his grandfather, nor of his father who died before he was born: he knew him only through a carefully preserved letter written from Paris in 1871, on the eve of the great siege.

So in his early home life there were these two women and no one else. For some obscure reason, due perhaps to economic difficulties or some private upheaval, they put all their goods, no great load, on a raft, and so floated down to the port of Orléans. The two country-women did not go up into the town, they stayed in the faubourg Bourgogne adjoining the port. Genetinnes faded out of their lives, and for Péguy it was never more than a name. The faubourg Bourgogne was his village, Orléans his big town.

Orléans has a number of trades and draws in workers from different parts of France. It is a travellers' town, an inn on the road from the central provinces to Paris: the bridge-head which lets them pass or holds them up. A travellers' town, we said, and a battle town too. So from all aspects it is a good spot for listening to France, to sounds from the fields and the clash of swords and staves.

Seventy years ago, there was no telling whether the faubourg Bourgogne was the first street in Orléans or the last village of the neighbouring country. Living in homes like village homes, the peasant-folk kept their own customs and dialect. Péguy's birthplace, as we see it in a very old drawing done by himself, is a simple cottage opening on to the road.

So the child Péguy grew to boyhood between his mother and his grandmother. His mother was very brisk, his grandmother stiff in the limbs ever since a day of heavy rain at the washing fountain, in her youth. The others had gone back to change. She stayed behind, saying: 'He who made me wet will dry me.' But He did not, and so she remained stiff in the limbs. His mother mended the rush seats of chairs in the borough which fate had made her home; she was not chairwoman at Saint-Aignan's church, as has been said, but merely doing the parish repairs. It had seemed to her a satisfactory job, and she had taught her mother to do it too; there were no idle hands in that home; work was continuous and pressing, up to seventeen hours a day, Péguy tells us. It was all for the child, for the future; it was habit and a vocation. In course of time, Mme Péguy was able to buy the one-storey house they had lived in from the first, to add another storey, and then to buy up the neighbouring houses. This peasant woman knew all about earning, saving and sensible spending. A valiant woman indeed.

In October 1914, I saw her home after Mass said for her son's intention. I walked beside her step by step and listened to her talk. She spoke like a peasant, to herself rather than to me. 'When I came back from the cemetery where I left my husband,' she said, 'I said to myself: "Soon you'll have a son; you've got to work and to live to bring him up; you won't marry again."' There was the same short sentence, the same tone of authority that I had known in her son. Struck by this likeness, I turned to look at her. I had recognised the tone of voice, now I recognised the blunt, square shape of the face.

We know the grandmother from a few words of Péguy's. She could neither read nor write, he says, and was none the worse for it. 'I never went to school,' she used to say. Or, better still: 'They never sent me to school.' Or, best of all: 'We didn't even know what school is.' Or, by way of explanation: 'I was working at that age,' or else: 'At that age everyone went to work.' With the result that: 'I can't even read the names of the streets. I can't read the papers'—admissions which reveal in their own way their secret pride in ancient modes of life. She was a great talker; Péguy tells us she loved to 'tell fine tales, and she was the first to teach me the language of France': the French of the Val de Loire, which, soil-bound as it is, thrills with the powerful, sensitive modulations of the language of the great masters.

At the New Year, this was the child's greeting to the old woman: 'Grandmother, I wish you health and happiness in the New Year and Heaven at the end of your days'—the usual greeting in the central provinces, though often with an additional clause that Péguy does not seem to have known: '. . . Heaven at the end of your days, if you deserve it.' We must not be deceived by this quaint old custom: this was not a particularly devout household; as in so many French families, contact with the Faith and the Church was maintained through the Sacraments, which everyone took for granted, and such customs as fasting on Good Friday and the Christmas midnight Mass. Morning and night, the child said his prayers. His mother saw to this, but he went to Mass under a neighbour's charge. 'My mother and I hadn't time,' she told M. de Poncheville, to whom we owe these details; 'there was the cleaning to be done.'

On nettoyait: here in a flash we have the key to the French peasant tongue.

This may count for little or much, according to the impression it makes on a child. It is clear that the prayer twice daily, and the yearly greeting, 'Heaven at the end of your days,' in all its simplicity, were not empty acts or words to the child we are considering: the soul of this child, so powerfully attentive and candid, yearned towards the mystery under the plainness of daily tasks that makes the glory of days and the glory of being. Heaven was a promise of glory.

Péguy said of the faubourg Bourgogne:

> . . . it was strictly old France and the people of old France. A world to which the lovely, beautiful term *people* can be applied with its full ancient meaning. In the strictest sense of the words, it is true that a child brought up in a town like Orléans between 1873 and 1880 has literally touched old France, the old people, the people in fact, he has literally had his part in old France, in the people. It is even true to say that he had a whole part in it, for old France was still whole and intact. The breakdown came, if I may say so, all in a rush and covered a very short space of time.

What began so quickly, next, is what Péguy calls 'the uncreation of the world.' Schooling, the daily paper habit, and the technical revolution are the cause of it.

•

The national character of Orléans was apparent to its children in the local monuments, and also by means of oral tradition which was very much alive in the times we are considering. In Paris, France displays her genius liberally; at Orléans, she is withdrawn, garnering her strength. In happy times, restless men from the central farmlands cross the town on their way to try their luck in the capital; in less happy times, Frenchmen from all the provinces come to Orléans; there, guarded by the river, curved to the shape of a bastion head, they gather their strength for the last battles. What can be saved is saved there: in the VIth century by the patron of the faubourg Bourgogne, Saint-Aignan, Bishop of the time of the barbarian invasions, who stopped Attila's advance. In the XVth century by Joan of Arc, who led the King's soldiers into the besieged town and changed the fortune of war. In the XIXth century, Orléans was still the same: after Waterloo, that is where Napoleon's soldiers came together again; in 1870, after Sedan, the honour of the countryside was saved by the band of volunteers and conscripts that fought so bravely before the town in Beauce.

In 1880 or so, the men who had fought in that unhappy war were still there, still young. The child listened while these wine-growers and artisans had their say. Péguy never forgot his neighbour the blacksmith who was so friendly to him. He would sit near the anvil listening while the soldier-craftsman told his tales. He was his first history master, he said, and his best. A teacher who had been on the spot himself, what a piece of luck! Péguy's interest in history was all for the tales of eye-witnesses, Joinville telling about Saint-Louis, Hauviette about Jeanne d'Arc. The blacksmith of the faubourg Bourgogne (a republican as well as a patriot) had fought all over the outskirts of the town, in the woods and along the river. It is through him that Péguy got to know the Chanzy campaign. And what a campaign it was: the Orléans men going towards Paris, the Paris men towards Orléans; the Prussians were to be caught between the two armies and forced to raise the siege of the capital. But the double battle was lost, the Parisians were not relieved, and the Prussians came into Orléans.

This blacksmith, whose name was Boitier, made a point of telling his tales with all due emphasis and feeling, for he had great ideas of the future of his young listener. 'We'll make him our Deputy,' was his simple and common-sensical ambition. He was the man to whom the telegram came in September 1914, telling of Péguy's death, and it was he who broke the news to Madame Péguy that her Charles was no longer of this world.

We know very little about the child's character. There is practically nothing but one very fine photograph, so expressive with its enormous forehead, candid, serious look, and steady concentrated gaze. Behind all this the man's impetuosity lies in germ no doubt, but it seems to have appeared only in zeal for work and strong reactions of conscience. On Shrove Tuesday, the calf was coming down their street and everyone ran to the window to see. 'Come, Charles, here's the calf!' called his mother. The child was sitting on a high stool, the better to reach all parts of a huge sheet of paper spread in front of him; 'I'm not coming, I've hardly time to finish my map of France,' and there he stayed, engrossed in his lettering. This may not appear significant, but to my mind it reveals the essential Péguy. The essential for a chronicler on the look out for significant traits. It shows his total indifference to whatever was not his immediate concern and, conversely, his complete absorption in what he was doing, that is, in his vocation, for whatever he was doing, it was always in line with his vocation. The map of France (*my map of France*), when he declined to go and look at the calf, demanded the complete attention of his hand, mind and soul.

'I was sent to that attractive little school-annex set in a corner of the first courtyard.... A sort of rectangular nest, official, solemn, sweet.' This little school, so tenderly described, tucked away in the corner of a playground, was an 'annex' in the sense that it was attached to the Training College for Loiret teachers. The primary school students in their belted school uniform, 'the black huzzars of truth,' were thus able to do their teaching practice without leaving the college. The republican primary school was in process of creation, and such was Péguy's early education. He was a marvellous pupil and delighted his teachers. Only one fault appears in a school report: he was too talkative. This good, dependable child had in him a spring which was to flow irrepressibly.

'On Thursdays we went to catechism,' he tells us. 'I expect it was so as not to disturb the time-table. It was a long way away, in the town, in our old parish of Saint-Aignan. Not everyone's parish is like that one.... The young priests taught us the exact opposite of what the young student-teachers taught us....' And it did not matter at all. The child was not concerned with reasoning things out, for him the two teachings did not clash. He listened to it all and believed it all. Nothing is more natural to a man than belief. As a child, he believes his parents and his masters as he believes the evidence of his own eyes. Péguy, a born believer, was never anything else. The assistant priests at the church, the teachers at school, all told lovely, stirring tales of the great wars and the Revolution, of Calvary and the Resurrection; all about greatness, sacrifice, and glory. How wonderful it was!

And yet between the two, parish and school, there was some difference, and the advantage lay with the school. For there, more spontaneously and more naturally than in the parish, his spirit warmed and expanded within him. It was largely due to the atmosphere of the faubourg Bourgogne which was not at all a religious one. The priests showed no surprise and paid no attention if a street urchin made rude noises at them when they happened to come that way. There were of course the Brothers of St. Vincent of Paul with their chapel in the district, and the good faithful old lady who, morning after morning, all through the snow and icy cold of the winter of 1880, never missed their early Mass. The housewives watched her go by: 'A lady so well off, up so early, in such weather as this!' The well-to-do lady fell ill of it, with acute bronchitis, and died so holy a death that the whole district talked of it. The child Péguy listened and ruminated. The early morning trek, the death of a holy woman, these were no light matters, he felt. But the general atmosphere of the faubourg prevailed, and there the child lived. It seems likely that the rather abstract definitions of the catchism, so conscientiously learnt and scrupulously engraved on his memory, were there like locked-up treasure to be opened at a later day. M. Bardet, the parish priest of Saint-Aignan, took note of this unusually gifted child and said to him: 'If you like, I will have you as a student in the seminary.' 'No,' said Péguy, shortly, 'that is not what I am planning to do.' He was always the sort of believer whom Barrès called '*croyant de la prairie*'; his work, rich as it is in reminiscences, does not, I think, contain a single religious impression of the stained-glass-window kind.

By the time he was twelve the stage was set: Péguy tells us so himself and tells it very well. The landscape of his life was always the plain of l'Ile-de-France, on the fringe of which he was born; there he was to live, there he was to die, on this single land with its double name: la Beauce, trodden by the child, la Brie, by the soldier; he came from the one, the other received him dead. The forms of his belief never changed: they remained those he learnt at school and in the parish. His devotion shifted from one to the other, but there was no innovation and nothing was discarded. Events, vocation, the invisible organist Grace, all played their own part on the different registers of the instrument: the response was always ready and assured. And affection and admiration were as assured then as later. There was Joan of Arc, whose May processions he followed through Orléans, he determined as a child to tell her story one day in dramatic form. There was Victor Hugo, whose immense verbal orchestration enchanted him. In school he used to stand up and recite:

Mes sœurs, l'onde est plus fraîche aux premiers feux du jour
—enchanted by the incantation. They did not all share his enthusiasm, some of the boys criticised Hugo severely. 'I always took his part,' says Péguy. And the tussles begun in the school playground were to go on all his life. He was always on Hugo's side.

The child contained the man entire. When, twenty years later, Péguy decided to found a paper and run it himself, he gathered his friends together and they started arguing about what to call it. A word from Péguy stopped them:

'*Les Cahiers*,' he said, 'that is the title.'

With this word in mind, which to-day has lost its freshness through over-much use, and in those days had the most restricted meaning, he was thinking of his school *cahiers*, always so neat, which his mother, who admired them as she admired everything her son did, had kept and still kept religiously in a cupboard. The schoolboy took

Péguy in 1888 (*Collection A. Martin*)

EDINBURGH UNIVERSITY LIBRARY
WITHDRAWN

infinite pains over them. Not a mistake, not a careless slip was allowed to pass; each separate letter, set exactly between the last and the next, like the rushes in the seating of a chair, had to be irreproachably straight. As author and publisher, Péguy was no different. The least printer's error on the sheets he published disturbed him gravely to the very last, and up to the very end of his stormy career he would cover page after page with this same slanting, conscientious, unfalteringly careful writing which filled the *cahiers* of his childhood.

So from every point of view the child was father to the man, and the child lived on in the man.

Life is dusty, tarnishing, corroding; Péguy's, like anyone else's. But there is no single moment in it when, if we choose to listen, we cannot hear the schoolboy's:

Mes sœurs, l'onde est plus fraîche aux premiers feux du jour.

II

FROM PRIMARY SCHOOL TO TRAINING COLLEGE

I live continually on two planes at once.—CHARLES PEGUY.

THE UNIVERSITY FULFILLED one of its functions as far as Péguy was concerned: it set him on the way to advanced studies. M. Naudy, the head of the school-annex, watched him carefully. His mother had obtained a scholarship for him to the upper primary school and asked no more. M. Naudy was more ambitious: 'Péguy must learn Latin,' he said.

Péguy must learn Latin: A profound saying, of ancient provenance. It may be some thousand years old. We observe that it would have very little chance of being spoken to-day: the heads of our primary education pride themselves on forming a separate body. If they pick out a child that they want to do well, his promotion will always be within the bounds of the primary school system, which knows no Latin. To-day, Péguy would have less chance of advanced studies than in any other centuries of French history, from the VIIIth to the XIXth. He would be further from Latin, and further from Greek to which he owes so much.

What would he have done? He used to wonder himself: 'I often wonder with retrospective anguish, unnerved at the very thought where I was going, what I was heading for, if I had not gone up into the sixth,[1] if M. Naudy had not rescued me at the Easter holiday. I was twelve years and three months old. It was high time.' It certainly was high time he got on to his Virgil and Sophocles, with all the religious devotion of a child who had never dreamed such dreams but who was destined by nature to drink the milk of heaven with them and through them. Without this initiation, cut off from classical studies, however would he have expressed himself? Somehow the obstacles would have gone up in smoke, of this we can be sure, but the damage would have been grave. Péguy might have become bad-tempered and this fertile flow of his been turned into a destructive flood. From such a sensitive soul the worst may be expected, as well as the best.[2]

[1] The lowest form, in a French school.

[2] In this connection, J.-J. Tharaud has something very different to say: 'Was Péguy justified in his pride in having learnt *rosa*, the rose? . . . It is not so sure that this studious life gave him more than he would have gained from any other sort of life.

On M. Naudy's recommendation, the scholarship was converted into a secondary school scholarship. Péguy went to the lycée d'Orléans and stayed there till he was nearly at the top of the school.

On these next eight years we have very little information. Péguy's work is full of reminiscences of before his twelfth and after his twentieth year. In between there is nothing, except indirectly. One has to find out from others, or guess. Péguy has nothing to show for these years that count for so much in a man's general development. We know that when he was about sixteen he drew and painted water-colours which show remarkable powers. We know this because we have seen them. Péguy never mentioned them. We know he left the lycée d'Orléans to do more advanced work at the lycée Lakanal, but that he had his scholarship withdrawn at the end of the first year, as a disciplinary measure, on the recommendation of the tutor in charge. This is probably when the inflexible temper of his character first appeared. Bursars are usually docile boys, and the bursar Péguy rode his high horse. This is only guesswork, however: Péguy never spoke of it, there is not a word from him about this accident to his studies. He was in an awkward position and joined up, starting his military service a year ahead of time. About this year, there is complete silence. Then he took up his studies again, thanks to the energetic support of two Lakanal masters (Rocheblave in literature, Noël in philosophy: both excellent men), who succeeded in getting him a scholarship at Louis-le-Grand and a grant for residence at Sainte-Barbe. We know this indirectly, not from Péguy, who never printed the names Rocheblave and Noël. All this is eight years of a life gone underground. At twenty, Péguy entered Sainte-Barbe; he was grown-up and terse, with a singular air of authority. How did it come about, and why this silence? We do not know.

We probe for reasons, and some come half to light. One very general one is that at the lycée he must have felt ill-at-ease and disturbed in mind. The atmosphere of his home in the faubourg Bourgogne and of the faubourg Bourgogne surrounding his home was integral, and Péguy throve and flourished there. But a lycée cannot be integral in this sense. Mixed classes produce their own complex atmosphere. From school to home was a straightforward walk for Péguy; from classroom to lycée, there were steps up and steps down. Steps in any case, meaning surprises and jolts. Péguy, whose own

---

It is clear that the finest and best parts of his work are inspired by the direct impact of things on his vision. If he had not gone up into M. Guerrier's sixth form, he might, one imagines, have followed his true genius with less sophistication, as chronicler and poet. Certainly, if Péguy had added to the experiences of his childhood those of an apprenticeship and the workshop, the results might have been marvellous. But when M. Naudy sent Péguy on to M. Guerrier's sixth form, he was not removing him from the workshop but from the upper primary school, which is a very inadequate form of schooling.

nature was so much all of a piece, had an imperious need for purity and integration. One can understand certain disturbing discoveries being passed over in silence.

We need only remember the types of crises which growing boys have to endure: those of adolescence, those of belief. To take the first: for Péguy it seems clear there was little trouble here. The impression of his fellows (and later of his friends) was that Péguy's spirit remained unscathed as far as sex was concerned. The child had been, the man was to come, but the intervening storms of adolescence do not seem to be there. We are, after all, free to see these things from the freudian angle, and to picture here how his mother, always and most admirably at work, completely filled his heart and soul from the very first, so that his attitude to woman was never impure. When he says to Lotte, much later on: 'There's not a single sin in my work,' he was no doubt thinking of sex, for he knows perfectly well that other sins, pride for instance, occupy conspicuous places in it. This exemption, as it were, going right back to early years, may help to explain all through his life the persistent and unweakened overtones from childhood.

The religious crisis was inevitable. As a child, Péguy had achieved a sort of candid doubling of mind, by which he was Christian in the parish and rationalist republican at school. It could not last: he had to choose between the two shining paths opening before him. Now he was a lay student, a University scholar; all the groups in Orléans to which he belonged after he turned sixteen were republican, of socialistic tendencies and masonic inspiration; eighteenth century philosophy held undisputed sway. It was a strong current for Péguy to enter, his youth was caught up in it. Our republic, accepted doctrinally as well as historically, leads inevitably to the Revolution. Péguy became a revolutionary and ceased to believe.

We may be sure that the difficulties that confronted him were not of the rational order. His was not a mind to exact compliance of this kind, his native sagacity must have made it clear to him that there was no less a paradox in the idea of Humanity being innumerable and one than of God being three in one. To accept a mystery was not his difficulty. It was another matter that disturbed him: at this forking of the ways, both leading to salvation and glory, he needed to know which promised greater salvation and greater glory.

Let us consider the history of humanity in the form in which his masters had instilled it into his mind. We may picture it as a diptych: the left hand panel represents the old times, cruel and dark; salvation and glory are there in short gleams only, reserved by the priests for the elect of God, by the kings for those who serve their power. The saints' halo, the crown of greatness, is a rare privilege. The multitude suffer oppressive poverty and tremble at the thought of one day wearing that headgear of flames by which the damned are burned in Hell. On the other panel, Humanity is shown in the glory of the new age. From the very beginning, its distant goal is clear and splendid. And the crowds set off with no restrictions on their hopes and expectations. Now Péguy as an adolescent was capable of belief, he believed whole-heartedly in eternal good. He refused to believe in eternal evil, it was impossible for him to do so. On one side, there was a mystery that was all darkness; on the other, a mystery of light. He chose light: his way was with the crowd.[1]

•

Let us follow him into Sainte-Barbe. Curiously enough, he was awaited there. The senior students had been told of his coming by one of their number, Henry Roy (a Senator of high standing and a near candidate for the Presidency of the Republic in 1939, Minister of the Interior in 1940). He had been at Lakanal and had known Péguy there; he was indignant at the withdrawal of the scholarship, and knowing that Noël and Rocheblave, his old masters, were petitioning for his admission to Sainte-Barbe, he put his new companions in possession of the facts. He told them about Péguy, saying: 'We must have him here, we must ask for him.' And they all went off to the Principal's office and asked for the admission of this student of whom they knew just enough to be eager to know more. The Principal of Sainte-Barbe listened sympathetically to what this very unofficial delegation had to say, and then announced that his decision was made, Péguy was admitted. A new student who was an infantry sergeant, one who had already made something of a name for himself: all eyes watched him cross the rose-coloured courtyard

One of these excited boys, Jérôme Tharaud, gave it this name. To-day it is a disappointing sight. It is said to have been rose-coloured on account of an attractive rough-cast which no longer shows rosy; half a century of weathering has sadly stained it and worn it away. And I have my own doubts as to whether this courtyard ever was lit but by the glow of eternal dawn shed by so many generations of youth interned.

Sainte-Barbe deserves a second glance. The pernickety censor of Lakanal had done his work well: Lakanal was a place of waiting temporarily useful, but on the outskirts of the town. It would have been a pity for Péguy to have stayed on there. Sainte-Barbe is Paris itself. It is an old college set on the very top of the Mont Sainte-Geneviève. Behind the buildings, right up against them, there are Louis-le-Grand, the Sorbonne, the Collège de France, the most extensive and most venerable city of learning in the world. On the same

[1] In 1900 Péguy wrote a well-known page on the rejection of Hell. We will quote it in its place: its tone is so violent that here it might appear an anachronism.

level there is the high ground where the Panthéon reigns supreme. This is where Paris and its thousand-year-old atmosphere are strongest. All the ages of France, all the successive Frances, France of the Merovingiens, of the Valois, of the Bourbons, Christian France and revolutionary France, all have set up their monuments on the crowded edge of the plateau: Clovis' tower, the lycée Henri IV, the church of Sainte-Geneviève guarding the body of the shepherd-girl whose devotion held up the barbarians, the library of the same name, built in the XIXth century. And at the centre, the Panthéon with its porch and dome. On the last page of *Eve*, his last poem, Péguy wrote these two verses in honour of Sainte-Geneviève:

> *La neige déroulait un immense tapis.*
> *L'histoire déroulait un immense discours.*
> *La gloire en commençait un immense parcours.*
> *Déjà l'humble Lutèce était le grand Paris.*
>
> *La neige découpait un immense parvis.*
> *L'histoire préparait un immense destin.*
> *La gloire se levait dans un jeune matin.*
> *Et la jeune Lutèce était le vieux Paris.*[1]

When he wrote these lines, he may have been thinking of the urban landscape before his eyes on the mornings he went out.

Sainte-Barbe takes its modest place among these noble buildings, in a corner just beyond the Bibliothèque Sainte-Geneviève under the shadow of the Law Faculty building. You cross the threshold, go down eight steps and along a dark passage; thirty yards or so bring you to the parlour, with portraits of the most famous past students on the walls: Ignatius of Loyola and Calvin first. And what curiously contrasting souls come next! At the time Péguy was admitted to Sainte-Barbe, fame rested on the name of a recent student, Jean Jaurès, deputy for Tarn. His portrait was not yet hung there. Now it is, the last of the series with Péguy's own. Jaurès and Péguy, both dead in the first days of the 1914 war.

The new student, in the throng of students all agog to welcome him, was no longer an adolescent, hardly even a young man; he was a man, keyed to a spiritual vision of which he himself was only half-aware. Happy novelists, who know all about their heroes! Biographers know very little, and must never forget it. What was Péguy? There

[1] The snow unfolded its carpet of state,
History, likewise, a far-flung argument
For glory to explore with tireless intent.
And small Lutetia became Paris the great.

Snow laid an approach to a sanctuary.
History pondered a destiny to prize.
Glory arose in early morning skies,
And young Lutetia was old Paris.

was a secret, several secrets even, in this awe-inspiring soul. Secret authority, giving him power to command. And another thing: a secret, a genius, of childhood, preserved intact. The young men round him were adolescents in the throes of puberty. Péguy was their senior—and their natural leader. Yet he was younger than they were, being more pure than they had remained. In the courtyard of Sainte-Barbe, Péguy was starting on an unforeseen chapter of his already distant childhood.

Questions were asked and answered; and so began what was to be one long-term argument, that of the *Cahiers*. The impressions of early childhood were deeply engraved on his mind, and so would be these few months of youth renewed, this interlude in his life's course. Those he always affectionately referred to as *les amis* are his friends of the *cour rose*. The Tharaud brothers and Porché, all from Angoulême, Jean Tharaud preparing for his entrance to Saint-Cyr, Jérôme, like Péguy, for the entrance to the Ecole Normale. Jean and Jérôme (I am anticipating by giving them so soon these apostolic names which Péguy was to bestow on them) were from the start the best of friends and admirable talkers, but their future fame as writers was unknown. Porché was his affectionate, subtle, mischievous self, the poet and essayist-to-be still unknown. Baillet (from Orléans, like Péguy) was liked for his kindness, respected for his seriousness; where would it lead him? He was to be a Dominican. Marcel Beaudouin, the silent, whom Péguy loved most of all, and whose sister became his wife, in two years 'time, Beaudouin will have died. Lotte, from Brittany, loved for his perfect heart; is it known what devotion, already shaping within these very walls, would crown his life? As a territorial in 1914, father of a family too, he petitioned to be given the place in the front line left vacant by Péguy's death, and fell himself almost immediately.

We must not leave out l'abbé Battifol, the almoner and the trusted friend of the busy hive. He listened to each and sundry, whether of the Faith or not. And when the young men went out into the slums with help for the poor, he went too. Lotte sang the songs on these expeditions. 'Now I think of it,' says Tharaud in a reminiscent letter to the priest, 'you heard those jolly sea-shanties too, on those winter nights when you came with us all the way to M. Enfert's, in the La Glacière district, where we went to serve soup to the poor of the quarter. Those are among the brightest hours of my youth. We were bursting with humanity and brotherly zeal. We came back through the cold nights along half-made roads, with planks and demolition works along the curbs, and here and there we caught sight of the sinister Bièvre and its awful banks. We were well and truly reforming society. Lotte, Péguy and I were the socialist, even anarchist voices, in this chorus. You were, as always, pure good sense, shrewd and kind. Baillet listened absent-mindedly, I believe impervious to our remarks. Only the pure song of his heart was audible to him. If Péguy spoke, Lotte immediately stopped his night-song. Although they were much the same age (Péguy a few years older), Lotte's feelings for his friend were those of a disciple for his master. Truth to tell, all Péguy's friends felt like that about him. His power was such that one could not meet him without acknowledging it.'

His power, all his friends testify to it, Lotte as well as Tharaud:

Péguy was a small, square-shouldered man, closely buttoned into his skimpy jacket, with huge hobnailed boots on his feet, a narrow soft felt on his head, and two keen bright eyes in his open peasant's face. 'I need money for the . . . strike,' said Péguy. There was always a strike somewhere and Péguy was always needing money. He went from group to group and everyone emptied his scanty purse, and Péguy passed on to the next, invariably solemn and concerned. He only had to hold out his hand for pockets to empty at once. It happened automatically. At that time, racing was all the rage at Sainte-Barbe. Once when an elegant Roumanian was just boasting that he had a first-rate tip, Péguy came along to ask us for money. I extolled the merits of the Roumanian's tip. 'It's not a betting matter,' was Péguy's simple answer: and there was I, speechless and ashamed, dismayed at the hold Péguy had on his fellows by his mere presence among them. This authority, spontaneous and so effective, is a thing I have come to understand since, it is the natural adjunct of a deeply lived spiritual life. . . . A saint has but to speak, no one argues: he is believed, and followed. And in Péguy, in his simplicity, gentleness and goodness, in his power, there were always traces of sanctity.

The mathematician and philospher, Charles-Lucas de Peslouän, writing with such precision and analytical power that not a word should be lost, says:

Péguy came straight from barracks to shut himself up in college: an imposition of restraint so unusual that I saw he was different from the rest of us. . . . You remember how cheerful he was then, quite light-hearted, and very funny, but with no malice. It was the only kind of funniness he admitted. . . . You know too how prompt and decisive he was. . . . None of his actions could ever be called reflex: between the impulse and the act, there was a decision, and a clear one. At Sainte-Barbe, life as a man, he decided, was to begin so. . . . At a very early stage he elected that the friendships formed during this year '94 should be those of his life-time.

The friends met in their free time. When it was fine, they paced up and down the courtyard, walking in step. Péguy liked it and to please him they conformed. When it was raining, they all gathered in a circle under a shelter and went on with their talk. One day Péguy expounded his theory of the ages of history, periods first, then epochs. Epochs were rapid and creative: it was a joy to belong to them. Periods were dim and groping, and to be entangled in the uncertainties of a period was sheer disgrace. Disgrace with no requital. Péguy trusted to the capacity of a man, a group of men working together, to counter the mediocrity of a period and break through to the glory of an epoch:

When we reach the age for self-revelation, we shall try to describe those two or three marvellous years of our youth, those ardent years. When everything was pure. Everything young. When young, new, grave socialism had just been born, rather childish (but this is part of being young). Ardent and, I must say it, profoundly Christian Christianity had been born again: deep, ardent, young, grave. It was fairly usually called social Catholicism too. In socialism, which was itself a sort of external Christianity through sheer proximity, in Jaurès himself, the jauressist infection had not yet declared itself nor spread its poison. The Dreyfus affair with its inconceivable destinies was still in embryo, in profoundest darkness. And France seemed to be in a joyful, intense, healthy, almost noisy, almost promising state of preparation.

•

The year at Sainte-Barbe we have told as eye-witnesses saw it: it is like reading a page torn from a golden legend. The witness is valid, the page is authentic, but the context is lacking. The friends did not know all that was going on. In the *cour rose*, so apparently clear and naïve, a secret was busily shaping which was the actual starting point of Péguy's life as a man. It was too serious in content to be told, the friends were too young, and it all needed to ripen before it could be truly thought and put into words. This brings us to a trait in Péguy's character which we must note: enthusiastic and emphatic as he was, he was also extremely concentrated, and capable of long periods of absolute silence. Psychologists are fond of distinguishing between extroverts, with quick reactions, excitable and easily roused, who are romantics, and those with slow reactions, patient and dogged, who are classics. If you try to apply these categories to Péguy, it is impossible to choose: he has all the characteristics. He is sanguine, and at the same time phlegmatic; easily roused (he became an angry man), and at the same time, long-suffering. He is a romantic and a classic. One of the sources of his great power is no doubt to be found in the way these different modes of being met and tightly knotted in him.

The origin of Péguy's secret is easy to grasp: some *barbistes*, he among them, decided to go in a band to hear *Œdipus Rex* at the Théâtre Français. Mounet-Sully played the part magnificently and people crowded to hear him. *Antigone* was given too: here Bartet was the star. *Antigone* was to come all in good time, but *Œdipus Rex* came first. They all clambered up and seated themselves in the gods. Péguy tells the story of this matinée in a *Cahier* called *The*

Suppliants, printed in December, 1905. That is to say, after twelve years of brooding.

What man of my generation, young in those days, does not remember the scenically sumptuous opening of the tragedy in its French version, with Mounet at the top of the steps, to the right, like a god receiving the supplication of a whole nation. . . .

. . . The rugged, burring tone of his voice still rings in our memories:

Enfants du vieux Cadmus, jeune postérité,
Pourquoi vers ce palais vos cris ont-ils monté. . .

He had a magnificent white robe in which he was draped like an ancient . . . and the least of his gestures has remained intact in our memory. . . .

Sacred initiation: let us consider these strongest of words, written with full knowledge by a man past thirty. The sacred initiation of which Péguy speaks is the initiation to tragedy.

Our university education has a strange habit of neglecting this conception. Human history is taught to the youth of France as though it were a rational development reaching a logical conclusion in the universal application of the solutions of XVIIIthe century philosophy and the French Revolution. A young Englishman keeps contact with a sense of tragedy through Shakespeare and the Bible; the young German is plunged and drowned in it through his native legends. For the young Frenchman, it is an exotic undertone.

No tragedy can enlighten him more thoroughly than *Œdipus Rex*. When the curtain rises, Œdipus is listening to the supplication of his people: he acknowledges it to be justified; the evils which have fallen on the city are too cruel, too constant, to have a cause of which the gods are ignorant. Assuredly a sin has been committed. It must be discovered and reparation made; Œdipus commands that this be done. The search is at once set on foot and it is soon evident that a great culprit lives in the city. The search continues, narrowing down till all is laid bare: the culprit is the unhappy Œdipus; all unknowing, he has killed his father in a nocturnal fight. All unknowing, he has married his own mother. Parricide and incestuous, he must punish himself and disappear. He puts out his own eyes, he proscribes himself and goes out with only his daughter Antigone with him. Instead of the suppliant nation, there is now the one Suppliant, assuming the weight of the sorrows of his city. Thebes breathes again; Œdipus is lost. *Tollit peccata mundi.* There is no change in the sum of sorrow, it is irreducible.

Œdipus Rex was Péguy's initiation to the idea of tragedy. With *Antigone* the idea bore fruit. In January 1900, in the second *Cahier* of the first series, after seven years of silence, Péguy was to tell of the impression made on him by the Théâtre Français performance. Antigone is the child who, after defying the law and remaining with her father, devotes herself to the salvation of the soul of her brother, Polynice, again in defiance of the law. Inside this tragic world where her own kin do such hurt to themselves, she fights on for the salvation of them all. *I am born for love, not hatred.* Creon, prince and guardian of the law, condemns her to be buried alive.

The tragedy of this stricken girl, led to her eternal tomb while the whole people present pity her and try to console her with the reiterated names of heroes who suffered before her, started Péguy's mind off on a track which it would nevermore cease to explore. Here was that same Hell which at sixteen he had refused to believe in. So it was not, as he had supposed, the perverse invention of the Christians and the Church; antiquity had had that terrible vision, and Sophocles, through the solemnity of his chant, had consecrated it. So the tragedy of the world does exist, it is not wiped out. Will the eloquence of Jaurès, with all its southern optimism, so prodigal of words and hopes, be able to overthrow this obstacle which neither olden heroism nor Christian sanctity could disturb? There is a vocation to tragedy in Péguy: Sophocles awakened it once for all. His less earnest companions were enthusiastic admirers of Mounet and Bartet, showing off their photographs in the college grounds. They were quite right, the actors were admirable. But their silent senior could not stop short there: from Antigone, the Theban maid, his mind was already on the track of another, Jeanne d'Arc, the maid of Lorraine.

For him, the two are closely linked; they are two sister heroines, vowed to a single task, which is to save souls by intransigeant bypassing of the laws of this world. Péguy never saw them apart, he was to meditate on their double, single destiny for years. For these sisters, girls of the same genius, are not girls of the same world, with good and evil sculptured in the one block of marble. Jeanne d'Arc is a girl of the Christian world, when the block has been split by grace. We may say, in Bergsonian terms, that Antigone's world is closed, Jeanne d'Arc's, open. Péguy did not know this use of the words, which came out in 1932, but Bergson is always a good clue to his thought. Between Antigone and Jeanne d'Arc, something shifted, if not in the visible universe, at least in the souls of men. It was a change which incurred a fresh tragic situation. After Sophocles' *Antigone*, in its wake, there was room for a *Jeanne d'Arc*, and Péguy was to write it.

Tradition holds that this project belongs to the last years of his childhood. Why not: where Péguy is concerned, we may assume the earliest origins to be the true ones. But there is no sign that the work was begun, or seriously considered, before the Sainte-Barbe year. On the other hand, we know for certain that he began it during the course of the year. His friends noted how diligently he was reading up the history of the reign of Charles VII by Vallet de Vireville. Péguy explained nothing: Jeanne d'Arc was his secret for some time to come.

It surprised them, too, to see how often he had Pascal's *Pensées* under his arm: was this the favourite reading of their master in socialism? Again, no explanation was given. Both occurrences were due to Péguy's concern with the problem of salvation, which he was making ready to consider as a whole, in the vocation and tragedy of Jeanne d'Arc. Jeanne d'Arc was condemned, like Antigone. When Antigone, the pagan maid, lost the light of day, she could only weep. What were the last thoughts of Jeanne d'Arc, the Christian with access to hope: that is what he had to find out.[1] And so begins the life-trek of Péguy the great.

•

In July, 1894, Péguy was admitted to the Ecole Normale, and this involved a change of perspective.

[1] There is evidence for the kinship of the two works: the opening scene of Péguy's *Jeanne d'Arc* is analogous to the opening scene of Sophocles' *Antigone*. Antigone, the heroic, converses with her sister Ismène, who is gentle and moderate. So Jeanne d'Arc converses with her friend Hauviette. It is not a coincidence: Péguy knew *Antigone* by heart.

III

THE STUDY CALLED UTOPIA

He knows too that Péguy is that ardent, gloomy, stupid young man of eighteen or twenty, whom he met on his first arrival in Paris.—CHARLES PEGUY.

THERE IS A story about Péguy's first day at the Ecole Normale. It was the custom then for the new students to be put through their paces; Péguy refused point blank to be bullied and let it be known that if anyone touched him he'd smash his face for him. The school administration, knowing their man, asked him to put off coming for a few days. He came in due course, took his place in his study and set to work. He had conquered and won the respect of all.

But it was a fruitless victory; Péguy was not happy at the School. The life was hard and monastic; there were daylight, pleasant expanses of grass, lively memories of past glories, but it was an enclosed life nonetheless, and the child of the faubourg Bourgogne, who had lived in schools or barracks for ten years now, longed for fresh air and freedom. The stress involved in the training of young Frenchmen is terrible. In any case, neither the atmosphere nor the companionship of the Ecole suited Péguy's temperament. The students were mostly studious young bourgeois, keen on their books and good at examinations. The *cour rose* friends were lively, spontaneous and unconstrained. At the Ecole Normale, the work was mainly concentrated on a rapid assimilation of texts and the art of making brilliant expositions of works or systems. Péguy hated these intellectual acrobatics. His method with any given subject was, first, powerful and personal concentration, then a decision and a judgment. His fellow-students at Sainte-Barbe and his study-mates at the Ecole all noticed the immense physical, almost animal, energy, with which he gathered his powers together before settling down to write, or in the case of a seminar, to speak.

We have an account of a piece of work Lanson asked him to do on Vigny. The Ecole Normale students as an audience are very critical and hard to please; each of them dreads having to face the rest. Péguy disarmed them with his terse, brusque, direct speech, but Lanson was not satisfied. Péguy not only explained Vigny, he judged him, and condemned his thought for its pessimism, egoism, narcissism. Such a condemnation was not in conformity with the traditions of university eclecticism, and Lanson criticised it severely, advising Péguy to approach the masters with an open mind and in a more liberal manner. Nor was this all. Like many lecturers, he quite enjoyed taunting young men and making a laughing stock of them for the benefit of the gallery. Péguy's manuscript was in his hand, written in that irreproachable handwriting, or rather calligraphy, which Péguy had learnt at school and kept religiously ever since. It was an explicit sign of his inflexible temperament. Lanson made fun of it and remarked: 'The work would have been better if M. Péguy had spent more time on preparing it and less on writing it out.' Everyone laughed. Péguy, silent until now, his arms crossed, very red in the face, broke out with a violent: '*I can't write badly!*' It was true, he could not, and never would be able to. Lanson had not foreseen a retort. Paul Claudel, forty years later, compared the fine and pointed letters traced by Péguy, all slanting in perfect order, to a forest of lances set for the defence. Lanson had met these lances for the first, but not the only time.

Péguy realised that his intransigeance was not acceptable. He responded to a sharp word with a show of temper. His study was his refuge where his solitude and his vocation were safe. He shared it with three others, one of them Mathiez, the future historian of the Revolution, and then already socialistic and quick-tempered. This study the normaliens lost no time in baptizing Utopia. A mocking hand cut the name on the door. Everyone knew that the renovation of society was being prepared inside, as well as the publication of a paper, *Le Journal Vrai*, which, by the two-fold method of rigorous truth and fraternal diffusion, was to transform society in thirty years. Money was needed for publication and the hat went round. The appeal was a comminatory one. Contributions were to be in monthly levies, and publication would start as soon as enough funds were in hand. The pioneers were to form a sort of secret society which, at a given signal, when all was ready for the great upheaval, would intervene *en bloc*, determine the course of the Revolution, and carry the day. Péguy was still determined to strike the flash of an epoch from the slothfulness and mediocrity of a period. From the study called Utopia came warnings, declarations, excommunications, which Péguy stuck on to the refectory door: *There are only three socialists in the School, me, so-and-so and so-and-so.—So-and-so is clerical* and a *worldling, I shall not speak to him*. And so on.

All this was quite ridiculous, and Péguy admits it in *Clio*, his last work, published after his death. He writes with scorn of the *ardent, gloomy, stupid young man* whom he remembers having been. A Normale student of 1897, whose own growing fame has not clouded his memory, writes to me:

> Apart from a handful of us, we all found Péguy quite impossible, he was so proud. Moreover, he was hard on our purses with his incessant demands for subscriptions to strikes and contributions to good works. But I must admit one thing, at the Ecole Normale he was the one subject of all conversation.

The subject of all conversation; and so it would always be; wherever he went, he commanded attention and set men talking about him. The students of Normale were quite right, for in the study called Utopia there was more than just the 'ardent, gloomy, stupid young man,' who was its chief occupant. They were aware of a creature different from the others, with his own manner of thought and speech, response and decision. It was a rare event.

•

Though still so raw that year, he nonetheless made three acquaintances which each in its own way played a great part in his life: Bergson, who lectured in philosophy at the Ecole Normale; Romain Rolland, lecturer in the history of art, and Lucien Herr, the librarian.

Bergson was at that time the young, already famous author of the *Essai sur les données immédiates de la conscience*. His mind was busy with the sweeping theses of *Matière et Mémoire*. He had recently been appointed tutor in charge at the Ecole, and had decided to give up all his own work for the time being, in order to devote himself wholly to the students. In their presence, on their behalf, by means of analysis, he transformed the whole conception of reality, and exposed the weak spots in the highly-considered dogmatics of rationalistic idealism and scientism. To have heard him is to know the quality of his spoken word. Written, though still admirable, it is but the shadow, scrupulously set down on paper. This marvellous teaching took Péguy by storm. He had studied philosophy under the hegelian Noël at Lakanal and the positivist Lévy-Bruhl at Louis-le-Grand. But for him philosophy began with Bergson. 'He will never be forgiven for setting us free,' he wrote later. He listened in silence, took no part in the discussions, did no written work. Such was the way of this 'ardent, gloomy, stupid young man.' Bergson took no notice, have been told this was a special case, and he might never have heard the sound of Péguy's voice, had he not stopped him one day in the School corridor: 'I know you have put aside your personal work to give us your whole time. You should not do this. You have a book to write, and that should come before everything else,' he said, and then passed on.

Romain Rolland was a very young master and a very beautiful young man. He picked Péguy out, saw what he was, and became his friend. The differences between them were marked: Péguy, thoughtful and resolute, digging and delving within, the true peasant busy on his own plot; Rolland, the man of ideas, restless, on the look out for models and refuges, drawn to all the arts in turn, in love with successive series of landscapes and places. The differences were to grow, until the ultimate contrast was disclosed: in 1914, Péguy died in Brie, lying on his face among the beetroots; and about 1935,

Romain Rolland received from Stalin the title of citizen of Moscow. In the early days, they had in common a thirst for greatness. *Memento magnitudinem* was the password of the two Normale students in 1910 who were the heroes of Jules Romain's *Hommes de bonne volonte*, forty years later. It would have done for Péguy and Romain Rolland in 1895. An essential trait would be lacking in his biography if we did not picture him talking to Romain Rolland in the windowed cloister at the centre of the Ecole.

Rolland's love at the time was for the old man whom all Europe venerated, Tolstoï, the last of the great men of the nineteenth century. He admired him but could not accept his summary aphorisms. He had written and told him both of his admiration and of his difficulties, asking: 'Why should manual work be one of the essential conditions of true happiness? Is a man deliberately to cut himself off from all intellectual activity, from science and the arts, which you consider incompatible with manual work?' Rolland wrote his letter and dropped it into the letter-box like a child writing to his guardian angel. Tolstoï wrote to him: 'Dear brother, I have received your first letter. It touched my heart. I read it with tears. . . .' The answer was a long epistle.

Tolstoï did not preach his uncivilising doctrine this time: to the young Frenchman who had written so reasonably he gave a reasonable answer, only trying to make him realise how much is factitious, vain and cruel in science and the arts as the moderns understand them. This is what he said:

True science and true art have always existed and will always exist side by side with the other modes of human activity, and it is impossible and useless either to deny or to prove their existence.

The false position attributed in our society to science and the arts is due to the fact that self-styled civilised men, headed by scholars and artists, form a privileged caste like a priesthood. And this caste has the faults of all castes. It degrades and lowers the very standards in virtue of which it came into being. False religion takes the place of true religion. False science takes the place of true science. And so it is for art. The caste oppresses the masses, and worse, it deprives them of the very thing it is there to propagate.

These were important words which sank deep into the mind of the man to whom Tolstoï wrote them. Péguy knew them through Rolland; they agreed with his own ideas and he appropriated them. The two young men thereupon decided to keep clear of professional castes in art and thought, and to work with the single intention of expressing as simply as possible the essential movements of humanity at work.

Now we come to Lucien Herr, Péguy's third encounter. Who is Lucien Herr? One difficulty in writing very recent history is that the people one consults think they know it, and in reality do not. If Hamon had been named in 1660 or so, or Doudan in 1895 or so, any French man of letters might have asked: 'Who is Hamon? Who is Doudan?' Yet Hamon has his recognised place in the history of jansenism, Doudan in the history of orleanism. So Herr has his place in the history of French democracy.

In 1896, he was librarian of the Ecole Normale. He had been there for ten years; it was the job he wanted and he settled down to it. His contemporaries considered him cut out for a brilliant career, with high honours in the University or the State. His own peculiar choice was for this not much coveted post, and there, invariably seated at his imposing desk, he watched the groups of young men go by, among the most intellectually distinguished of the country. He supplied them with reading matter and laid his own immense scholarship at their service. He welcomed the new students and watched the seniors develop, going through their theses with them. How many books this man, who put his name to none, read and re-read and enriched with his commentary! He won respect by his spiritual as well as his physical stature, equally exalted and excellent. In the twelfth century he would have been a monk in a monastery or a soldier on a crusade, and it would have seemed quite natural to see him with helmet and coat of arms at hand (how well he would have looked in them) rather than piles of papers. Lucien Herr was born to serve a church and to propagate a faith, he would have made a good Catholic; actually he was one by origin and early habit and practice long maintained. But he had given it all up; when he was about eighteen, he threw over both belief and practice and (perhaps the first of the French university men to do this) put his name down for the Socialist Party. This throws some light on his choice of a career: at the age of thirty, he realised that the library in the rue d'Ulm was an admirable spot from which to convert the University to socialism. He did not of course say so, in so many words, when he applied for the post, and there is nothing to cause surprise in his appointment to it by a radical minister.

Lucien Herr soon measured the worth of Charles Péguy. He subscribed to *Le Journal Vrai*, he visited the study called Utopia as a friend, and it seemed to Péguy that he was, for once, meeting a man of his own kind, one capable of boundless devotion. Hitherto socialism had meant a vision, the vision of the cour rose and an ideal, the ideal of the study called Utopia. Herr brought about a complete change: he spoke of the Party as alone endowed with strength and reality: it was a man's duty to support it. Péguy listened and obeyed.

It was a mistake which brought both Herr and Péguy great suffering. Péguy was not a man you could enlist.

IV

JEANNE D'ARC

THIS FIRST YEAR at the Ecole Normale echoes, in more bitter tones, the first year at Sainte-Barbe. It too has its double aspect; it is a page which you must read and turn over and read on the other side; there are two tellings of it. We have told the first, now let us turn the page and start at the top again.

At the beginning of the session, in November 1895, M. Perrot, the Principal, had a visit from Péguy in his study.

'There is something the matter with my eyes,' he said. 'I can't see clearly. I think I had better go home.'

M. Perrot tried to get to the bottom of the trouble, but could not make it out. To all his questions Péguy replied by reiterating that as his sight was bad, he had better go and spend a year at home with his mother at Orléans. M. Perrot put it to him that a year's absence would very seriously interfere with his studies, but without success: Péguy simply said again that the leave he was asking for was necessary. M. Perrot looked steadily at the young man and his gaze met his clear lucid gaze, keen as the sharp edge of steel, calm as the calm of waters, distant as distant skies. Contrary to regulations, he gave his consent.

So Péguy went off. Why? He couldn't see properly. What was the matter? It is true that Péguy did sometimes complain of his eyes. This did not stop him from working, nor ever would; all his life long, indefatigably, missing nothing, he corrected proofs. The excuse of eye trouble for so long a leave of absence is inadequate, and none of his fellow students accepted it as it stood. Some of them concluded (M. Félicien Challaye tells us) that Péguy was going because he had been sent to coventry by a certain number of them and wanted to shake it off. Others (says M. Joseph Aynard) assumed that Péguy had gone back to Orléans for direct contact with working life and to help his mother mend chairs. Another theory was that Péguy was going to learn type-setting in Orléans and would combine this with founding a socialist group there.

All these different theories can probably be traced to passing conversations of which the thread is lost. All have their point. At the Ecole, Péguy was fond of talking about chair-mending as a craft; he said that with all its different processes it was a real art. It was natural that he should think of giving his mother a hand if he was going back home. It was equally natural that he should think of learning to set type. The indivisibility of craft was a notion to which he was, and would always remain, deeply attached. It was one he would put into practice himself to a very large degree. It seemed to him normal, in fact honest, for a writer to be also a typographer. As for revolutionary propaganda, it is quite true that he was ardently engaged in it all through his leave of absence. His mother, that most hardworking and unrevolutionary woman, gave vent to her displeasure in no measured terms, and when he went back to Paris rumour had it, in the faubourg Bourgogne, that the local authorities had asked for his recall.

So all the stray accounts may each have had their grain of truth, while none was sufficient to account for this serious interruption in studies and complete change of life. Péguy was not impulsive, far from it. Tharaud's explanation is different and better than the others because it is confirmed by fact and places us at the quick heart of things. He tells us that Péguy kept in his study, under the table, a long, narrow black box like a coffin, on which he had written in his firm writing: *Not to be touched*. In the box was an imposing manuscript. No one, not even Tharaud, knew what it contained. On leaving the Ecole Péguy took box and manuscript with him, and the whole of the next year was spent in finishing it.

It was a play, or more precisely, though Péguy did not yet use this word, a mystery, in prose and verse, about Jeanne d'Arc.

So the Sainte-Barbe secret had been carried on into the study called Utopia; and this brooding over Jeanne d'Arc and her voices and vocation had been silently maintained by Péguy even as an intimate of Lucien Herr's circle. If Herr had known, what would he have said? 'It makes me laugh to think of it,' writes Tharaud. 'This project, which came to Péguy from the very depths of his being, seemed a challenge to what he allowed to be seen of himself, and was so contrary to the spirit of the place that he felt he had to go away in order to make room for it and give it a chance; he had to get out of reach of too over-shadowing influences.'

So here we have once more the phenomenon of the two planes of existence. Behind visible activity, incited by contacts, there is silent activity, over which Péguy, at the warning of some unknown instinct, maintains the strictest secrecy. He must have had the feeling, or rather the conviction, that this activity, involving as it did more than himself, demanded quantities of time and quiet to mature.

So there were two Péguys: one, the young student, embracing a doctrine, and defiantly and as a point of honour giving it the most rigorous practical interpretation imaginable; the other, Péguy the man, with this unnamed ferment in his soul.

Now we can perceive the undercurrent of his thought, we are no longer surprised at his leaving the School. In the thick of the crowd of young men, his genius for action took possession of him, his vocation for leadership, which he kept all his life, was too much for him at this stage and got out of hand. In reality, he had other things to do, and his appointed task was to consider the problem of evil through the trials that beset Jeanne d'Arc.

This is the subject matter of the mystery play born in the faubourg Bourgogne. And a mystery play it was, already; there is no break between this first work and the ones that were to follow. This one, written as it was by a socialist, is in a certain sense wholly revolutionary; Jeanne the peasant girl is led by her voices without the guidance of a priest, and it is the people who discover her and make the King accept her. At the same time, it is wholly Christian; Jeanne is a saint-like child whose vision and desires go beyond the visible world. Péguy makes one picture of the girl of the fields and the budding saint. He is aware both of the French landscape and the mystical horizon; the two things fit. He tells of great human acts: their greatness is due to superhuman action. The peasant girl he shows us is alive, very touching indeed in her humanity; she would be less real, less touching, but for the hidden springs of sainthood working in her. She is a child of Lorraine mourning over her plundered village and her ravaged countryside; she is, too, a Christian suffering for the incursion of evil in creation. She is both, serving both reigns, time and eternity; the two-fold task is not one, but concerted. Towards the close of his life, Péguy was to write these profound, pregnant lines:

Et l'arbre de la grâce et l'arbre de nature
Ont lié leurs deux troncs de nœuds si solennels,
Ils ont tant confondu leurs destins fraternels
Que c'est la même essence et la même stature.

Et c'est le même sang qui court dans les deux veines,
Et c'est la même sève et les mêmes vaisseaux
Et c'est le même honneur qui court dans les deux peines
Et c'est le même sort scellé des mêmes sceaux.[1]

It would be no shock to find them in the early work.

There is such varied promise in this juvenile work. At this stage Péguy had barely crossed the threshold of a hard and troubled life, the struggles that were to darken it had not begun. The pure clarity

[1] The tree of grace and the tree of nature
Have let their stems so intimately mate,
Have so interwoven their two-fold fate,
There is but one essence and one stature.

The same blood runs in both their veins.
The self-same sap for single weal,
One honour at the heart of all their pains,
One single destiny, sealed with one seal

of the inspiration is something exquisite. He tells Jeanne's whole life: her departure, her battles, her triumph; her captivity; her death. All this is a tale told; a great tale, too, with a vocation taking shape. And the vocation is part of the tale. 'Who is to be saved? How are they to be saved?' asks Jeanne, and all we need to know is there, in the reiterated cry of hers. As a child, Jeanne looked after the sick and visited the neglected, and the village people called her happy because she shed happiness. They were wrong: she grew up without happiness, with no release, constantly inveighing against the evil which cropped up again wherever she looked and was so much stronger than she was. Her friend Hauviette tried to comfort her, as Ismène, in Sophocles, tried to comfort Antigone. There is no doubt as to Péguy's intention: he quietly placed himself under the patronage of the elder, leaving to scholars the task of pointing it out. Hauviette says:

Look, here, Jeanne, you're not to get annoyed. . . . Listen to me: For nearly fifty years now, or so the old folk say, the soldiers have been reaping where they choose; for nearly fifty years, they have been wilfully crushing, or burning, or stealing the ripe harvest. Well now, after all that long time, every year, come autumn, the good labourers, your father and mine, the fathers of our friends, always the same, still go on working the same land with the same care, always those same lands yonder, sowing them with seed. That is what keeps things together. They might have turned into soldiers too, it's quite easy: you don't get half so knocked about, since you give knocks as well as taking them. And then as soldiers they could have harvested without sowing, too. But good labourers like to see the land well worked and the sowing well done; every year, at the same time, they do the same thing with the same good heart: that is what holds things together; it is they who hold things together and keep things going, and who save all that can be saved; it is because of them that everything is not yet dead, and God will surely end by blessing their harvests. . . .

Jeanne cannot accept this, she cannot listen to this sage advice.

For nearly fifty years now, Hauviette, the good labourers have been praying to God for the good of the harvests: and for eight years now I have been praying with all my strength for the good of the harvests . . . God answers us less and less, Hauviette.

Hauviette: That is God's business: our corn is His. When I've done my job properly and said my prayers properly, then He answers me in His own good time. It's not for us, it's not anybody's right, to go complaining to Him. Really, Jeanette, your suffering must be very great indeed, for you to go grumbling to God like this.

Jeanne: It is true: I am still now suffering pain, a nameless pain, beyond anything you could imagine.

Jeanne took her secret to a nun, Madame Gervaise, who was very highly esteemed in the Lorraine country. But it was useless, Madame

Gervaise understood Jeanne no more than her small friend Hauviette. 'Do what the rest of us do,' said Hauviette; 'pray, and don't worry.' —'Pray, and submit,' said the nun. To submit, for Jeanne, is impossible.

If anyone will point out a piece of work to be done, she will do it if she can; but it is no good talking to her about resignation. 'Do you know,' she said angrily,

'Do you know, Madame Gervaise, that everywhere the soldiers are taking the boroughs by storm and breaking into the churches?'

'I know, my child.'

'Do you know they make their horses eat their oats off the altar where we worship?'

'I know, my child.'

'Do you know, Madame Gervaise, and may God forgive me for ever daring to mention such things to you, do you know that the soldiers drink the wine that makes them drunk out of the most holy chalices?'

'I know, my child.'

'Do you know they go junketing with the most holy consecrated hosts?'

'I know, my child.'

'And I know damnation rises like a rising tide where souls are drowned.'

'And I know your soul is sorrowful unto death when you see the eternal damnation of souls.'

'Do you know, Madame Gervaise, that when we see all this happening under our very eyes and do nothing about it now but useless acts of charity, not killing the war at all, we are accomplices of it? When we let the soldiers do what they like, do you know we too are engaged in torturing bodies and damning souls?'

Madame Gervaise knows that Christian ardour must fight evil without hope of abolishing it; that it must be in constant travail, and yet unruffled; that Jesus Himself knew of His own experience how evil stands its ground; that He went down into Hell but could do nothing for the damned. This defeat and sorrow of Jesus Himself are told by Madame Gervaise in lines that are as sinewy as any in French religious poetry. Péguy incorporated them in his mature work and they are often quoted. They may have been written in the study called Utopia and hidden at once in the black box that no one was to touch.

Jésus mourant pleura sur les abandonnés.
Comme il sentait monter à lui sa mort humaine,
Sans voir sa mère en pleurs et douloureuse en bas,
Droite au pied de la croix, ni Jean, ni Madeleine,
Jésus mourant pleura sur la mort de Judas.

Etant le Fils de Dieu, Jésus connaissait tout,
Et le Sauveur savait que ce Judas qu'il aime,
Il ne le sauvait pas, se donnant tout entier.

Et c'est alors qu'il eut la souffrance infinie,
C'est alors qu'il sentit l'infinie agonie,
Et clama comme un fou l'épouvantable angoisse,
Clameur dont chancela Marie encore debout.

Et par pitié du Père il eut sa mort humaine. [1]

Madame Gervaise added:

'Sister, what is the use of wanting to save the dead condemned to eternal Hell, and wanting to save better than Jesus the Saviour?'

The determined girl would not give in. If Jesus' last cry was a cry of agony, is it not a Christian's duty to repeat this cry?

Madame Gervaise left her question unanswered; Jeanne went on:

'Well, Madame Gervaise, who is to be saved? How are they to be saved?'

Again and again the same cry unanswered, the same call unechoed. So she must shatter this hostile thing herself. As evil goes armed, she must be armed; she will do what no Christian girl has dared to do before, what no Christian girl will dare do after her, she will go with the soldiers and fight evil with a sword. And so she goes and the soldiers follow her, she delivers Orléans and has her king anointed and crowned. Most wonderful it is, her mission succeeded. And then after victory she looks over her booty: what has she saved? France, but still incomplete, still a prey to sin. Her old enemy evil has taken one step back, that is all: it has not yielded. Should she perhaps put down her arms, her saints' voices give her no more advice. She makes no definite decision, but goes on with the war, here and there, with little luck. The English take her prisoner, Jeanne la Pucelle for them is Jeanne the Witch. They hand her over to the Church authorities, and now it is against these that she has to make her defence. She is sure of the rightness of her inspiration, but less sure of other things; she allowed herself to be made angry, she told lies, evil found footholds in her, too. How little she had done, wishing to do so much; how badly she saved! Her last night is sad and anxious:

[1] Tears for all lost souls fell from His eyes.
There stood His Mother, weeping, sorrowful,
John, and Magdalen, at the Cross's foot.
Mortal death upon Him, Jesus saw them not.

Son of God, He knew all things, and gave
Himself entire, knowing, sorrowful,
Judas whom He loved He could not save.

This to Him was utter suffering.
This to Him was worst of agonies.
Hearing His cry aghast to Heaven ring,
Dauntless Mary swayed and caught her breath . .

Pitiful Fatherhood granted mortal death.

. . . How much I need to know,
My God, if it is true that I have damned myself. . . .

There is the essence of Péguy's first work. I have passed over the unfolding of the plot, which is very skilfully done. Andler it is who in his book on Herr says so rightly: 'Reading this play, one is struck by the discovery of something greater and simpler than Hebbel, more moving than Gerhard Hauptmann, more tender than Bernard Shaw, it is in fact the revolutionary drama that Romain Rolland was looking for and had not found.' Having finished it, Péguy dedicated it:

To all men and women who will have lived
To all men and women who will have died
in trying to remedy universal evil.

In particular,
To all men and women who will have lived their human life
To all men and women who will have died their human death
in trying to remedy universal human evil;

And among these,
To all men and women who will have lived their human life,
To all men and women who will have died their human death
to establish the universal socialist Republic,

This poem is dedicated.

Now to everyone who chooses, his share in this dedication.

The whole of Péguy, as we shall come to know him, was in this juvenile dedication: Péguy who seemed to be repeating himself and never repeated himself, for he proceeded like the sea, his thought driving on in long waves, one rolling over the other and progressing line by line. And at the end a dig in the ribs.

•

Péguy went back to the Ecole Normale in November 1896, greatly eased, it seems, by his long absence. Some of his fellow students were none too pleased to have to make room at their table in the refectory for the awkward customer of 1894, but relented when they heard it said: 'Péguy has changed a lot, he is now a very pleasant fellow to have about.' So he had taken himself in hand about his tiresome behaviour in his first year.

He gave his play a last look over and finished it in June 1897. Then there was the question of getting it published. To talk of the difficulties of the undertaking is an understatement: it was not difficult because it was impossible. Péguy had no cash, and no publisher would conceivably accept it. There was no solution to the problem. So Péguy set about finding his own solution. He considered the writer to be a craftsman who should be familiar with all the processes of his craft from beginning to end; the intention, the writing, the printing and the distribution are his jobs to be done in due order.

So Péguy sent the word round. He had completed a considerable piece of work, it must be published, and it could not be published without their help: they must get down to it. Here was this determined beggar begging for himself this time. His method was not to ask, that would be derogatory; in a perfectly calm, steady, measured tone of voice, he put the facts before them. And they all listened.

Tharaud has admirably dissected this phenomenon of obedience in those who came within Péguy's orbit: 'When Péguy asked for anything,' he writes, 'no one raised any objection. One would not have thought of doing so, even if one had a vague feeling that his request was not wholly reasonable, and there was no sense of constraint, for your own will seemed to go out from you to join his.'

Marvellous power of penniless youth! Two thousand francs were needed, quite a large sum of money in those days. And Péguy got it. In December, 1897, his fellow students were handling an imposing in-quarto volume. The impossible had happened.

It was imposing both to look at and to hold, and most surprising to open; the text seemed to be drowned in blank spaces. Great blanks, which sometimes went on for pages on end.

You turned a few pages over, and a bit more of the text would appear; a reply, a few prose sentences; a stanza, a dozen lines of verse. The first edition of Péguy's *Jeanne d'Arc* is a unique phenomenon in the history of books. To some, these empty silent pages said: 'Ponder and wait. We have set out on a long trek. Everything cannot be said at once.' . . . But Tharaud is speaking for the very few. Péguy's fellow students hadn't emptied their pockets for such a waste of paper. They took it as a joke. It is natural for people to laugh at what they do not understand. The laughter came rocketing over the Montagne Sainte-Geneviève to the right bank of the Seine, and that is how in spring 1898, probably, I first became aware of the existence of the astonishing *normalien* named Péguy.

Fèlicien Challaye asked him:

'Why so many blanks?'

'To give you time to think as you turn over the pages,' was Péguy's brief reply.

In actual fact, these blank pages were the sign of a very remarkable psychological phenomenon. Considered after a lapse of forty years, they reveal a meaning which could not possibly have been guessed by the scornful students of 1898. In the *Mystery of the Charity of Jeanne d'Arc*, which appeared in 1909, the text of the original *Jeanne d'Arc* is retained, word for word, with lengthy additions. Péguy had filled in the unexplained blanks of his early work, which figured the space of his life and discoveries-to-come. Ponder and wait, as Tharaud put it so well. How far was Péguy conscious of what he was doing? We cannot tell. What we do know and must point out is, that here we have a signal instance of that faculty of foreknowledge which was so singularly Péguy's, and which will more and more distinctly strike across his life like a flash from the unknown.

On the last page you may read, in lovely slanting letters called Egyptian type, the names of the twenty compositors who set the type. Péguy wished their part in the work to be stated: Claude Briand, Eugène Bridault, Théodore Chevauchez, Emile Daviot . . . I stop at this name, because for many years Emile Daviot it was who set up the type of the *Cahiers*, a real friend to Péguy and all of us.

St. Paul counsels us to let life absorb all that is mortal in us, and this applies most satisfactorily to the first *Jeanne d'Arc*, where life (to be understood as St. Paul has it, of the free and glorious activity of man) has absorbed everything. No commercial considerations intervened between the birth and the final setting out of the idea. Inspiration, zeal and friendship did it all: what a victory over evil.

The eight hundred beautiful in-quarto volumes were deposited at a socialist bookshop which had opened at the Croisel passage-way. One day a stranger came in and bought a copy. An unheard of event which never occurred again.

V

THE DREYFUS AFFAIR

PEGUY FINISHED HIS book in June. It was high time: the Dreyfus Affair was starting: Scheurer-Kestner, president of the Senate, was at that very time warning his colleagues that he was going, fully documented, to demand the revision of the 1893 trial. By October the news was common property. It is clear that if Péguy had embarked on this storm six months earlier, his *Jeanne d'Arc* would not have been written and his work would have lacked this essential foundation. He would not have gone home to the faubourg Bourgogne. He would have thrown himself whole-heartedly into the fight.

As far as public opinion was concerned, initiation came slowly; there was a long period of twilight. But for the Ecole Normale students there was nothing of the sort: Lucien Herr knew all about it and kept them informed. The rue d'Ulm library became one of the focus points of the dreyfusard movement. Clémenceau tracked Herr down among his books; Jaurès dropped in to chat, glad to find himself back in this building where he had belonged, among the young men whom he always regarded, in his powerful kindliness, as his fellows.

Dreyfus, Esterhazy, Picquart, ghosts of a forgotten drama, were to all those young men, mistaken innocence, glorified treason and downtrodden loyalty incarnate: what a cause to serve, one and threefold, a gift dropped from heaven!

Péguy never hesitated: the cause was his own. *Who is to be saved? How are they to be saved?* Now, he knew. The *Affaire* was startlingly clear to him and his friends: in the place of a *period*, an *epoch* was opening out before them. Herr was the leader, Péguy his lieutenant, and together they hurled all the youth of the Latin Quarter into the battle.

Once more, Péguy felt cramped in the narrow framework of the Ecole Normale. It was too narrow for all that was going on now: his seclusion was becoming intolerable. It was too narrow for all that was going to happen too, for he felt no attraction for the careers that the Ecole made available. A man needs to produce, not annotate: he must dare to take responsibility and never fear to strike out along fresh lines: this was his conviction. The customs of the faubourg Bourgogne fitted this picture well: during his year's leave Péguy had seen his childhood friends and neighbours, young men getting on for twenty-five, marry and settle down, with a workshop or small business of their own. Had he been other, he might have boasted of all the important examinations he was going to take in his stride and the careers available to him. But Péguy felt no particular pride in his prowess in the obstacle race; faubourg custom was good enough for him, he intended to conform to it. He knew he was master of his own craft. His *Jeanne d'Arc* was a fine, stout piece of work: he had supervised every detail of the printing and putting together of the book, and had proved his worth at once as a proof-reader. So he was admirably qualified for setting up as writer-printer-publisher, according to the best rules of the indivisibility of craft. As for the home, he knew where to find his wife: his dear Marcel Beaudouin, dead at twenty, had a sister; he would marry her. Such was the custom of the faubourg, and his own vocation to a life of heroic standards required it too.

So his path lay clear before him, he had but to follow it. For the second time he went to see M. Perrot, the Principal of the Ecole Normale. This time, it was not to make a request, but simply to inform him that he was going to change the course of his life, and must begin by leaving the School. M. Perrot was astounded. No such thing had ever occurred before. He spoke most seriously to this foolhardy, rash student of his: he was only a few months from his final examinations, there was no doubt that he would pass, and as an *agrégé*, his life and career were assured; there would be no more difficulties in his path and it would be in order for him to marry and bring up a family. But not till then! 'My marriage and my business will not stop me from taking the examination,' said Péguy (and he did sit for it). 'Your marriage and your new concerns will prevent your passing,' said M. Perrot. And he did, in fact, fail when the time came. But the conversation made no difference. M. Perrot pointed out the dangers, Péguy asked only to be allowed to tackle them; M. Perrot pleaded in the name of common sense, Péguy had ears only for his imperious private injunction. He said good-bye to the Principal and then paid another call. He was still very fond of l'Abbé Batiffol, the almoner at Sainte-Barbe. He had made an important decision, and felt the need to tell him about it. For the priest's benefit he added that Mlle Beaudouin was a revolutionary socialist like himself, and that their marriage would have no religious sanction. Now it was the priest's turn to express surprise and concern. M. Perrot had pointed out the dangers as they are met in ordinary social life; l'Abbé Batiffol showed the dangers in the supernatural order. Again, without success: in both the natural and the supernatural orders, Péguy was ready to take risks. L'Abbé Batiffol's words had as little effect as M. Perrot's: he found himself up against a sort of absolute, invincible resistance. He pleaded in vain, nothing could be done. So he promised prayers and all good wishes. Years later, Péguy wrote:

'Fathers of families, those great adventurers of the modern world....' It was an adventure he was embarking on, risking all shipwrecks the better to save and save.

Rid of his studies and married, he only had to settle himself in a business. Mlle Beaudouin had a small dowry of forty thousand francs or so. She agreed with Péguy that this money ought to be invested in an independent concern in support of the Revolution. Now in the rue Cujas, under the shadow of the Sorbonne, there was a bookshop of which the owner was having to sell out. Péguy bought it up, summoned his friends, the *cour rose* group, Lotte, Tharaud, Henry Roy, Peslouän, Riby, and a few more recent ones, Challaye, Litalien, Berth, Lagardelle, and together they swept the shop and put it into shape, and it became one of the most lively spots on the Montagne Sainte-Geneviève. Herr was a frequent visitor. Like M. Perrot, he had done his best to put a stop to the scheme. But now it was on foot, he watched it with interest.

This first undertaking of Péguy's has been chronicled by Tharaud, and after so admirable an account I have no desire to go over the ground again. But the page must be written. Bookshop, editorial office, publishing concern: it was all this at one and the same time, just as Péguy had planned. And also, cutting across the too narrow rule of the indivisibility of crafts, it was the guard-room of a militia. In those years, 1898 and 99, clashes were frequent in the Sorbonne corridors a hundred yards off. Péguy was constantly on the alert, ready to intervene and to throw his friends into the fray. A voice shouted: 'Durkheim is being attacked, Seignobos invaded!'—'Rally!' said Péguy, who had a liking for military terms. If he was in the Ecole when the call came, he immediately set out down the corridors, opening study doors and shouting 'Rally!' They all seized their sticks and raced after him to the Sorbonne. Ça ira, ça ira, Péguy went humming—he knew no other song—and Tharaud ran up the hill beside him. Péguy's stick was a stout one which he held by the middle and brandished at arm's length. Inside the Sorbonne, he was captain of manœuvres: 'Your group up the stairs—Yours down the corridor!' He knew victory and defeat. He was once beaten up by the police: everyone has his bad days. Fifteen years later, he wrote: 'The great captain is not the one who is never beaten, but the one who goes on fighting.' He was that man.

The militia were covered in glory, but business was bad. The eight hundred in-quartos of *Jeanne d'Arc* had been brought from the Choisel passage-way to the rue Cujas, and built up into the same formidable block. The general public were showing no interest in Tharaud's *Coltineur débile*, and Péguy's *La Cité harmonieuse* was no more successful.

Bellais, who had lent his name to the concern (Péguy as a University Scholar could not go into business), was growing anxious. Péguy remained unperturbed. 'Wait a bit, old friend,' he said, pointing to a passing Hachette van, 'we shall have our vans, too!' Bellais was not so ambitious, all he wanted was a little light to be shed on muddled and disquieting account books. Jaurès, as soon as he became aware of the difficulties, authorised Péguy to publish a selection of his articles. Péguy, who liked to do things in style, put together a stout volume and printed ten thousand copies of it, according to Andler, twenty thousand according to Tharaud. The sales accounted for only eighteen hundred. Eight thousand (or eighteen thousand), unsold copies, piled up in the shop, had their use (with the *Jeanne d'Arc*) as seats for the militia. Bellais took expert advice and bankruptcy was declared. The predicament was serious, for on the head of the innocent Bellais fell the threat of a condemnation in court. He had to be extricated. Péguy went to Herr, who listened attentively. Bellais' downfall was Péguy's, too; and with Péguy would go the shop, the guard-room of the dreyfusards, to the delight and derision of the opposite side. It couldn't be left at that. It was a matter of cash, and the dreyfusard party was not impecunious. Herr promised to see what he could do. His intention was friendly, there is no question about that, it was in his nature to come to the rescue of his friends. But the enterprise itself was of interest to him, and the idea of getting it going again attracted him. So the plan he set up had a two-fold purpose, first, to save Péguy; secondly, to save his scheme and take his publishing concern in hand. Herr's idea was that Péguy as a militant artist had ruined his chances. It was worth while to see what would happen if university socialists took his place and worked along the same lines, not wasting time over publishing a *Jeanne d'Arc* or tales by little Tharaud. The moment was most opportune; Jaurès' ambition was to ride on the tide of emotions roused by the *Affaire* and unite the divided fractions of French socialism, so creating that one revolutionary party which was the dream of people like himself and Herr and Blum. The 'New Bookselling and Publishing Society' (as Herr called it) would be a very powerful means of action in their hands.

It all came out as Herr had planned. The debts were paid off and the business was straightened out. Péguy was kept on as 'publishing delegate,' and as initiator of the scheme received shares to the value of twenty thousand francs.

To all appearances, the two-fold purpose was brilliantly achieved. In actual fact, the combination was complicated and delicate. The bookshop was a joint stock company, with five trustees, who were Herr, Symiand, Léon Blum, Mario Roque and Hubert Bourgin. Hubert Bourgin is now on the opposite side to his old collaborators; Mario Roque is a philologist and now professor at the Collège de

France; Symiand was a sociologist, and died while a professor at the Collège de France; Léon Blum was a Councillor of State, a writer, and a man of the world; a disciple of Barrès before the *Affaire*, of Jaurès since, but always a man of the world. Péguy was their employee. Those responsible for such an arrangement were shocking psychologists. The consequences emerged in due course, and very important they were. That is why I went into these details.

Now, all energies were dedicated to the *Affaire* and its final surge. The *Cour de Cassation* in full session (after how many reverses) decreed the revision of the 1893 trial. The opposition refused to accept the situation, and violent manifestations were expected. Great strikes broke out and lasted an unconscionable length of time; anti-Jew thugs arrived in Paris from Algiers. The nationalists counted on the support of the President, Félix Faure. The police were engaged in a game of their own, and by the spring of 1899, things had come to such a pass that the whole situation rocked dangerously. A death by accident brought on the crisis: Felix Faure died of an attack of apoplexy on February 16th, in the bachelor's establishment he had set up on the ground floor of the Palais de l'Elysée to entertain his lady friends. The unexpected news trickled through to the theatres, drawing rooms, and newspaper offices of Paris, throwing the forecasts out. When it reached the Ecole Normale, 'the news was so welcome,' says Andler, 'that a soundless jig of joy made its way down the corridors, emptying the library, dormitories and studies.' In night-shirt or work jacket, barefoot or in slippers, the cream of France's youth danced upon its way.

The nationalists did not give in. A military *coup d'état* was expected on the day of the funeral. The dreyfusard leaders made up their minds to offer stiff resistance. 'The republican forces,' says Andler, 'were organised by Herr and under Péguy's command in the street.' Péguy, in his sequel to *l'Argent*, tells a rather different tale: 'Herr was in command of the republican forces on the days when there was no fighting, I took over on the fighting days.' Actually, something did happen, but nothing serious. What worried the dreyfusards was not so much a military *coup d'état* as an intellectuals' day-dream spun in the minds of Barrès and Déroulède. The *Affaire Dreyfus* was a very literary affair. On one side there was Lucien Herr, doctrinaire-disciple of Hegel, and Péguy the poet; on the other, Maurice Barrès, novelist-disciple of Hegel, and Déroulède the poet. *Coups d'état* are conceived on another plane. Déroulède and Barrès seized every opportunity for action: with the support of the *Ligue des Patriotes*, they tried to hold up General Roget's brigade returning to barracks after the funeral ceremony, and to divert it towards the Champs Elysée. General Roget pushed them gently aside and continued on his way. If he had fallen in with their plan, Déroulède and Barrès would have come up against Péguy somewhere in Paris, between the Place de la Bastille and the rue Saint-Honoré.

It all came out, and the dreyfusards were the winners. The fashionable crowds seethed at the Auteuil races, and at Longchamp the masses demonstrated. The *Affaire* was, to all intents and purposes, over now. The valiant group that led it disappeared in the crowd of those wearing the new emblem, the red rosebud. Something else was on foot, sprung from the *Affaire,* but no longer part of it, and which we may fairly accurately call by a name that has frequently been applied to it: the Dreyfus revolution. In September, 1899, Captain Dreyfus was set free; on the 11th of November, the Senate condemned the fomenters of the failed *coup d'état* in the High Court; on the 16th the Chamber, which had not hitherto declared itself, voted 317 in favour, 212 against, the '*actes de défense républicaine du Gouvernement.*' The radicals were becoming dreyfusards: a sure sign of victory. The socialist leaders claimed the honours of victory for their troops, and it was decided that on November 19th, the people of Paris should themselves inaugurate a bronze statue by the revolutionary sculptor Dalou, symbolising the triumph of the Republic.

It was a colossal day. Almost exactly half-way between 1848 and 1936, the famous manifestations of old were staged afresh, and the new manifestations of mission-conscious France foreshadowed. Péguy was at his place as a militant. He has described the events of the day in the opening number of the *Cahiers.*

He was actively engaged wherever he went; his thoughts were coloured by what he saw; nothing escaped his notice as the people sang, shouted and surged around him. This was his first active part in a crowd. And his last; he never took on the part again. He went down the boulevards, round the colonne de Juillet, through the faubourg Antoine (it was revolutionary custom to laicise the mediæval term), till he came out at the Place de la Nation, with Dalou's triumphant *République* standing high above the sea of heads. Péguy could not see the crowded figures around her triumphant chariot; nor the blacksmith, nor the reaper, nor, as he puts it quaintly, 'madame la Justice and her grandchildren.' He did not mind. He saw *La République,* all alone, looking towards the sunset in the fading light, and saluted her as he will always salute her.

He had come out with the crowd, and with it went back to Paris, and the account of this homeward journey is given at the end of the *Cahier:*

I shall never forget what was the loveliest part of that day: coming down from the faubourg Antoine. Evening was falling, night was coming on. Ignorant though we may be of the history of the past revolutions which are the beginning of the forthcoming social revolution, we all know the glorious legends and history of the old faubourg. We were treading the paving stones of their glory. The bearers of the *Petite République* walked with measured pace at the head of the new procession. The people of the faubourg came and looked, spelt out the letters, read: *La-Petite-République-Socialiste; Ni-Dieu-ni-maître;* applauded, cheered, and joined the crowd. There was nothing to show who were spectators and who were demonstrators. The people came down into the crowd and took fresh life from it. The old *Marseillaise* was sung again, though recently disqualified among socialist revolutionaries by its favour among the nationalist bandits. The whole faubourg came down into the night, a mighty surge, with no trace of bitter feeling.

I have myself kept a strong impression and clear memory of this homeward trek. I was not, as Péguy was, part of the crowd. Standing at the doorway of the Adult School which Deherme had recently opened in the district, I watched for a long time, probably for hours on end, this endless stream of tired faces under the soft shade of the evening, and banners with symbolic inscriptions. In the group where I stood there was young Emile Labeyrie, some years my junior, whose destiny it was to be Governor of the Bank of France during the disastrous storms of the Front Populaire, and the elusive Paul Desjardins, inextricably divided between the 1848 creed and very acute critical dilettantism. Suddenly the word *Emancipation*, traced in golden letters on a garnet-red poster, surged into sight and vanished again.

'The point is,' said Paul Desjardins, 'to know what that word means to those particular people.'

This penetrating remark threw so much light on all the perplexities we were facing that it has remained in my mind ever since. Let me repeat once more that the *Affaire Dreyfus* was over.

VI

THE ORIGIN OF THE CAHIERS

A STORM WAS brewing at the *Société nouvelle de Librairie et d'Edition.* And the cause of it was the publishing delegate, Péguy. Andler tells us that 'Herr was insistent that the whole group should be in close relation with the Socialist Party.' The five trustees (we shall call them the Five, for short) were with him. Péguy was not. He considered socialism to be a tendency, and a federation of groups brought together by their individual tendencies and by the unity of a common movement, not a party.

Behind the word there loomed, for him, a compulsion, which he had no idea of accepting. Herr and Blum were in favour of the compulsion, and whoever was not was immediately relegated to the category of 'enthusiastic amateurs.' I know what I am speaking of, having myself been so docketed by Herr. 'The theoretical freedom of the members remains entire,' he had written. But who shall say where theory ceases and practice begins? It was to be feared that this freedom *as to theories* would rapidly degenerate into an abstract freedom valid *in theory*. On September 15, 1899, Péguy published in the *Revue Blanche* an article in which Herr and Blum read the following words:

> If someone were to propound this simple statement: that Guesde does not know what Socialism is, he would to all appearances either be making an insolent remark, or amusing himself with an obvious paradox. His statement would nonetheless be as rigorously and precisely true as a statement, during the Armenian massacres, to the effect that Pope Leo XIII does not know what Christianity is.

Now Guesde was looked upon as an authority in French socialism. It was he who had introduced the marxist doctrine into France; and between 1878-88 he had built up, in the cloth factories and mines of the North, in the Champagne clothing industries, and the Bourbonnais iron-works, a closely-knit, powerful party. Jaurès witnessed his genius for organisation and his power of speech with some trepidation. Guesde was a man to be approached with all due circumspection. The Five warned Péguy that as a functionary of a socialist institution he must mind his words and not treat Guesde and Leo XIII as equivalent cases. Péguy protested in some surprise. Herr and Blum pointed out to him where he was wrong: the freedom he had been promised and that was guaranteed to him did not permit him to criticise personalities. He had mentioned Guesde by name and spoken of guesdism. It was a double error. The party vulgarly and currently called *guesdist* had an official name: it was the French Workers' Party. Charles Péguy, attached to the *Société Nouvelle* in the capacity of publishing delegate, was requested only to use official terms in future.

There is no difficulty in imagining the tempest which this rebuke roused in him. So ideas were only to exist in their discarnate, depersonalised state. Such were his orders. And he, Charles Péguy, the most personal of creatures, compounded of affection and mistrust, deeply persuaded that the principle of any occurrence or human story lay in the quality of the people inspiring or conducting it, could only answer: 'When the dictatorship of the proletariat has been proclaimed, shall I be able to mention the dictators by name?'

He saw now what they were about, and pondered his revolt. The occasion came when a motion was voted at the Socialist Congress in December 1899. Here it is:

The Congress declares that none of the socialist papers is, in the present state of affairs, the official organ of the Party.

But all papers claiming to be socialist have definite obligations which increase with the importance of the paper and the assistance given by the active members throughout the country.

There is entire freedom of discussion on all matters regarding doctrine and method; *but as regards action to be taken, the papers must conform strictly to the decisions of the Congress as interpreted by the General Committee.*

Furthermore, newspapers are asked to refrain from all statements of a polemical nature or likely to incur the displeasure of one of the organisations.

One can only laugh, reading this Congress prose in this context. The absurdity is in the very act by which Herr enlisted Péguy and Péguy accepted to be enlisted. Péguy attached immense importance to every act of his. As a member of the socialist group of Orléans, he had asked to be its representative at the Congress. Defeated by five votes to four, he remained in his own town the leader of a minority whose creed it was up to him to maintain. He examined the motion on the liberties of the press minutely, accepted the first item, passed the second, questioned the third and rejected the fourth. As a dreyfusard, he had fought State-truth; as a revolutionary, he would fight party-truth. Moreover, he had to stand up in his own defence: he had taken his pages on the *Triumph of the Republic* to a review Lagardelle had recently founded, and they had been refused, the reason being that he had named Guesde and once again denounced guesdism. And the refusal was due to Herr's *veto,* of this Péguy was sure. He sought out the Five (Athens had the tyranny of the Thirty; Venice, of the Ten; the Montagne Sainte-Geneviève, in 1899, felt the full weight of the tyranny of the Five) and declared his intention to publish at the *Société Nouvelle* a fortnightly bulletin in which he would provide the public with information about revolutionary action.

Was he really so simple as to imagine that his proposal would be acceptible, as Tharaud makes out: all things are possible where such choice souls are concerned, in which simplicity and violence, sagacity and candour live side by side. The refusal of the Five was unanimous. Blum, always courteous, said to him:

'Péguy, there is no point in thrashing it out, it is just that your proposal seems inopportune. You are too late with it, or too early, maybe.'

What he meant was, the freedom you claim was valid yesterday, during the *Affaire*; it will be good to-morrow, when we have reformed society. But to-day it is not to be thought of, in the very thick of the political struggle in which we are engaging.

Symion's remark was sardonic and sententious:

'I know what you want, you want to start a review for fatheads.' Meaning, for the simple-minded who do not know the hard facts of politics, and suppose that a band of free-lancers can reform a State.

Lucien Herr had the last word:

'Hitherto we have followed you into too many disagreeable adventures out of sheer friendship. All that is over. We are agreed in believing that you are about to turn against all we did together, and we are agreed in not accepting this publication. You are an anarchist.'

Péguy retorted that he was not afraid of the word, and Herr repeated, emphatically and with much sadness:

'That is what it is, you are an anarchist. We shall oppose you with all our might.'

I can still see his massive forehead wrinkled with care, and hear his fist thump the table; I understand both his expression and the gesture. Herr was a man of feeling. Violence was as natural to him as kindness; his literary taste was excellent, and he had certainly loved and admired Péguy. But above all he belonged to the domineering kind of men who conceive it to be their duty to crush all resistance to their imperious doctrine.

So Péguy withdrew, 'Léon Blum's icy lorgnon upon him.'

'I was stunned,' he tells us in his account of the interview. And no wonder. Once and for all he had lost the flowering illusion he had so far kept intact: he had lost his sense of the friendliness of his fellow-creatures. He had read dislike and enmity in the eyes that met his, and for the first time. And this loss of friendship incurred the loss of everything; he had given up the University to devote himself to the publishing business, and now the business was gone; he was having to leave the concern he had himself started; he had nothing left at all but his sense of distress and emptiness. He had a wife and already a child. *Fathers of families, those great adventurers of the modern world....* Péguy had now begun to appreciate the hardships of the adventure. There was no question of giving in. And yet he had neither backing nor cash. This meant that everything had to start from scratch and carry on from there. That was how Jeanne managed things, she carried on, regardless: Péguy saw her mission in these terms. And his own, too, as her faithful follower. To carry on, regardless: *Passer outre:* it is a good slogan. He resolved to follow it implicitly, side-tracking misfortune and founding a new publication; and the publication, his wife and child, the children to come and all, would live and last and grow by his single effort, and would see him through life, him and his life's work. It was a matter of destiny, discipline, and a job to be done. His sacred calling: a leap in the dark.

The first thing was to find a roof. Jean Tharaud and Poisson, both *cour rose* friends, had a small student's room in the faubourg St. Jacques; Péguy requisitioned it and came along with his files. The room was tiny, and a plaster cast of the Victory of Samothrace took up most of the space. There was just enough space for a gathering of the faithful few whom Péguy wanted to found the new publication with him. All the *cour rose* friends came and some from the Ecole Normale. Romain Rolland was there. Péguy held forth and described his new scheme. There were to be no definite rules, sections of work could be delivered when they were ready, at frequent or rare intervals as occasion demanded; the subscription would vary, too: each giving according to his means; and there was to be no restriction on collaboration, Péguy regarded himself as a mere manager. 'I am opening a letter box,' he said. The manager would open and read the post. And then he would publish the articles or books. Books were not to be brought out in serial form, as in other reviews, but published whole. Péguy had already published *Le Coltineur débile* by the Tharaud brothers, and *Les Loups* by Romain Rolland. He would continue along the same lines. Romain Rolland, who warmly supported the idea, promised to contribute. As for a name, it was to be the simplest one of all: *Les Cahiers.*

We have already said where the word came from. At this crucial moment of his life, Péguy remembered his school *cahiers*. Or to put it perhaps more precisely: at this moment, so decisive in the life of the man Péguy, the hurt child rose in him and opened his beloved, beautifully neat exercise books. On these he would write his lifework.

The friends listened approvingly and undertook to keep the letter-box well fed, and to do their share of begging and recruiting for the

Cahiers. They had all the light-hearted youthful enthusiasm and simple joy that were needed: their glorious *Affaire* had fizzled out with an act of grace and an amnesty. And with the *Affaire*, the glow had gone too: or so they might have feared. But here was Péguy, their friend and their leader, bringing it all back again. It was a godsend and a new lease of life. For Péguy it was that and much more: it was his leap in the dark.

A thousand-franc note, an opportune gift from a friend's mother, supplied the first necessities, and the first *Cahier* appeared almost at once, early in January 1900. So we read the beautiful pages on the *Triomphe de la République*, then the series of letters to a provincial. Pascal, in 1650, had written to a friend in the provinces to enlighten him as to the dealings of the Jesuits; there is always the danger that one's country friends will not know all they should know, and they must be informed. Péguy made it his job. His imaginary correspondent is liberally visited by all the personalities that Lucien Herr had refused to have mentioned.

It is within our powers and it is our duty, within the order of knowledge, to comment upon all the personalities that events bring to our notice.

All the personalities and the whole truth. The Five were preparing to issue the official account of the recent socialist Congress. Péguy had had it taken down in shorthand and printed it forthwith. An honest factual account was an unique occurrence in the history of political parties; a revolutionary one, which the revolutionaries never forgave him. The same directive is in all his work.

To tell the truth, the whole truth, nothing but the truth, to tell flat truth flatly, dull truth dully, sad truth sadly; such has been our programme for the last twenty months and more, not only in so far as doctrine and method are concerned, but also, and above all, as regards action.

Here is a Péguy still entangled in academic bickering. But only superficially so, and it is well and truly Péguy himself who has got to work at last. *People must be saved; but how?* We always come back to the same statement, followed by the same question. And first on the list of those to be saved are the would-be saviours, the professional saviours, pedants who envy the preachers their pulpits, and 'permanent civil-servant heroes' as he calls them later. A low-grade complacency, and still more, sloth and inertia, an unavoidable downhill trend, are constantly undermining the most exalted causes. This low-grade state is called, in the vulgar tongue, evil, the old enemy whose accomplice Jeanne had refused to be, still untiringly pursuing its policy of widespread degradation. Here is the enemy to be fought, and from this degradation people must be saved. A confirmed republican and socialist still, as much as ever, but after his own manner which is no one else's, Péguy was always offering the

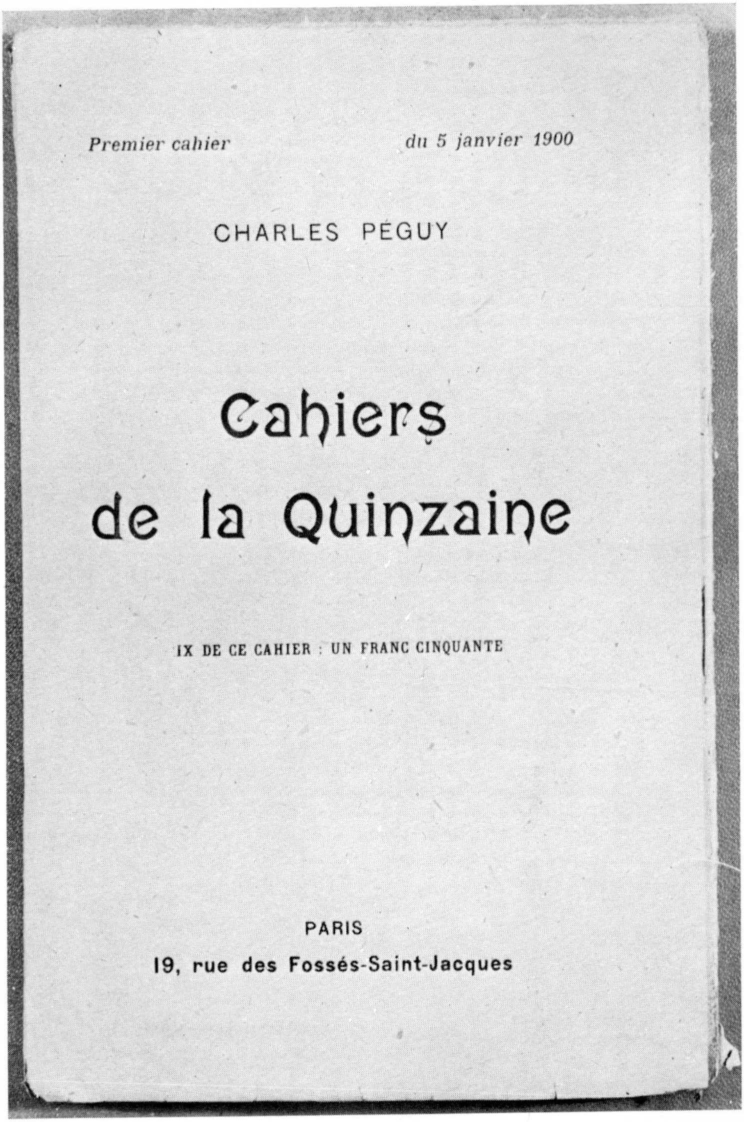

Premier cahier *du 5 janvier 1900*

CHARLES PÉGUY

Cahiers de la Quinzaine

IX DE CE CAHIER : UN FRANC CINQUANTE

PARIS

19, rue des Fossés-Saint-Jacques

Cover of the first Cahiers (*Collection A. Martin*)

republicans and socialists his distrustful collaboration.[1] There they went walking in step, in orderly ranks, along their chosen route.

•

Péguy wanted to go in the same direction, but apart, alone or with only a handful of friends. His job was the survival of the *Cahiers*, and survive they should.

The account we have just given of the origin of the *Cahiers* is the one Péguy has given many times over. The Five and their interpreters agree about the facts, so the description is valid. This does not, however, mean that it is complete. And once more we must start the story all over again, having told this phase of his public life, in order to discover what was going on inside him.

Between Péguy and the Five, there was more than patent disagreement on a Congress motion. A second bone of contention had appeared as early as October, on quite a different plane.

A manuscript called *Jean Coste*, signed Antonin Lavergne, had been handed in at the *Société Nouvelle*. Péguy considered it a remarkable piece of work. It was the story of the unhappy life of a school teacher's family, constantly subject to ill-health, bad luck, the clumsy handling of their affairs and official discrimination; and finally driven to family suicide, which is not so rare in our country as might be supposed; such was the tragic eclipse of a group of people who, by common consent, attempted to find in death a solution to their hopeless misery. To Péguy it was quite evident that *Jean Coste* must be published. He told the Five so, and they examined it and, to his great surprise, decided against it. They did not find these family troubles interesting. 'No,' said Léon Blum, 'it's not a book to publish, people are never as unhappy as all that.' Blum has denied that he said it, while Péguy has quoted him as having said it. The fact remains that *Jeane Coste* was turned down.

He was terribly upset. He could not understand the chilly disfavour of the Five, whose attitude to Jean Coste's life-story was so depressingly like the official attitude to Jean Coste the man. '*People are never as unhappy as all that*,' was what Blum had said. What on earth was a man to make of a statement like this? Péguy saw daylight at last. If you get a big business man to read a tale of sordid workaday life, he doesn't like it. 'No,' he says, 'it's exaggerated; among my work people, no one is as unhappy as all that.' And so it was with the Five. Blum, Herr, all of them were capitalists in their own way, aspiring capitalists. They lusted not for money but what is worse, *for men*. It was their ambition to rule the socialised masses. Dealers in men, *capitalistes d'hommes* is Péguy's strong expression.

[1] I find this phrase, which is so right and so characteristic of the first *Cahiers*, in a study of André Spire's on André Chénier, published in *Les Pages Libres*, January 5th 1905.

Human misery could wring the hearts of the Five only if it was born of class strife. In that case, it was useful propaganda and deserved to be set in the limelight. But if it was a matter of misery among people already socialised, the whole thing was different and should be left to fade away in the greyness and silence that stifle the cries of unhappy men. This was clear to a man of sense: if his attitude were questioned, he would say the case appeared to be merely an unfortunate accident. Such was the fate of Jean Coste.

But Péguy was no sort of a capitalist at all, neither for money nor for men. Nor was he a man of sense, in this sense. The more the Five looked the other way, the more keenly he looked at what lay before him, and the significance of the miserable Jean Costes grew and grew in his eyes. The Jean Costes are lost, said their friends. It is the very word theologians use to designate the damned: their souls are lost. The similitude of the words corresponds to a similitude of situations: the downfall of the Jean Coste's is the transposition and, precisely, the reappearance of Hell. They are the victims of a sort of social damnation.

Hell, again: Péguy couldn't avoid it. First of all he had held the Church responsible for inventing it out of spite. This he had proved to be wrong, as it occurred in Sophocles. Both antiquities, pagan and Christian, agreed in their evidence of the power and permanence of evil. And Péguy was discovering in one of those state administrations which are the prefigurations of socialised humanity, the prefiguration of a fresh hurt and a fresh Hell.

It is true we have here a tremendous working up of a very simple case. Péguy was the sort of man who saw what he looked at very large indeed. Things, as such, disappeared, being merely occasions and signs, valuable only for what they signified. When a man falls into the water he disappears altogether, and then hair, shoulder or arm emerge, and the man on the bank makes for the hair, shoulder or arm by which he can catch hold of the man entire. So it was with Péguy: his vocation, his hidden faith were brewing in him. *Who is to be saved? How are they to be saved?* Péguy took charge of the manuscript. It is of no importance, said Blum. It is of immense importance, was Péguy's retort, seething with indignation.

Now the socialist revolution, as those who had enlisted him saw it, appeared to him in all its vanity; no political or social organisations can conquer human misery, of this he was convinced at last; there is no common measure between the evil to be tackled and the remedies they apply. *The social revolution is moral, or nothing*: this brief formula, so often quoted anonymously, was the one Péguy printed in fine sensitive capitals on the fly leaf of his first *Cahiers*. What a wide gap there was between his way of thinking and that of the Five! The dissonance came from so deep down, and aroused such manifold reverberations, that it is impossible to explain it away in a few words. Péguy had to go on pondering, letting this hidden life-giving stream well and surge within him, past master as he was in the gentle art of waiting, as we shall see.

•

But he was in such a state of effervescence that he could not wholly conceal it. The veil was lifted in the second *Cahier*, which is called *De la Grippe*.

The influenza in question caught the author in January and nailed him to his bed. It was a great surprise to him. Having hitherto escaped illness, he thought he was immune. He had to change his mind rapidly, for it was a malignant brand of influenza that had settled on him. The doctor was called, he examined the patient and declared him to be in poor health for a man of twenty-seven. Professional opinion was wrong: there was nothing the matter with Péguy but overwork. And so it was for all the fourteen years he still had to live, he was always overdoing it, always on the move, always ready for the next exploit.

This influenza was another sign. Everything was a sign. Having politely listened to the doctor, Péguy made his own plans. Illness had taught him a lot and he felt almost grateful for it. Formerly everything seemed to contribute to a hopeful outlook; that is over now, the outlook is miserable. *Sub specie mortalitatis:* under the species of death. Otherwise, *sub specie eternitatis:* under the species of eternity. Mortality, eternity: which is hiding the other? Does mortality, with its appearance of reality, mask eternity? Or does eternity, with its appearance of surreality, mask mortality? This was the substance of Péguy's feverish imaginings. Everything has its uses, he said to himself: when the doctor has cured him of his influenza, he will be a less simple-minded sort of a fellow. Péguy wished the same cure to others, too. For instance, to that revolutionary humanity with the movements of which he was recently so closely concerned. It suffered from the same complaint as he was being cured of by the 'flu. Like a child who was promised a brightly coloured toy, revolutionary humanity was rushing to what it called its 'emancipation.' There was no knowing but that, propelled by quite different forces, it might not stumble into one of those snares, social disease or pestilence, which history so readily lays for unwary people. Who can tell what to-morrow will bring?

On Péguy's bed, among the morning papers, the *Petite République*, the *Aurore*, there was a book: Pascal. Jérôme Tharaud had lent it to him: he had re-read the *Prayer for the good use of illness*, and hoped Péguy would do so, too. Péguy then recommended it to the doctor. They chatted about it, and the easy flow of their conversation seems akin to the conversations which Anatole France was bringing out at that time. Not really, though: on page after page, a word, or a few lines, ring a powerful note with resonances to which Anatole France never aspired. Not more than a word or two, or a few lines: Péguy's prose had still not found its full rich cadence.

Doctor and patient discussed health and disease, good and evil, from the physical, moral, and political point of view. There are so many different kinds, how are they to be sorted out? The doctor was rather surprised, he was not used to this line of thought: his customers' ailments were enough to keep him busy without going any further. But customers we all have: Péguy's were the *Cahiers'* readers and subscribers. They were his customers, and to some extent his patients, too, whose peculiar affections were commonly called democratism, socialism, Christianity. Ample material for a pathology of souls. We may well ask what he meant, and what preoccupations the words reveal. Péguy would have found it hard to name the peculiar affection of his own mind. Was he a democrat? No. The mechanism of the majority vote held no interest for him. He believed in man's activity, in his work, in a sense of vocation which is the very soul of his work. He did not believe in democracy. Was he a Christian? He had Christian friends, he liked and respected their goodness, their belief appealed to him. Why did he not side with them? What was it that prevented his sharing their faith? He came out with it in a sudden explosion of violence: If the vocation of believers is the salvation of men, then he was a believer, if he did not side with those who believe, it was because the salvation of men meets an obstacle, a limit which he refused to accept, in Catholic dogma:

So I shall attack the Christian faith. What seems to us so strange, let me say outright, so barbarous, the thing to which we can never assent, and which has haunted the best Christians, the reason why the best Christians have gone away, or turned silently aside, master, is this: that strange combination of life and death which we term damnation, that strange reinforcement of a presence by absence, which eternity makes entire. No man whose lot is cast with humanity can give his assent to this, or who cast his own lot with humanity. No man whose lot it is, or who has taken upon himself, to have a profound and sincere sense of togetherness. No citizen living in simple solidarity with his fellow. As we must live in solidarity with the earth's damned:

Debout, les damnés de la terre,
Debout, les forçats de la faim.[1]

so, not with merely verbal assent, but basing ourselves on reality itself, we live in solidarity with the eternally damned. We don't admit that any citizen should be treated uncivicly. We don't admit a state of affairs where men are refused access to any city. There you have the movement

[1] Stand up, you damned of the earth;
Stand up, you slaves of hunger!

in depth for which we live, that great movement of universality which breathes life into the Kantian ethic, the driving force of our just claims. We don't admit that there should be a single exception, nor that anybody should be forcibly shut out. In heaven or on earth, we don't admit that there should be bits of the city outside the city. Convictions, probabilities or dreams (for those of us who dream) [1], we are just as perfectly insistent on togetherness in our dreams and yearning as we are in our acts and teaching. We shall never give our assent to the long-term exile of any unhappy man. With all the more reason, we shall refuse our assent to eternal mass exile. It is not only individual, particular, national, international, political and social events which set the socialist revolution up against church reaction.

But these events are the expression, I might almost say this opposition is the symbol, of an invincible fundamental discrepancy. The idea of an exile is the most repugnant of all to any form of socialism. We shall never agree to the supposition, the proposition of this living death. An eternity of living death is a perverse, inverted conception. We have got quite enough with human life alone.

What a wind blew through that sickroom, with what gusty currents. Péguy had suddenly found his own great prose, with its characteristic repeated words. The doctor must have thought him a very surprising new influenza patient with his metaphysical turn, now recommending Pascal, now chanting the *Internationale*. Then Péguy told of that production of *Antigone* when he first saw the world *sub specie mortalitatis:* and he wouldn't let his companion go till he had read him a long passage from Pascal. I picture this doctor coming out of the isolated house at the bottom of the Osray slopes in the Chevreuse Valley, and asking the neighbours: 'Who is this M. Péguy?'—'A Parisian, who settled there with his wife and mother-in-law some months ago. Quiet folk, nothing is known about them.'

Before leaving these strange pages, let us stop at a couple of enigmatic lines to which we should pay serious attention: 'I was busy with thoughts that I will tell you of later. They were very long-term thoughts.' Some of them may appear in the essay on *Jean Coste* which Péguy published in 1903, after publishing the book itself; or it may be that he never found the occasion to put them down and we must guess what they were. Péguy is not a hurried author. His work is a colossal system of time-bombs. Or to use another metaphor, it is a tree laden with fruit which falls in due season and is gathered even at the latter end of a late autumn, which, after forty years, is still not over.

•

When those two dialogues called *de la Grippe* appeared in the

[1] These are the titles of the three parts of Renan's *Dialogues Philosophiques*, which Péguy was reading at the time.

Cahiers, I did not know Péguy very well, and I have no idea what his friends thought. I am inclined to think they thought very little. All of them (Lagardelle, Berth, Guieysse, Aubriot) were entirely taken up with studying and putting into practice working-class society and culture; their masters were Proudhon in the past, Sorel in the present, and their work brought them into contact with men for whom Christian pessimism and its views were non-existent. I do not think I read them myself. Taken all in all, they made no impression at all and that is hardly to be wondered at: the prose of *de la Grippe* is like those very young wines of the great Bourgogne cultures, with violent, discordant savours which scorch the mouth and make you spit them out. They are, like the thoughts whose hidden existence Péguy mentions, very long-term cultures.

In his account of his break with the Five, Péguy is very amusing about the unanimity of these five important personages in their censure. 'They are five,' he wrote, 'and they are unanimous; happy men, to be unanimous; all by myself,' he said, 'I am never that.' The fact is that Péguy in 1900 was all at sixes and sevens with himself.

For a moment we saw behind the curtain in the pages of *de la Grippe*, but that is all. He sternly refused to let his distress appear, determined to hold it at bay and fight it if need be; he even went so far as to write (which is the height of absurdity) that Christianity had passed over him leaving no traces. Although at sixes and sevens, he did not intend to let it be known. 'It is unworthy of a great-hearted man to let his distress be seen,' wrote Clotilde de Vaux, and so thought Péguy.

•

At the end of their first eighteen months, the *Cahiers* were firmly established and recognised as a sectarian publication. It was a great victory for Péguy and a hard one. Herr's declaration: '*We shall fight you with all our might*,' had not been uttered in vain; all Péguy's efforts met with opposition. I had a proof of this myself: I was greatly moved by the pages on the *Triomphe de la République* and wrote a short article about it which I took to the bulletin of the *Union pour l'Action Morale*. I read it to the committee, as was their custom. There was a discussion, and a university socialist of Herr's persuasion said with much conviction that I was mistaken, that Péguy's intentions were not such as I had propounded them, and that my article would do more harm than good to the cause; briefly, it was preferable not to publish it. This opinion was accepted, and as to the sort of thing that was being concocted against Péguy, I was the sadder and wiser man.

Notwithstanding the obstacles, Péguy had launched his ship and successfully ridden over the first breakers. He reminded the Ecole

Normale people who had undertaken to support the *Journal Vrai* of their promise. 'The paper still exists,' he told them: 'it is my *Cahiers de la Quinzaine*; and subscriptions are overdue.' He did get some cash in this way. At the same time he was methodically organising the recruiting of subscribers, as the militia-to-be of his freedom. The first on the list were his friends; then the friends' friends; then he made an attempt to get into touch with each and every one of the ex-militant dreyfusards. He sent circulars to the members of the *Ligue des Droits de l'Homme* and the *Union pour l'Action Morale*, and to friendly associations of teachers. There was a good deal of enthusiasm among these different groups at this time. The crisis had created a state of expectation which no subsequent events or political results had come to satisfy. The brief formula printed by Péguy on the fly-leaf of his *Cahiers: 'the Revolution is moral, or nothing,'* was in itself something of a magnet. And on another plane, among the dreyfusards, there was an element of disappointed curiosity. The *Affaire* was magnificent from the polemical point of view, but its sudden cessation had left a void. And behold, all was not over, for here was this whimsical creature Péguy, whose every step raised a cloud of incidents. He was untameable, he was the freelance who goes on shooting after the cease-fire has sounded. To this must be added an unaccountable element, which is the authority which a chosen few can exercise over their fellows, far or near. Péguy was to a marked degree a man of this sort. He got his subscribers.

He had at first given out that the finance of the *Cahiers* was to be free, each contributor to give according to his good will. It was expecting a bit too much. So the new rule was that there should be three categories of subscribers: a small number to pay a hundred francs, the greater number to pay twenty francs and a very small number indeed to pay variable sums as fixed by Péguy, modest for those of modest means, increasingly large for the well-to-do. No one got it for nothing.

So the four or five hundred subscribers whom Péguy gathered in fairly easily, meant an assured income of about fifteen thousand francs. The thousand-subscriber mark, reached after four years' hard work, would never be sufficient to pay all the expenses and keep the family. His brother-in-law's savings (probably about twenty thousand francs) were swallowed up; his wife's dowry had already gone. The Beaudouin's were admirably generous folk. Twenty thousand francs were retrieved from the *Société Nouvelle*, not without friction: little is known about this incident, but it seems to have been unpleasant. There was a law-suit in which the *Société Nouvelle* came off worst. Charles Andler writes of this episode, in his *Life of Lucien Herr:* 'In Péguy's knotty character, there was a good deal of the sour, crafty Beauce peasant, an awkward customer.' There is some truth in this: to defend his *Cahiers* Péguy drew upon the peasant instincts hidden in him. *Pour ma maison* was the name he gave one of his pleadings against Lucien Herr and the *Société Nouvelle*. His *Cahiers* were his house and holding: worthy of a peasant's defence.

More money was needed, more and more money. Péguy got it by asking and by personal approaches. His early life had trained him to it: he had always begged with simplicity and pride, and as though doing honour to whomever he approached; at Sainte-Barbe and at Normale he went with outstretched hand as calmly as the sidesman handing the parochial plate from pew to pew. Now it was for some poverty-stricken family, now for some strike, for the *Journal Vrai*, for the *Jeanne d'Arc*. He seemed to have been trained from the start for the line of life which was to be his without respite. The young beggar of the *cour rose* was unwittingly undergoing his apprenticeship for the hard trade that he had taken up for life. January 1900 saw the beginning of this collection on behalf of the *Cahiers*, not in a school playground but in Paris itself, which was to go on for fifteen years. He drew up a list of likely contributors and started knocking at doors. In the poor man's hooded cloak, once or twice a week he set out from the Montagne Sainte-Geneviève towards the XVIIth or XVIth *arrondissement*, the Paris of insolent doorkeepers who, more than once, took one look at him and showed him the tradesmen's entrance. Barrès gives us a picture of him thus engaged:

> . . . when he came so simply, like a pilgrim, like a mendicant friar of old France, to beg for his *Cahiers*, and not so much to beg as to do us the honour of informing us, with his monotonous voice and dim face, so level-headed, serene, and proud, that he was paying us his fraternal respects in asking a favour of us.

No one ever heard him utter the smallest complaint, not the least word, on this account, and though we all knew of the terrible reality of his hardship, a sort of instinct made us not think of it at all, going on with our own unharrassed daily round.

•

The flowering season of the *Cahiers* lasted ten years. From 1910 to 1914, we shall have Péguy in his solitary grandeur, borne by the *Cahiers*, but towering above them. From 1900 to 1910, we have to do with the *Cahiers*, that is, Péguy in a certain setting, with work and eager friendly collaboration in full swing. After camping for some months in Jérôme Tharaud's room, he transported his files to the rue de la Sorbonne, where a certain Mme Dick May, a Dreyfus enthusiast, had started a School of Journalism. The *Cahiers* had a desk and a special department on the first floor. Next to Péguy's papers, there were Guieysse's with his *Pages Libres*. The Dick May School started a connection which was to be long-lived.

In October 1901, the *Cahiers* and the *Pages Libres* moved together some twenty yards from the School, to a shop still bearing the inscription which recalls its original use. The shop was long and narrow, boarded off into sections. On opening the door, a passage (or a sort of slip-way) took you to the back regions, where you found Guieysse; a door on the left led to a small space which was Péguy's domain. His shop.

Guieysse came of a good republican family in Brittany; he had trained at the *Ecole Polytechnique* and been an artillery officer, but had left the army to side with the Dreyfus supporters. His manners were charming, his heart was in the right place, his mind was keen and swift, but he had the failing of many *polytechniciens:* he thought by rote. In the XIXth century, this fine specimen of a Frenchman would have come under the spell of Fourrier, a strict disciple of Proudhon. In 1902, he paid allegiance to Sorel. As a gifted man he had chosen well. He remained a soldier at heart and still had by him two of his ex-subalterns, Moreau who to-day edits the *Revue Universelle*) and Dujardin. Like Péguy, and in fact among the same set of people, he had recruited contributors. Things had gone smoothly for him, partly because he was, compared to Péguy, a very simple soul. He very rapidly got together a thousand, two, three thousand subscribers, whom he addressed weekly, directly, in frank military and republican tones. This went on for some ten years and was thoroughly useful work.

Compared with the *Cahiers*, the *Pages Libres* do not cut much ice. They had however a distinguishing trait which the *Cahiers* lacked rather conspicuously. Guieysse, a pure bourgeois by birth, had a sense of working-class life, in factory and workshop. Péguy, so magnificently of the people though he was, belonged to them by instinct and childhood only, though that is immense in itself; but it is not all. The scholarships to the University, and even the Ecole Normale, had left their mark on him more than one might have expected. He had been a socialist for two years with Herr, and for two years a socialist against Herr, in violent dispute with him and his. Quarrelling binds men as closely as other things. A minute critique of the *Petite République* which was Jaurès' paper at that time, and the detailed accounts of Congresses, occupy a considerable, in fact ridiculous, amount of space in the first two series of the *Cahiers*. Jérôme Tharaud one day dared to say: 'Is all that any good, really?' To which Péguy answered: 'It's a very serious matter, old chap.' What a sudden, odd, and indeed all-too-schooly idea of seriousness, to come from a man like Péguy! When Péguy ceased to give his mind to socialist congresses, it was because the battle of the *mystiques* was engaged. He never knew anything about the most remarkable work done by the trade unions in the first ten years of our century, with Ponnard de Saint-Claude in the Jura, Malebranque at Amiens, Bernard at Bourbon-l'Archambaud, Emile Guillaumin, the great Ygrande peasant, in the Bourbonnais, all men of great worth whom I used to visit in turn, to gather news for the subscribers of the *Pages Libres* and for my own private information; their co-operation would have done honour to the *Cahiers*.

Péguy's kingdom was minute. His tiny office was about ten feet by six: a mere pocket handkerchief, but the scene of very lively happenings. Thursday afternoon was the great time for people to meet there. Péguy was 'at home.' This is perhaps not quite the right term to use: he opened his door, and let his friends flock in. Meanwhile he sat at his desk signing letters, searching through registers, the least loquacious of hosts. Even so, he was editor still more than manager, editing the conversation but not attempting to lead it. I expect his guests were like children to him, his own children, chattering away. What a lot of idle talk! I remember one Thursday he said to a newcomer, 'Let us go outside for a moment, I want to talk to you. They've been rebuilding the cathedrals for the last two hours.' Meanwhile, he had been busy putting notes in order. There was no stiffness about this procedure, not even absent-mindedness I think. He listened more than one might have believed, looking up from time to time to catch an exchange of remarks, and the speakers would notice the serious gaze as of an attentive child turned on them, or else the merry gaze of a mischievous child. For a friendly childishness flowed on and on like a brook under shady trees, in this exalted creature. The Tharaud brothers have given an excellent description of this trait in a single phrase: speaking of 'the charm of childhood in this man of such profound maturity.'

Facing Péguy, seated on a chair which none of us would have dared to usurp, was 'M. Sorel.' That is what we called him, out of candid respect. M. Sorel had not yet become venerable, far from it. He was in his early sixties. But his beard was white, his experience immense, and we were not yet thirty and our experience was nil. So we looked upon him as an old man. An old student of the *Ecole Polytechnique* and an ex-civil engineer, he had retired early in order to settle in Paris, with his astounding stock of knowledge garnered, ripened and, as it were, mellowed by forty years of reading, observation, and no time wasted in idle talk. Each day, at Place Saint-Sulpice, he got off the tram which he had taken at Boulogne, and walked towards the rue des Ecoles, where he was a familiar sight with his overcoat and top hat, for the latter was already going out of fashion. The Latin Quarter was the Forum of this new Socrates of ours. He sat in the Collège de France and listened to a lecture. Then he made a round of the bookshops, the modernist Nourry's, the revolutionary Delesalle's, and Péguy's as soon as he had set up shop. And wherever he went, there was always an eager crowd of young men around this elder. 'Socrates is not to be taken seriously,' said some eminent patricians of Athens, 'he spends all his time with the young people.' 'M. Sorel cannot be taken seriously,' said the Sorbonne authorities, 'he spends all his time with the young people.' They had no great use for the exuberant author of the *Devenir Social* or for the philosophical mathematician who, nevertheless, was given a liberal welcome in the pages of the *Revue de Métaphysique et de Morale* and the *Société de Philosophie*. (This came to an end: after 1910, Sorel was turned down as reactionary in University circles.) They mistrusted his ready, scathing wit—and went in constant fear of what he might say next.

Andler, in his biography of Herr, accuses Sorel of inciting Péguy to rebellion in 1899. 'It is, to my mind, a fact, that this civil engineer, become such an amazing pamphleteer, egged Péguy on.' But the rebellion did not need inciting, Péguy was quite capable of forging ahead without any urging from outside; though we may be sure Sorel was delighted when it occurred and applauded heartily. Andler adds, 'this strange man, so hail-fellow-well-met, was full of bitterness and went stark staring mad when he sat down to write.' Our University men are professionally unaccustomed to contradiction and inclined to attribute to base passions any inimity they meet. Only bad men would oppose them, is their idea. According to Andler, Sorel roused Péguy against Herr because the latter 'had, very rightly, cut him to pieces in the *Revue Critique*.' Andler is simplifying the facts and leaving out the human factor. What bitterness there was in Sorel's soul was due to scorn, not spite. Mad with scorn I have known him myself: scorn for a democracy where the popular vote as manipulated by verbal skill elects a pseudo-élite of pseudo-statesmen; scorn for an intellectual society where the examination system, meaning book-knowledge, recruits a pseudo-élite of masters of thought; and finally, scorn for what he amusingly calls our 'doorkeepers' civilisation,' and for France vulgarised by the presence of its pseudo-élites and the reign of the second-rate. From the time he first began writing, in 1880, Sorel had taken his stand, and it is not surprising that at the opening of our century he immediately recognised in Péguy a militant after his own heart.

He liked being in the *Cahiers* bookshop nestling under the Sorbonne, fastened like a firebrand in its side and under its shadow. Facing the talkative crowd in the tiny office (with a bit of good will, if most were content to remain standing, it could hold ten), crouching in his corner like an old faun, besieged by a pack of friendly young people who fired questions and conundrums at him, Sorel improvised rapid answers, always and all the time speaking impromptu. If one of them put forward an idea of his own, he might expect to see it turned down: 'you must take something else into consideration,' said Sorel, throwing back his great head. The *something else* was produced in a flash, and it was always daring, sometimes risky, and infallibly and singularly fresh, clear-cut and stimulating. This constant *something else* enchanted me, and I used to enjoy provoking it by making some wild statement which would produce the inevitable flash. Sorel's 'something else' was his own private domain, the sky-line of the born investigator. A single word of his swept our minds clear and opened up the still-to-be. Not that he prophesied, that was not his line, but he shattered the scaffolding of unreality with which the intellectual crazes of the dying nineteenth century were cramping men's minds. And still to-day, so near ourselves, they continue to cramp many minds.[1] Such was the man of whom Andler wrote, in 1935, that Herr had 'rightly cut him to pieces.' Those who listened to him forty years ago owe it to him that a changing world did not take them by surprise.

This office, the size of a second-class cabin on a transatlantic liner, was the scene of other, even more interesting, interviews, not on Thursdays. On ordinary days, when Péguy sat in solitary state with his files and registers, Sorel used to come in and sit down, and there the older man sat facing the younger one and unfolded the treasures of his experience. Péguy respected Sorel's mind, Sorel admired Péguy's creative power. He regarded it as a most suitable sharp tool for fraying a way through the stuff of history, and he admired its potentiality. The history of ideas is always written too late and neglects these bonds by word of mouth which holds the generations together; it overlooks the direct play of mind on mind, so superlatively fruitful of ideas. There are certain phrases in Péguy where I can positively hear Sorel's voice over the printed words; this one, for instance: 'By far the greatest number of historians is to-day recruited among the ranks of the teaching profession; and as there is nothing more contrary to the profession of scholarship than the profession of teaching, scholarship requiring as it does an open and enquiring mind, and teaching on the other hand imperturbably demanding an admirable assurance, it is not surprising that so many teachers of history have not acquired the habit of meditation on the proper limits and conditions of historical scholarship.' This is not Sorel's curt, abrupt manner, but the essence of his thought. When I read the critique of historical method as Péguy expounds it, and when I see what a *reductio ad absurdum* he makes of it, showing up the meagreness of the results obtained, and when I see him knotting his nets of impossibilities with which to ensnare his opponent, it is Sorel's dialectic that I hear through his words; and when, under

[1] These words were written in January 1940, and have to-day ceased to be quite so true. But I cannot say more than this. (October 1940.)

Sorel's name, I find in a *Cahier* a clear-cut denunciation of the 'politico-scholastic Party,' I can see in outline Péguy's coming attack on what he calls the 'modern intellectual Party'; when Sorel asserts, in this same *Cahier* and in the same passage, the survival of the mystical faculty into the present age of human existence, I feel how near is that famous page where, six years later, Péguy will give the word '*mystique*' a meaning which our language could not now be without.

I can ferret out affinities even in his sallies. When Péguy speaks of Renan and tells me that the important question, as far as Renan's thought is concerned, is not to know why he gave up Catholicism; there are serious difficulties there, and many have given it up and more will do so; no, the important thing is to discover why such a mind as his, having 'ceased to subscribe to the old review, at once became a subscriber to the insipid review published by the modern world, which we all find such a bore,' well, reading those words, I can, if I choose, hear Péguy's short, even tones pronounce them, or Sorel's jerky voice.

Friday was the day when Bergson was lecturing at the Collège de France, and Sorel never failed to attend. At a quarter to five, he walked up the rue de la Sorbonne and came into the shop. There were nearly always others present at the rendezvous: Berth, Benda, Peslouän and myself. His arrival was a signal: we all stood up; at the sound, Guieysse came in from his den at the back, and we set off together to the Collège de France. Seated on one of the upper seats of the hall, we listened to the master's wonderful, subtle, precise language, always so simple and always straight to the point. We were all ears, and all eyes too, for Bergson's teaching was a sight to be seen. He worked at his philosophy under the public gaze like a craftsman alone at his bench. The whole man was employed. In the throes of intense concentration, he leant forward, then drew himself up to his full height, sometimes as though really surprised at the difficulty that had just emerged. At the end of a minutely detailed analysis, he would produce an image as though by inspiration. What marvellous lectures they were! In about 1910, society women began to attend, sending their servants ahead to keep seats for them, and soon after Bergson withdrew before this elegant and imperious invasion, which could not be restrained in any way by the liberal rules of the Collège de France. At the time of which I am speaking the word had not yet got round to the ladies, and the audience was exactly what it was supposed to be; a strong lamp lit up the master's massive skull and slender body, and there were three hundred motionless listeners in the shadow. Among them Péguy.

•

We have seen Péguy in outline only, in the last few pages. This is no accident: he kept himself to himself at this time.

The curtain had been raised for a moment in January 1900, and not again since. The quibbling, quarrelsome Péguy of early days seemed to have settled down.[1] From 1902 onwards, the *Cahiers* became less controversial, and more general publishing work was done: so we have *Beethoven* and the first volumes of *Jean-Christophe* from Romain Rolland (they were a great success and kept the *Cahiers* going for some time: *Dingley* by the Tharaud brothers (still unknown); *Gobineau* (still unknown) by Robert Dreyfus; *Catholicisme et Critique* by Paul Desjardins; *Marée Fraîche* by Pierre Hamp; *l'Affaire Crainquebille* by Anatole France: a collection of articles by Jaurès called *De la Raison*. Péguy, as editor of the *Cahiers*, was therefore a very busy man, and the Péguy of controversy no longer ruled the roost. Not that he was out of it altogether, that was not Péguy's way. In the spring of 1902, the voters were preparing, for the first time since the end of the *Affaire Dreyfus*, to elect and crown the victors, and for Péguy this was the occasion for dipping his pen in the murkiest ink to pass judgment on the way politics were coming to be conducted in France:

> Whatever one thinks and whatever one might think of one's duty as a voter, it is in actual fact impossible to deny that the practice of universal suffrage in France is, with rare and honourable exceptions, an overwhelmingly vicious system. And in exactly the same way as barbarian nationalism, drunkenness, barbarian anti-semitism, a certain kind of colonialism, africanism, industrial oppression, prostitution, syphilis, racing, and in the same way as and as much as, all forms of parliamentarism, electoral parliamentarism is a disease.

He insists that it is a form of prostitution because it is selling a sacred act. That is why it is so intensely serious: our universal suffrage is 'essentially, the vilification of a great human love.' Péguy wonders:

> Is one to believe there is some ruling of religious or metaphysical fatality by which all human effort is damned? Is one to believe that all the good things of the earth, so good to have, are bad to keep? Is one to believe that it is always good to acquire, and always bad to preserve? Is there no sense in it at all?

'*Tout cela n'est il qu'un immense divertissement?*' is what he wrote, and thereupon quoted at length some of Pascal's famous reflections on the subject. Man is always avoiding essentials and slipping off to pastimes. The most powerful of men, the king himself, gathers

[1] Péguy,' said Anatole France, ironically, 'is a monk; he is Brother So-much-the-Worse; it makes him furious to see Brother So-much-the-Better smile; he objects to Brother Glutton helping himself to beans again; he bewails Brother Greedy's licking a honey-cake. As to the horrors of the wide wide world, Péguy never even notices them.'

round him a society of friends whose task it is to keep him diverted. The republican people, heirs to the kings, inherit their courts: courtiers are succeeded by candidates, and so prospers the eternal kingdom of evil. To those old words of Pascal's, Péguy observed, it was given to anticipate events in a prodigious manner.

The typographical lay-out of this political manifesto under the ægis of Pascal is noteworthy. Two-thirds only of each page are covered with print: at the top there is a huge blank space. This odd arrangement is not to be condemned as freakishness. We must remember that for Péguy typography was a language. Witness the blank pages in the first *Jeanne d'Arc*, a whole series of them together, causing great amusement to the author's fellow-students; we were able to explain them, however, and the meaning of these blank spaces over Pascal's *Pensées* is no other. They are there to warn us that the passages which we are reading are even more laden with thought than we realised, and that the overtones are just as important as what lies formulated before us; beside the text itself there is the extra-text, and our reading should therefore leave us attentive and alert.

After the May elections in 1902, the Combes régime ruled the day and was so little to Péguy's liking that he extricated himself rapidly and radically. He asked Bernard Lazare to contribute a defence of persecuted congregations, and printed a protest against denunciation in the army. There was no doubt as to his own views. He broke with the heirs of decaying dreyfusism. But without that tie, it was hard to see what would become of him and what affiliations would claim him. He grew more solitary, and people noticed it. Such withdrawal always has its hidden cause: few, if any, knew the secret of Péguy's, and these few remained silent.

In 1901, he had published *Jean Coste, ou l'Instituteur de village*, the very book which the Five, led by Léon Blum, had refused, finding the story too gloomy altogether. It caused quite a sensation when Péguy published it.[1]

In 1902, Péguy published an article called *De Jean Coste*. It contains grand pages on poverty and destitution and the sort of perdition which the latter inflicts on its victims.

In her *Souvenirs*, Madame Favre speaks of the 'great revolutionary sweep' of this article. It is easy enough to say revolutionary, but we

[1] The University authorities always hated the book and were prejudiced against the author, who was in the teaching profession. Although he had a gift for writing, he wrote no more. M. Gilbert Maire was a colleague of his in a school in Paris, in 1915 or so, and, struck by the name, which everyone else had forgotten, he asked if he were not the Lavergne who had written the *Jean Coste* which had been much talked about in its day. It was he, but M. Gilbert Maire was warned that he did not care to be reminded of a book which had brought him difficulties. For his peace of mind, it would have been better for him never to have run into Péguy's stormy wake, and for the verdict of the Five to have stood.

must agree about the meaning. Mme Favre was a very intimate friend of Péguy's; he had lunch with her every Thursday with Jacques Maritain (her son), Maurice Reclus, Pierre Marcel and a few others. She herself was a daughter of Jules Favre, the 1848 republican, and certainly gave the word a socialistic meaning. The statement is neither insistent nor emphatic, but it is made. It is however clear to anyone reading the work to-day, in the full light shed on it by Péguy's later development, that his *Jean Coste* is not a socialist work at all, and not to speak of Christian belief at this point, it is drenched with pessimism about human nature, which is one of the ways Christianity often takes to reach a man's heart. It is the way of Pascal, which Péguy had chosen for his own. Destitution, as he describes it, is the token of an essentially tragic universe of which the nineteenth century socialists had no idea. Remember the query: 'Is one to believe there is some ruling of religious or metaphysical fatality by which all human effort is damned?' It is marginal to the *Jean Coste*, and Péguy is haunted by it.

Then we have another preface, called *de la Raison*, written for the set of articles which Péguy asked Jaurès to let him have, and which Jaurès gave. Jaurès undoubtedly had a great gift for admiration and a kind heart. 'Sloppy, rather than kind,' said Péguy, who was soon to become the merciless judge of this man whose friendship had been very profitable to him. The preface is a fine piece of work, all the more weighty for being even-paced, and laden with warnings, not to say threats. The writer of these preliminary pages was a dangerous disciple to have. Could he be called a disciple at all? Péguy knew which way Jaurès inclined and where he was allowing himself to be led, towards what rationalist religion served by what priesthood. He told him: 'I am not coming.' In fact, 'You will find me opposing you.' Soon he will say the same to others whose murky ambitions and turgid pantheism he detested. Péguy examined and honoured the good tool of all honest work: Reason. The tool was what concerned him, not God or the soul. Péguy did not speak of God nor did he print this ancient word. But he intended, with a singular and most significant vigour of will, that the august seat be left empty, and that no upstart God be ushered in to the heart of this topsy-turvy universe.

The seat must be left empty: perhaps this is, after all, the best way to express what Péguy was looking for; not to say a clue to one of those decisions made on his sickbed in January 1900, and mentioned enigmatically: 'I was thinking thoughts of which I will tell you later. They were very long-term thoughts.' Now it is possible (even probable) that Péguy there and then decided to keep in reserve this sacred domain, this Christian ground to the edge of which he had once come. One day, perhaps (doubtless: but did he know, and do we know?), he would frankly face it, and face it in order to dwell in it. That is still hidden in the future. For the time being, he was a self-appointed knight of the land he had caught a glimpse of, roaming around, prosecuting for disrespect or trespassing, and keeping a constant watchful guard. He had no illusions about the sheer inanity of scientific ideologies, and with his own foreboding of truth so different, his present practice (which he imposed on his readers) was a sort of metaphysical asceticism. He was moving away (and his readers with him) from the springs which had fed them hitherto. A void was forming in his soul (likewise in the souls of his readers), ready for a belief to fill. Nature abhors a void and so does the soul. A dramatic vision of the void was part of Pascal's torment. And what Péguy was trying on himself and on his readers (or so it appears) was a cure by void.

I had a conversation with him which confirms this. It was about a tale called *Un épisode* which I had written, and which appeared in the *Cahiers* in 1908. Péguy discussed the wide Christian bearing of the tale, which surprised me a good deal, for I had no idea of it. 'What do you mean,' I said, 'the people in the story have no idea of Christianity, they are so completely unaware of it that they do not even attack it.' 'That is just the point,' he answered. 'What is apparent in your tale is a terrible absence of God.' He made some remarks which I have rather forgotten, but the gist of it was (these may be his very words), 'Absence of God, presence of God, it is always God.'

We never dreamt of the therapy which was being applied to us. Nor did we need to, for the régime our editor imposed on us consisted simply in depriving us, it was a sort of fast. So without the assistance of dialectical operations, we were to be changed and given new health. We, that is, and the thousand-strong battalion.

We did admire Péguy for this unique destiny he was offering us by his own example: as head of a family and of a business; as printer, publisher, bookseller, bookkeeper, and on busy or rushed days, general factotum, sweeping out the shop and the pavement in front of it; as philosopher, essayist, pamphleteer, poet, and all the time such a magnificent writer; *poor as a poet, more free than a king* was this young hero around whom we gathered, faithful to intellectual and moral powers whose hidden springs we never tapped and whose secrets remained unknown to us.

These fitful, changing impressions are so difficult to seize after a lapse of thirty-five years that I should not attempt it, had I not re-read an article of mine published in *Pages Libres* in 1904, which brings back to me my frame of mind at that time. The article was about an essay called *Israël Zangwill*, where, dealing with a different set of facts, Péguy was again working at the central theme of the preface to Jaurès' articles, attacking Taine and Renan as historians anxious to reconstitute by scientific method the whole of human evolution. In other terms, to re-create and resurrect, by means of the intellect, what we know by intuition.

Here was Péguy up in arms again, against presumption. The essay, magnificent for its force and liveliness, analysed the insufficiencies of history. It was a pamphlet against history itself.

I praised it, but was nonetheless disappointed to be left with a question mark. Péguy tore away with great wolf-like fangs, and it was a sight to show in an arena. But were the *Cahiers* he had organised for our benefit and welcome, and to which we came as to a workshop, to be the arena for a gladiator? Péguy gave us no clue as to the source of his ardour, nor to the colours of the banner he bore. Keeping watch around a void: was this the finest use for such energy, eloquence, poetry and wit, a wit so joyous in its strength and kindness of heart? Péguy was visibly striving to free himself from the impediments that had closed in on his youth, and to discover some fresh aspiration and make it his own. What was it to be? He kept mum. The subject of my article was this double sense of admiration and of disappointed expectation.[1]

See our Péguy run; having duly jostled Taine, he lets him lie, shakes a fist at historians in general, and pleased at such a throng of enemies, he rises to the height of his form and dubs their learning puerile, their science utopian. With what an abundance of well-controlled improvisation he goes, from Taine, left for dead, to Renan, the ambitious man who really believed in scholarship; and here Péguy stays, feeling his way, quoting him at length, and Péguy's language pales not at all in such high company. On it goes, sinewy as ever, and its full, rapid flow bears us along with it to unexpected turns and mellow scenes; it widens out, and then, in familiar, almost filial mood, reaches back to the old masters, Taine and Renan, surrounds them, and shows them motionless with the water rising about them, like a couple of islands with time-old dawn upon them, half submerged by the swelling tide of a young river; Péguy rough-handles them a little, examines them side by side, and then, without disrespect, starts knocking them about. But the time for indulgence is passed. Our Péguy now gathers himself up to hurl his whole weight against these men's pretention to infinite science, efficacious scholarship, and creation re-created by a total application of intelligence. Péguy exults, because experience is against them to-day. I overhear strange tones, a Christian, puritanical cruelty in his joy at overcoming them: There is no such knowledge, he proclaims, and no such future for humanity; no science of history or of man exists; there are only tentative suggestions to be drawn from the countless facts. We must read, and

[1] Péguy was so much feared after this, that Guieysse thought it advisable to warn him before printing my article. I had forgotten this but am reminded of it by a short note from Péguy to me: 'That's right, my dear Halévy, go straight ahead.'

love, and understand; it cannot all be done by intellectual attainment alone.

Then surprise and the question-mark:

This Péguy frightens me. He drags me along and pushes me about, and I am filled with admiration and remonstrances; it annoys me to be so fond of this sparring warrior. Let him get on with his insults and destruction, I know it has got to be done. But I don't see why he need enjoy it so much, and I fear that is an essential part of him. For him, to fight is to plunge into regenerating waters and issue twice the man he was. Where does the sheer joy and wit of his *Zangwill* come from? Most of his joy, perhaps all of it, comes of trampling under foot an impressive and long-honoured piece of reasoning. What imp of mischief possesses you, Péguy? Why is it such joyful news that so many men are wrong, and with them Taine and Renan, our own true masters?
. . . What hopelessness is it that makes love impossible to you? How deep down in you is this evil thing? Is your life to be all tension? This I will not admit. The language our gloomy, zestful friend has at his command is too fine a thing; there are too many years and victories ahead of him; maybe his sadness will remain: we must wait and see.

These lines show the mixture of right and wrong and the lack of decisiveness characteristic of a mind on the search, all agog at every move of another seeking mind. The last word was right: it was a matter of waiting.

Georges Sorel's impulse struck and stung like a seaborne wind in sudden gusts; it was exciting to the mind, a tonic to the will, but it did not touch the heart. Bergson's was wholly intellectual: the movement of a naked, lively mind, eager to reach its bounds and its own strange fading out. Péguy's was something quite different.

But what was it? To what end would this force, now held suspended, bend and expand?

VII

ROMAIN ROLLAND: *BEETHOVEN* and *JEAN-CHRISTOPHE*

I HAVE HARDLY mentioned Romain Rolland: we did in fact take very little notice of him. Yet he played an important part in the institution of the *Cahiers*: I should not be surprised if, for eight hundred out of every thousand subscribers, Péguy was not an indescribably obscure scribbler who had the merit of printing Rolland. It is only right to say that Romain Rolland's disinterested collaboration saved the *Cahiers*.

We told how the two men met at the Ecole Normale. In spite of great differences of temperament, they were bound by common tastes. The bond was to last and the divergences to become more marked. For Péguy, life was a plot of land in which he was digging a furrow; for Rolland, it was at times a fatality to be endured, at others, a landscape with scope for his dreams.

About 1902, he was, like Péguy, flotsam from the Dreyfus crisis. The French people had been stirred by the *Affaire*, and he had attempted to give them a national civic theatre. Péguy had published his *Quatorze Juillet*, his *Danton*, his *Loups*. The people had not put themselves out to the extent of coming to witness the performance of these pieces, and the audience of the first nights had been frankly bored. There were the readers, but elusive.

This for Rolland meant disappointment and strain. His tension of mind was a personal instance of a general state of affairs. All the enterprises that sprang into being under the inspiration of the *Affaire Dreyfus* were dying of inanition: adult schools and revolutionary reviews faded away; the workers, who were nationalists in their own way, withdrew into their own class and chose to fight their own fight, bidding their intellectual counsellors be off. All by itself, like a smoky torch, the small firebrand of the *Cahiers* burnt on. Things were in ferment all around: there were the solitary spiritual crises of Claudel and Henri Brémond; and the enthusiastic town-wide activity of the monarchist Charles Maurras, challenging Paris to collaborate. What line would Romain Rolland take? He was without creative force, but he was ambitious, in fact we may say he was nobly ambitious and sensitively aware of greatness where it sprang; he was inspired to fall back on the great of the XIXth century, that line of great men who maintained such an exalted standard for more than a hundred years, from Beethoven to Tolstoï. It was dying out, but he was able to restore its brightness and soon deservedly basked in reflected glory. 'The air is so heavy all around us,' he said, 'old Europe has grown numb in this oppressive, poisonous atmosphere. A low-grade materialism hampers thought. . . . The world is stifling. Let us open the windows and let the fresh air in. Let us breathe the air the heroes breathed.' These lines, weak and breathless as they are under the majestic weight of words, are part of the introduction to the *Beethoven*, which was published by the *Cahiers* with such astounding success.

I have here a copy of the first edition: I can admire that air of decent poverty which Péguy was able to give his *Cahiers*. The print is a bit crowded, very clear and black; the paper has a yellow tinge but is strong and lasting. 'Cheap and honest,' said Péguy. Beethoven's name is on the cover, on the fly-leaf a quotation from Dante, then comes the book itself. Such simplicity and severity were not omens of success. But success is a mystery. Without any advertising (and Rolland was still practically unknown), as though by magic, the copies of the life of Beethoven went off one after another. A whole world of unknown readers, men and women, countless faces without names, crowded into Péguy's little shop, to buy, pick up and carry off the small book of which the papers made no mention. How did they know of it? A second edition appeared and disappeared in the same way. At last Rolland had made himself heard and put his aspirations across; speaking through Beethoven, he had managed to put into words the secret principle of his own life and of so many other lives: suffering, love, courage. Bitterness at bay, hope crowned.

We may add that this biography was the first of a countless series of similar books published in France during the last forty years: so it has a place in the history of our literature.

What was the value of this success? Was it just a wave of general emotion called into being by one man's emotion conceived in solitude? Or pure sentimentality? A strange woman once came into the shop, bought her Beethoven, and went straight out with it under her arm; and Benda observed drily: 'These creatures who buy Rolland are women who haven't the courage to take a lover.'

A smile passed over Péguy's face. Benda's hard wit amused him, and he did not much like either Rolland's pathos or his success.

•

One of the rather attractive doubts this little book aroused was whether one was listening to Beethoven or Rolland. The question was, what Rolland would say unsupported. He wanted it to be known, and brought Péguy the manuscript of a short novel called *Jean-Christophe*. 'That is all right,' said Péguy, 'I will publish it.' Romain Rolland explained there would be a sequel. 'I will publish the sequel,' said Péguy. Romain Rolland added that there would be a third, and a fourth volume. In fact, he did not really know how many parts there might not be. Any other publisher but Péguy would have shown his author the door. He merely said: 'That is all right. I will publish it all.' So, from the coming together of two daring souls, sprang the first of the novels in serial form, *romans-fleuves*. Others, later on, were to make a lucrative business of it.

In a small German town, a child was born. He was Jean-Christophe. He was born alive. But what is life? Pain suddenly seized and held the tiny body. The child cried out, and so it all began. Each man is judged first of all by the lustiness of his first cry.

The child grew, crawled across the room, dabbled with the wide world; Rolland followed this child's every movement, and as he grew, so the book grew too, just as simply and touchingly. On and on it went, with nothing to stop it; like a stream, shrunk in winter, flowing freely in spring. What would it lead to, a glorious high moment of open sea, or the slow meanderings and shallows of a delta? There was a sense of unknown distance, quite different from the curiosity aroused by an ordinary plot, which had its charm. There were diverse opinions as to the quality of the work. The style itself was worthless with its dim vocabulary and weak syntax, so flabby and non-existent. How much had Rolland intended this? The Russians say that Tolstoï's telling of a tale is admirable but he has no sense of style. Rolland may be a similar case. Behind it all was his sensitiveness, which was his substitute for genius. If the emotion slackened and he tried to set down his ideas, there was a general collapse. But as the tide of his emotion rose he kept steadily at a fairly high level, the work became operative, and few could resist his spell. All this belongs to the past. The day for such books is soon over, they are the fashions of the heart.

Jean-Christophe was written negligently and put together negligently. No one quite knew why the episodes turned up as they did, yet they were linked by life's secret logic and hidden commands. Rosa was a plain, dull, good-natured girl, clumsy too; she seemed to be true to life. And what reader of *Jean-Christophe* ever doubted the reality of Sabine? She must have lived and died just as Rolland said. I know that no one knows these names now, they are only tenuous memories to me. I wonder if a reader with an independent mind would find, on glancing at this old story, that Rosa and Sabine are as we knew them; or would the printed page only show him traces of a smudged charcoal drawing.

One episode in this *Jean-Christophe* throws light on Rolland's conception of his art and art in general. Jean-Christophe was a child musician, and from the age of eight or ten, as inspiration moved him or as he had been taught, he composed minuets, songs, sonatas and jigs. The grandfather, an old musician, was filled with admiration at everything the child wrote. But the child liked, and perhaps even preferred, another judge of his work, an uninitiated and severe one, who was his Uncle Gottfried. He knew nothing about music. He was a poor relation in a family with no rich ones, a countryman who dropped in sometimes when he came to town. Young Jean-Christophe played him his tunes and at the end Gottfried usually remarked: 'What did you write that for?' 'But it's a minuet,' said the child; 'a minuet is a dance, and grandfather . . .' 'Why so many notes?' Gottfried went on, obstinately; 'what did you write it for?' There's no point in writing notes and notes like that; you don't need so many notes to make a song. . . .'

Now no one ever asked Rolland why he wrote so many words and so many pages: the book might be boring, it was never artificial.

Jean-Christophe became a professional musician. So Rolland wrapped his readers in that equivocal, dangerous musical atmosphere in which nineteenth century romanticism found such delight. He became a great musician, of course: one always has to take the author's word for that. An insubmissive German, he quarrelled with his family and professional friends and created a scandal in the small princely court of his native town. So he had to go. He came to France, which had always attracted him. Beethoven's Germany had been Rolland's spiritual harbour during his time of crisis; Jean-Christophe's was to be France. Rolland brought him to Paris and stayed there with him.

He was wounded in feeling, and his first act was an act of revenge. The Paris critics had set his nerves on edge; his hero was made to meet them. Jean-Christophe, the penniless musician, was introduced to life in Paris through the doors of editor's offices and hack work for the theatres. He came to know the men who had hurt Rolland's feelings and passed verdict on them accordingly, with their despicable ways of life and paltry ideas. And he met the Parisian artists and listened to them attentively. He admired their good taste and exquisite technique, and wondered at their lack of life. They were mannered, fidgety, finicky sectarians. If only that simple soul Gottfried had been there, how he would have asked them all: 'Why did you write that?' Listen to Jean-Christophe (or Rolland: it is the same thing):

What they chiefly lacked was will-power; they had every gift except one: powerful life itself. And there seemed in the main to be an immense misuse and squandering of effort. Rarely were these artists sufficiently aware of their true nature to co-ordinate their efforts faithfully towards a given end. It was the usual outcome of French anarchy, which spends its enormous resources of talent and good will on self-annihilation through incertitude and contradiction. It was almost inconceivable that any of their great musicians, Berlioz, or Saint-Saëns, for instance, not to say more recent names, would not become bogged and bent on self-destruction and treason for lack of energy and faith, and chiefly for lack of a sense of purpose.

The craft remained, an honoured, cultured one; but what is a craft with no soul, merely the cloak of death. 'The more progress he made,' said Rolland, 'the more precisely was he struck by a certain taint in the atmosphere of which he had been half-conscious from the beginning, increasingly clinging and suffocating: it was the taint of death. Death: it was pervasive, under all the display and clamour.' Death, what death? Rolland stated it in black and white: *Christophe heard the rumbling of the big guns grow nearer that were going to crush this outworn civilisation, this little dying Greece. . . .'*

Rolland's mind constantly returned to this tragic thought. He drove it home with episodes and sensations taken on the quick:

One fine evening, when the sky hung over the dim city like an eastern carpet in light, rather faded colours, Christophe wandered along the embankment, from Notre-Dame to the Invalides. The towers of the cathedral rose through the falling night like the arms of Moses raised during battle. The golden, chiselled spike of the Sainte-Chapelle, that holy, beflowered spire, sprang skyward from the thicket of houses. Across the water, the Louvre displayed its royal façade, and the reflection of the sinking sun put a last glow of life in its tired eyes. Beyond the plain of the Invalides, over its moats and proud walls, the deep-golden dome soared above the august sweep of ground like a concert of distant victories. And up the hill straddled the Arc de Triomphe with the huge stride of the imperial legions, like an heroic march.

And suddenly Christophe felt that it was indeed a dead giant whose immense limbs sprawled over the plain. Fear clutched his heart and he stopped, contemplating the gigantic, fossilised remains of a fabulous species whose steps had once made the earth resound: with the dome of the Invalides for helmet, the Louvre for girdle, stretching to the sky the thousand arms of its cathedrals, with the two triumphant feet of the Napoleonic Arch buttressed over the world, and to-day's Lilliput seething under its heel.

•

Jean-Christophe lived in a state of wonder. He went about this busy, bustling town with a watchful eye. He pictured the country that lay beyond it with its thousands of families, forty million souls. He knew the artists of Paris; but did he know the French people? In a flash, he saw clearly: '*This art is a people-less art.*' And one night he said to Sylvain Kohn who was piloting him through the streets of Paris:

'This cannot be all, there is something more.'

'What more do you want?' asked Kohn.

Christophe stuck to his point.

'*La France.*'

'France is us,' said Kohn, with a burst of laughter.

Christophe gazed at him a moment, shook his head, and said again: 'There is something more.'

'Well, old chap, you had better hunt it out,' said Kohn, more and more amused.

Christophe could hunt to his heart's content, they had hidden it most thoroughly.

This is the way a Sylvain Kohn might speak: he was a Jew fresh from Germany. Rolland did not care for this type of person, and he showed it. That improvised ballad of his called *Jean-Christophe* is a gathering-place for all sorts of feelings: germanophilia and germanophobia (very little of it); gallophobia, gallophilia, and anti-semitism. And now a new France appeared in this work and a new conception of France. Jean-Christophe (and we must always remember that this German is Rolland himself) became involved in the struggle into which so many Frenchmen have thrown themselves: a struggle and escape towards the people of France, turning to their healthy popular ways of life and their sturdy manner of speech. Molière and Boileau lead the same struggle against the *marquis* and the *précieuses*; Diderot lead it against artificiality; Balzac against the critics; Zola and Brunetière against the parnassians and the decadents. Rolland leads his against the coteries of æsthetes and theory-mongers and against the fashionable press.

At last Christophe succeeded in his search. It is one of the finest things in Rolland's work: this evocation of the unknown people, the old, valiant, courteous, honourable nation, of which one example after another stepped forward for Jean-Christophe's enlightenment, revealing those truly French features which he had felt must exist. So we meet Sidonie the Bretonne, Antoinette, Olivier . . . Rolland's accounts of them deserve reading and re-reading. When he described Germany, he saw it through books; when he described Paris, he saw it through mishaps; but when he spoke of Sidonie, Antoinette, and Olivier, Rolland was a child of Clamecy remembering his boyhood. What grateful pages these are.

A young student, Olivier, introduced Jean-Christophe to hidden France. They had become friends, and Rolland found in them the symbol and realisation of his hope: the collaboration of the French and German spirit. This friendship and collaboration he did achieve through his own culture and friendships, and the hope was one he never lost. The very choice of names was no doubt symbolical: Jean-Christophe stood for Christian inspiration; Olivier, for the Latin inspiration of peace.

It is a great misfortune that Rolland, for all his powers of conception, work and production, and with his eager, ardent public (the *Cahiers* group created by Péguy), produced nothing but dreams, pursuing them in defiance of the times he lived in One day he tired of dreams and the urge came to settle down, somewhere right in his own times, and the result was that well-known plunge into Moscow waters. Olivier was a charming creature, but exceptional as a Frenchman: hence that rapid friendship with the exceptional German Jean-Christophe. Olivier was an almost disincarnate Frenchman with aspirations Germany-wards. Together they were but a couple of restless souls, the living shadows of their author. They were not capable of founding a new Europe.

Time will show how their destiny was to work itself out.

VIII

TOWARDS BELIEF

A DECISION WAS provoked by outside events. In July 1905, something occurred which changed everything. Since the *Affaire Dreyfus*, people in France hardly realised the existence of an outside world and a dangerous Europe. All the distances appeared blocked by the pacifist dream trailing behind the Dreyfus business like a heavy mist, and effective only in its proscriptions and denunciations. The storm broke suddenly, dispersing the mist. Is it so long ago that the facts need recalling? The Emperor William landed at Tangiers and declared that the Moroccan question was not to be settled without reference to him; the minister Delcassé had presumed to do so, and Berlin insisted first of all on his dismissal; if he were not dismissed, the Metz garrison would march into France.

Nothing was ready, the arsenals were practically empty, the war tradition was dead among the masses of the people. So Delcassé was made scapegoat. This sacrifice availed nothing, however, for all Europe was afoot in a few hours, and the twentieth century, in its fifth year, was looking as Nietzsche had described it to an inattentive world twenty years earlier: 'The twentieth century,' he said, 'will be the classic century of war.'

The event acted on Péguy as a liberating force. Long ago he had shed the ideologies which conceal the true destiny of nations and put false hopes in the place of courageous resolutions; and with clear vision he had for a long time been pondering over the tragic vicissitudes of nature, scorched by summer, racked by autumn, crushed by winter, to be born again in spring. The threat of danger was neither a surprise nor a source of depression to his sensitive soul.

In a few days (just long enough to write it down) he put together a small book, very lovely in its simplicity, and yet so mysterious: *Notre Patrie*. It was not a dissertation on foreign affairs nor a commentary. Delcassé was not mentioned at all, Germany only here and there, all that being merely the stage for an event that took place in men's inner consciousness. Péguy described the plain working week of a busy man in Paris, not the one following the Kaiser's threat but the one preceding it. The King of Spain had paid a visit to Paris; he had come right up to the Latin Quarter, with his fine cuirassiers trotting alongside; the town had decked itself out, smiling and sunny, to greet the young king: 'We don't have the King of Spain here every day.'

But after the party came trouble:

How in the space of a morning everyone knew that France was within an ace of a German invasion, that is what I want to put on record first of all.

We had come along with something totally different on our mind; there is so much to do at the beginning of a week, especially after a slight break; life is so laden; we are not of those great geniuses who have always got one eye on the czar and the other on the mikado; the destinies of empires are of enormous interest to us, but we are bound to earn our poor living. We work from morning till night; our days are much more than eight-hour days; like all honest folk and plain citizens, we have a lot of private cares; one cannot always be thinking of babylonian revolutions, one has honestly to live one's daily life; it is drab, and woven of coarse common thread.

If a man has no wish to be better than his fellows, his life is much like sackcloth.

So everyone, on this count, everyone at once, knew that the threat of a German invasion was present, was there, was really imminent.

It was not a piece of news that went from mouth to mouth, passed on laterally, like ordinary news; what people passed on to one another when they met was not the news, but the confirmation, each for each, of news come from within. The knowledge of this truth did spread from one to the other; but it spread like a contagion of inner life, inner knowing, recognition, and almost platonic reminiscence and certitude before the event, not like ordinary verbal communication; in truth it was within ourselves that each one of us found, and received, and rediscovered the total, immediate, expectant, ominous, motionless, whole knowledge of the threat that was upon us.

The spread and expansion of this knowledge, gaining from man to man, was not the dissemination in dusty discontinuous particles of ordinary news by verbal communication; but rather common inner recognition, deep ominous knowledge, and a single sound of wide-reaching resonance; as though a spring gave way with a ring, from that moment every man could hear within himself, listening to something he was rediscovering, seeming known and familiar, that deep resonance, that voice that was no outward voice, that voice of memory buried and as though heaped up there, no one knew why nor for how long.

That is all. Péguy stopped at the discovery of a voice of memory beginning to stir. 'People who lived through those days and understood the meaning of them,' he says later, 'know what a revolution is: a transfiguration of the world and of man's instincts.'

Péguy had far to go along this track. The others did not all set out on it at once as he did. If we consider the small society formed by the *Cahiers*, with its contributors and subscribers closely gathered round Péguy, we witness the surprise and dismay which Rolland depicted so well: we must never overlook the fact that for the subscribers he was the great man of the *Cahiers*. Péguy was just the peculiar editor.

In writing his *Jean-Christophe*, Rolland had first intended to symbolise the future of Europe by the whimsical romantic friendship of a Frenchman and a German. Running full tilt into the 1905 events, he stopped short, held up his tale, and set to work on a study of solitary genius; he wrote a life of Michael Angelo growing old, a scarred and disappointed man in furious revolt against his times.

After that he came back to his major work and tackled the problem of how the Frenchman Olivier and the German Jean-Christophe would react. Bound as they were to one another as well as to their countries now enemies, they could not help suffering. As Europeans nourished at the same sources, they would not consent to separation.

Could their friendship be saved? Rolland intended that it should. They did attempt to save it but it was a miserable failure. So here were these two heroes, the Frenchman and the German, witnesses of wound-inflicting days. They might become revolutionaries or nationalists; they went from one extreme to another, tempted by all in turn. But they could not make up their minds. The reader grows weary of these lengthy pages with neither aim nor object, and finds this lamenting pair, isolated among their kind through incapacity to adhere or to create, very boring.

The whole thing drops to pieces around Jean-Christophe. This escaped German was only tolerated in France; Olivier got himself killed in a brawl in which he became involved only because his nerves were on edge. A death due to impulsiveness. Jean-Christophe left France and went to live in Switzerland and Italy. Romain Rolland assures us that his hero never lacked lovers and that his genius never failed him. We must take his word for it.

On the first page of his last volume, he states:

> I have written the tragedy of a disappearing generation. I have not tried to dissimulate its vices or virtues in any degree whatever, nor its oppressive sadness, chaotic pride, heroic efforts and distress under the crushing burden of a superhuman task; a real *Summa* of the world, with a new attitude to life and to art, a new faith, a new humanity to be found: such were we.
>
> Men of to-day, young men, trample us under foot and go forward: be greater, and happier, than we were.

What does this confession and exhortation mean? Was Rolland giving his assent to anything that might come, anything young, brave and sincere, whether success was to lie with the monarchists or the trade-unionists? Had he shut his eyes to utter a fervent *amen* to whatever destiny might produce? And what about this muddle-headed *Summa*? It is the mediæval Latin word for the entire intellectual heritage of mankind. It would appear that Rolland considered that this heritage no longer existed, having been laid waste; he said so: 'A new humanity to be found: such were we.' So he gave us a humanity all to pieces, living only on aspirations. A *Summa* was announced and all that was produced was the balance-sheet of a bankrupt.

All through this lengthy confession ran that pathos peculiar to Rolland, which many of his readers found so moving. They read him believing they were listening to an authentic great solitary and a real explorer in the field of feeling. They were mistaken and there was quite a different reason for their enthusiasm. True inventiveness is wearisome and graceless to most people. They were attracted to Rolland because of his lack of it. In the order of celestial bodies he was of the lunar kind, reflecting the after-glow of the much-loved, still near nineteenth century. He awoke memories and echoes of Michelet, Ruskin, Tolstoï, striking chords of sincerely moving quality. He stirred the ashes of a tired hearth and made one last flame to flicker. The acclamation that greeted the work was as short-lived as the flame. Thus Rolland took on the likeness of a worthy captain, beaten but not cowed, covering by his faithful work the retreat of the grand old days.

For a 1940 reader, there is nothing in all these volumes of an old story but paltry eloquence with undertones suggesting escape and failure. Rolland's intention was to preserve what was good. But that will not do. The need, in all circumstances, is for increase. But this was beyond Rolland's scope. The man of increase was Péguy, who was so little understood and so badly understood by those of us who were nearest to him. Our merit, and no negligible one either, was that we were all the time passionately interested in the enigmatic process that was working itself out, the spade-work going on under our eyes for some unknown harvest.

•

Henceforth, Péguy was no longer the man of negation who had some months earlier distressed and baffled me. By writing those two words, that simple title, Péguy was once more in possession of a wide stretch of country from which his stunted civism had excluded him. As a revolutionary, he wanted the people to be great, with honour available for all, and that remained his desire. But how were the humble to be great and honoured if the ground under their feet was subject to outsiders? People and homeland are one and inseparable, whatever the expounders of the proletarian revolution may say.

Based on the honour of the home, Péguy's patriotism was no threat either to honour or to hearth. It was militant love of a land, a source, a flame, and all that supports and feeds and gives growth. The function of the homeland is not to complete a man, as Péguy knew, but to shape and shelter him for a higher destiny.

We may be sure that the voice of buried memory so newly awoken spoke of this destiny. *Notre Patrie,* our homeland, as now revealed, was the emergence of a universe with deeply hidden roots. He turned and took a few steps on it, knowing what there was under the ground that bore his weight. The harvest was not yet ripe, nor was the soul master of its convictions, but certain thoughts were all ready. The proof is in a couple of lines that occur in this little book, and we should pay attention to them.

It is the soldier who measures the amount of temporal earth, which is *the same* as the spiritual earth and the intellectual earth.

So much said, in so few words. Too much, in fact. The reader cannot understand, he cannot penetrate the density of the language. Péguy was referring to a world of thought, the space of which is filled with the three mysteries and *Eve.* A development now would be premature.

André Bourgeois remembers a brief exchange of remarks which confirms what we have just said. Towards the end of 1905, sitting cheek by jowl with Péguy, correcting the proofs of *Notre Patrie,* he came across a clumsy sentence: 'May the event decide that if ever battle be waged in the forest of Soigne again, it may be an inverted Waterloo.' 'That sentence of yours isn't good French,' he said. 'Not French?' said Péguy, indignantly. 'No. *May the event decide* doesn't mean anything; an event hasn't got a will, an event can't *decide* things.' 'In a couple of years,' Péguy answered, 'I shall write: *May God decide.* . . . Not now. They would not understand.' *They* being the subscribers.

A couple of years was rather short counting on Péguy's part. It was not till 1909 that he published the *Mystère de la Charité de Jeanne d'Arc* and printed the word in black and white. Four years later.

Four years about which we know very little. All the ripening took place in silence. The same curtain that Péguy let fall in January 1900, will rise only at the end of nine years of meditation. All the visible signs were external ones. From the beginning of 1900, his ardent desire to be free, utterly free, was manifest. The *Cahiers* were a burden which he longed to be rid of. He was hampered right and left, and the thousand-strong army of subscribers were a heavy load to drag along. Yet he could not live without them. They wasted a lot of his time, too: out of every three days, he calculated that he only had one for his own work. If war had broken out in July, and he had fallen then, what should we have been left with? One youthful dramatic exercise, the *Jeanne d'Arc* of which he alone knew the worth because he alone could read into the blank pages. Apart from that, a few essays, corner-stones for future building. If Péguy had been killed in 1905, he would have remained, for future curiosity as for his friends, an enigma. A gift for words, fiery ardour, but sterile, would have been the common verdict. One of the curiosities of literature.

Péguy, in his eagerness to be free, was chasing and nursing a variety of dreams. At times he thought of being a teacher in a small school, with a small number of boys, a small salary, but comparative freedom. This was pure phantasy for a man of his kind. His old fellow-student Lebeau said, 'After three weeks of it, Péguy would strangle the inspector.' At other times, he turned over in his mind the idea of a University Chair, and actually delivered to the Sorbonne the title of a thesis: '*De la situation faite à l'histoire dans la philosophie générale du XIXe Siècle.*' This too was phantasy. It is not at all sure that the Sorbonne professors would have discovered in Péguy's writing the technical qualities they are accustomed to require. He would have done it all against the grain. And moreover it is inconceivable that they would have consented to place on the register of Doctors eligible for University teaching posts the name of this unfriendly controversialist who had not even passed his Agrégation examination. At the root of these insistent day-dreams was the desire to be rid of the *Cahiers*. Péguy made contact with the Plon publishing house, and negotiations were set on foot and might well have come to something, but an undertaking like the *Cahiers* is tied up in half a hundred different ways; there was, for instance, Péguy's gratitude and affection for his manager, André Bourgeois, his employee in fact, to whom he was bound by a mutual trust of a very rare quality. Bourgeois had given up everything for the sake of the *Cahiers*. If the house of Plon were to take them over, what would happen to him? That was a problem Péguy could not solve, and Bourgeois was not unaware of Péguy's unspoken scruples on this point. Some little time later, in 1910, a rue de Grenelle civil servant attached to the Steeg ministry came to Bourgeois with a proposition: 'The *Cahiers* are going to fall off; come back to the University, we will smooth things over for you.' For Péguy, Bourgeois' departure would have been a disaster. Bourgeois answered: 'No, I cannot leave Péguy like that.' Péguy never heard of the suggestion, which he would, perhaps rightly, have considered a case of enticement. Politics use crooked paths. Péguy gave up the Plon idea and started on a scheme for reforming the *Cahiers*: he wanted to make a limited joint-stock company of them; the stock holders were to appoint an administrative council. We all received a circular letter as well as personal letters asking us to subscribe. The only part of this scheme that materialised was a crop of subscriptions.

I alone was concerned in Péguy's final attempt. In spring, 1908, he asked me to take over the direction of the *Cahiers*. I was a long way away when his letter reached me, in Tuscany, where I was putting the finishing touches to my *Vie de Nietzsche*. Péguy was asking me to change the whole course of my life. And what bristling difficulties would lie ahead! It was no simple matter to be Péguy's successor; the whole thing might turn out to be quite impossible, and there was always the fear that quite soon after persuading me to take over the *Cahiers*, he would start accusing me of robbing him. So I declined. I am not sure how much I was aware of the significance of what was going on, though the work which engrossed me at the time had its bearing on it, for there is a connection between Péguy's and Nietzsche's solitude. But one seldom gets an impression of greatness from anything very near to one. My refusal tossed back on to the high seas the adventurous bark that had come so near me for a moment, and which was to bear Péguy along the path of his destiny to the very last.[1]

This feeling round for new openings was the result of strained circumstances of which very few of us appreciated the gravity. There were money difficulties, which complicated his home-life and affected his temper. His mother-in-law and brother-in-law, an unemployed engineer who had given his modest all, as his sister had done, to the *Cahiers*, lived in the same house and he had to keep them. These few words tell a long story. For Péguy, money was an increasingly harsh master and foe. At the same time, on a different plane, conditions of work were increasingly difficult too. Péguy had no peace of mind when he most needed it. Here, we are on the fringe of that inner region on which he himself throws no light. We must nonetheless explore it. At this stage, Péguy was a Christian again in thought and feeling, but not through the clear operation of an act of faith. The act will come later, with tears and by grace, and Péguy will be overcome by belief. But not until two long years have gone by. A

[1] Here is the letter: 'In one year's time, accidents apart, I shall have taken my doctorate, meaning that I shall be eligible for a lectureship and an appointment shortly after in the honoured solitude of a provincial University Faculty, with 4,500 francs to start with; it will be a great temptation to escape from prison, and some very close friends are urging me to turn professor and start writing again.

'If I were to follow their advice, you, Halévy, would be the successor I should most welcome. If you were in Paris I should not tell you yet. But you are far away. You can write to others about other plans which we could discuss and which can't be written. I don't want to remain in the dark about you through over-discretion on my part.

'What I would be offering you is, as you know, from the moral point of view, the highest situation and position in Paris, as well as an admirable instrument of fifteen years' good testing.

'Of course, no word of this to anyone. Put it away in your heart till we meet again. I shall not have the viva for my thesis before the beginning of the next academic year.

'At the end of the tenth series the Cahiers show a profit of three hundred francs a month. For me it is perpetual drudgery. For a man like you, it would be a magnificent chance to have a perfectly free hand.'

great many people go on living in this half-and-half state, but for Péguy it was impossible. He loathed any sort of symbolism or mythologism. He was getting ready to go back over his juvenile *Jeanne d'Arc* and to fill in the blank pages of his first work after a lapse of ten years. His inspiration would have been paralysed if what was supernatural for *Jeanne* were not equally so for him.

In my own experience, I find a memory of a visit I paid to Orsay in 1907 or 1908. Madame Péguy and her mother, Madame Beaudouin, were having a wash-day in the open air; Péguy was playing with his children, and everyone was chattering about Saint Catherine. Just as though she had only gone out ten minutes ago, and might be back any moment, and be seen on the road or in the garden. I myself find this rather surprising, when I remember what rifts occurred in this home when the religious problem emerged. But there it is, a clear picture because of the surprise it gave me, for after all it was Péguy I had come to see, and not Saint Catherine.

When it was time to leave, Péguy came with me as far as the heights of Saclay between the two valleys of the Yvette and the Bièvre, in which we had our respective homes. 'For us,' he said, as we walked along, 'the *Imitation* is a holy book, in the same way as the Gospels.' The two first words, *for us*, struck me at the time, they contained a profession of faith of which this was my first intimation. The idea struck me too, it appeared to be related to the modernist movement which was then in its hey-day, and proving very attractive to the young of the rue de Vaugirard and to many of their betters too. It was but a passing remark, however, and the friendly terms with Saint Catherine may have been part of a lively game. In any case the *Imitation* never was one of Péguy's mainstays, it was too monastic in style to suit him.

We parted half-way home, on the crest of the hill-top. Soon after he left me, I turned round and watched his black figure walking away with a firm tread, seeming so small already in this wide stretch of open land where he so often went walking. What intimacy there was between him and it, what thoughts and scenes and lovely, inspired pages. More than once, in reading a book of Péguy's, I have seen the lie of the land at Saclay in my mind's eye; or walking there, I have done so with thoughts or verses of his running through my head. There is a gentle roll of hill half a league long: Péguy would imagine a division of cavalry hidden by the fold in the ground. Between the Orsay slopes and the village of Saclay, there is a strip of lane with trees along it, running cross-country to the sturdy square copse like a rampart, around the buildings and outhouses of *La Martinière* estate. This rural setting of the Ile de France found a place in the *Mystère des Saints-Innocents*.

. . . The Old Testament is that fine, slender,
Uniquely faithful avenue of poplars,
All by itself in the flat open country,
But the New Testament is the well-made park round the house:
And the belt of oak-trees, sturdy and straight,
Snug behind the foursquare lofty walls.
And all the ground in use.

As for the spot called *Christ de Saclay*, a crossroads in the middle of the plain, the site of a lost Crucifix, the less said the better. Now there is a modern set-up of signboards with red arrows on a white ground which has destroyed all trace of its original character. It was the arresting image of this site left empty that Péguy was always so eager to point out.[1]

•

The Péguy of the mysteries and hymns must ripen undisturbed. We know that meditation is to turn into song and prayer. If we cannot detect how it happened, we need not be surprised. The first of the mysteries of belief is, for every believer, his own belief. There is a region beyond the thought that can be told, as there is one beyond the measured scales of sound or light. It is here that we lose sight of Péguy.

Not entirely, though: beside that solitary Péguy walking at Saclay, there is the rue de Sorbonne Péguy, the writer and controversialist. We see side by side the believer on the road and the busy publisher-editor poring over his books and his post, the mettlesome manipulator of battle-words.

One particular case stands out clearly to show us the complex activity of this two-fold life, when the inspiration of the solitary once took control of the hammer-and-tongs of the controversialist, imposing first a halt and then a guiding hand. This is what happened: immediately *Notre Patrie* had appeared, Péguy gave his mind to the publication of a poem by Porché on that terrible day, January 22 1905, when the first blood of the first Russian revolution was shed. Led by the monk Gapone, the workers of St. Petersburg had delivered a supplication to the Czar in his palace. The Imperial Guard had received them with salvos of fire and mown them down at the palace railings. There were a thousand dead, two thousand wounded on the spot. The double character of the event, religious and revolutionary, priestly and popular, had struck the imagination of a Europe grown unused to ritual and grown unused to bloodshed. It caused a considerable stir. Paris had not forgotten it eight months later. Porché's poem was very short, and to make a whole *Cahier* Péguy had to fill it out with a preface. His first aim was a critical

[1] Here the author quotes a long poem by Charles-Lucas de Peslouän called *La Route de Saclay*, addressed to Charles Péguy, which is omitted in the English translation. (*Tr.*)

analysis of revolutionary ideology, and with this went a lively and direct attack on Jaurès (the first, others were to follow), who was in Péguy's eyes more and more clearly the incarnation of the false prophet, the accomplice of the weaknesses of the people he misled. It is a good essay, that is all. The writer-publisher had done a good piece of work and nothing more.

But the Slav episode merited something else. Péguy evidently realised it, for he laid aside the pages he had just written and wrote a second preface in quite a different vein. Such a change of mind, so exceptional in this career where nothing is left to chance, needs some explanation. It can be found in the fact that Porché himself changed the title of his poem, which had been called *L'Icône* and was then named *Les Suppliants*.

One word changed everything: instead of a material image with Slav local colour, Porché evoked a whole attitude to life, religious and moral. *Suppliants* is an age-old word with an undertone of echo from ancient tragedy.

Péguy may have suggested it himself, I do not know about this and it may be so. Vision took on new depth, inspiration soared higher. Anyhow, the controversialist of the rue de la Sorbonne no longer had his shop to himself: the solitary of the Saclay plain was sharing the work, and wrote out in his clear hand the text of the workers' supplication which the monk had carried to the Czar:

Sire! We, the workers of the city of St. Petersburg, our wives and children, our old invalid parents, come to you, Sire, for justice and protection. Terrible distress has befallen us: we are oppressed, weighed down with work, insulted; we are not recognised as men, we are treated like slaves who have to bear their sad, bitter lot patiently and without complaining!

That is how it opens. Let us go on to the closing lines:

These, Sire, are our chief requirements which we have come to lay before you. Command, on oath, that they be executed, and you will have made Russia happy and glorious and your name will remain engraved for ever in the hearts of our grandsons and of your great-grandsons. But if you will not, if you make no reply to our distress, we shall die on this very spot, in front of your palace.

There is nowhere for us to go, nor any reason for going.

There are only two ways open to us: one leading to freedom and happiness, the other to death. Tell us, Sire, which we are to follow: we will go without a murmur, even along the road to death. Our life shall be a sacrifice to Russia in her death-throes. We shall make it willingly and without looking back.

Was this text to be a prelude to a discussion of French ideologies and invectives hurled at Jaurès? It was not a good idea. The first preface fell very short of the mark. In the one Péguy then sat down to write, the name of Jaurès (with Lucien Herr's) occurred only once, in a sentence which stated that it was a name not to be written, and that both names, and both men, should be ignored. The supplication of the Russian workers had awoken a grand memory of the distant day—twelve years ago—when as a student at Sainte-Barbe he had seen Sophocles' *Œdipus Rex* at the Théâtre Français. When the curtain rises, the people of Thebes fill the stage, and bowed down at their Prince's feet they make their long complaint. Their suffering and lamentation is like that of the workers of St. Petersburg:

> O Œdipus, master of my country, here you see us whatever our age may be, bending low at your altars; some are not yet strong enough for long flights, others are heavy with old age, and here am I, priest of Zeus, and here are these, chosen among the young men; and the rest of the people, wearing crowns, are sitting in the squares and at the double temple of Pallas and on the prophetic ash of the Ismeus. . . .

There is no pause to underline a point; the humble, strong supplication goes on and on. 'It is the poet's function,' says Péguy, 'to seize in a word, to gather in a word, the whole reality of an event, the essential reality of a tale, in a single movement, an individual or collective gesture.' Porché, in his new title, *Les Suppliants*, had found that word.

For Péguy, it opened up horizons of thought which amazed him. Nowadays, a suppliant, a man pleading, is taken to be in a humiliating position. In the ancient world, there was no such feeling. If misfortune has turned a man into a suppliant, that man is great, according to the ancients, and to be feared and respected by the powers themselves. The suppliant is a man who is bent, *bowed under*. But not under another man: under misfortune, that absolute misfortune which marks the presence of the gods. They it is who sent him his suffering to try him by travail. Coming from the gods, it is fruitful. When they have broken him and moulded him by their blows, by some cruel means the suppliant comes to life again as their own child, and when he speaks, it is in their name. Hence the deference due to him and the religious attention which the powerful are bound to accord him. To all appearances the man who receives the supplication is above the suppliant. In reality, invisibly, the reverse is true: the suppliant is above him to whom supplication is made.

> We need to read one of those admirable ancient supplications very closely, the one of the entire people at the feet of Œdipus, or the even finer one, the finest of all, which is the supplication of old Priam at the feet of Achilles. Clearly, it is not he to whom supplication is made, but indeed the suppliant himself who commands the situation and in fact orders the course of the dialogue. In every ancient supplication . . . the man to whom supplication is made seems to be living in the lap of

fortune: he is a king; a tyrant; a chief; a conqueror in war; . . . one of the powerful of the earth; in peace time, he is a wealthy man, powerful and with prosperous herds; briefly, he is a fortunate man, a man who seems to be, and is, fortunate. And that is exactly why, when the meeting between him and the suppliant takes place, the occasion of the supplication, it is not he who orders the course of the conversation. He is a fortunate man, so, for the Greeks, he is to be pitied. In this dialogue, the man to whom supplication is made can speak only in the name of his good fortune, or at least in the name of general good fortune. It is not much. It is nothing. Less than nothing. In fact it is the opposite of an advantage. Good fortune. . . . It is the suppliant, whoever he may be, the beggar along the roads, the miserable blind man, the man proscribed, or crushed. . . . It is always the suppliant who, in reality, holds the upper hand, orders the course of the conversation, commands the situation.

All this, which is very much abridged, is only a first exposition of the situation. Péguy returns to it, underlining and engraving every point:

The man to whom supplication is made has a grand, exalted situation, humanly speaking. But it is never other than a quite miserable human situation. Whatever his situation may be, he never has anything but that situation. And that is all. It is nothing. Especially in comparison with other forms of greatness. And the comparison is imposed by the very operation of the supplication. What makes him weak, and small, is that he is only himself and his little bit of human situation. He doesn't represent.

The suppliant represents. He is no longer only himself. He is no longer himself. He no longer exists, himself. He is not concerned. And that is why the other man must look out. Stripped of everything by this same occurrence which brought about the dangerous good fortune of the man to whom supplication is made, a citizen with no city, a head with no sight, a child fatherless, a father childless, a belly with no bread, a back with no bed to lie on, a head without a roof, a man with no goods, he no longer exists as himself. And that is what makes him fearful. For what he represents.

Because he has been handled, kneaded, manipulated by the superhuman human fingers of the gods, he has suddenly become dear to the superhuman human heart of the gods. Because he was wax in the divine superdivine hands of fate, he has become mysteriously dear to the divine superdivine heart of fate. Because the powers on high laid a heavy hand on him, by a singular return—not at all a compensation—by a sort of filiation, rather, of exalted childbearing, of particular adoption, he became their protégé, their son. The gods, and over them, behind them, fate, took his father from him. But the gods became his father. The gods, and behind them fate, the gods took the city from him. But the gods in a manner conferred their own city on him. The gods, sub-orders of fate, took his gods from him. But these same gods gave him that good thing which no goods can replace, the gods gave him that first of all good things: to become the representative of the gods.

There is no question of compensation, nor even of justice: that would be a Christian idea, or at least a relatively recent one, in a certain sense a modern one; of course there is no hint of romantic antithesis. But the idea is much deeper, it is a much deeper and truer perception, as far as one can see one's way among these mysterious, deep, true perceptions; a perception of life, art and workmanship; that these men have given proof that they were malleable men to the statuary fingers of fate.

The gods, fate, have become his father and mother; he, the orphan, has become the son and representative of the gods under fate. Indeed it is true that for the ancients, for the Greeks, by a second generation, by a second childbirth, he has really become as a son of the gods. All that was needed was that he should be to their fingers plastic material, of proven plasticity. He became their son as the statue is born of the statuary. With the enriching, exalting added factor that the statuary is a god, more than a god, fate-guided.

So Péguy swung full-sail into religious meditation. Sophocles who, long ago, by the opening scene of *Antigone*, gave him the impulse he needed for his first *Jeanne d'Arc*, the inspiration of all the others, had now unveiled for him one of the secrets of prayer. Péguy was writing with no sense of constraint, for he was moving in the setting of the ancient world, and his flock of subscribers were tolerant of religious terms so long as they were free of Christian taint. So he had no fear they would grow restive. Supplication, he explained, is a prayer: the ancients gave it ritual form. The suppliant asks nothing, he has no voice, no strength. As the blind man shows his extinguished eyes, the cripple his stumps, the man with scurvy his sores, so the suppliant shows his destitution, and that is enough. Woe to the strong man who scorns him! He offends the gods and his punishment is at hand.

To bow silently, and then to wait, for hours, for days, such was the ritual of supplication, the ancient form of prayer. Others were to come, ripened in another light, lit by another hope, aspiring to a renewal of created being. Péguy knew them but refrained from mentioning them. 'We will not speak of creation, of second creation,' he wrote, 'for we must be careful to keep Christian terms and the Christian language in reserve.' What he was keeping in reserve was the realm of the mysteries he had in mind to write, and especially of the second one, which was to be about the second creation: it appeared six years later. More long-term thoughts.

Let us add that Péguy's Christian conversion never diminished his attachment to antiquity. He was advancing, but the ground he covered was sound and he always revered the sites among which his journey led him. What is holy cannot be effaced, there it stays at the spot where it first appeared. The 1905 declaration is no Good-bye to all that, far from it; it is a token of fidelity. On the other side of his conversion, at difficult times, Péguy without question turned to forms of prayer so utterly simplified by imminent despair that they strangely resemble the supplication of antiquity.

Only a title was needed now for the inspired pages Péguy had written, *Les Suppliants* was Porché's suggestion: Péguy liked the word, and with Plutarch's *Parallel Lives* for model, he wrote: *Les Suppliants Parallèles,* deliberately underlining the connection between the Slav crowd at St. Petersburg and the Hellenic crowd at Thebes, one stroke tracing a short-cut through the ages.

•

The fine pages of the *Suppliants* were written without premeditation. When Péguy started writing his preface to Porché's poem, it was a tussle he had in mind. The delay was no loss to his opponents: they had their fight and a battle royal it was.

The way Péguy attacked and set about him is one more proof of his will to increase the scope of his work in all directions. The day of private quarrels and prefaces was over. In the space of two years there were to be three essays, or rather one essay in three parts: *On the position ascribed to the intellectual party and to sociology in the modern world* (1906); *On the position ascribed to the intellectual party in the modern world* (1906); *On the position ascribed to the intellectual party in the modern world in relation to the accidents of temporal honours* (1907). Péguy loved long and dignified titles and enjoyed the game of setting them out on the page in three, or if need be, four lines. Their effect on the reader's patience was the last thing that occurred to him.

Nothing had changed at all, fundamentally. One man has one war to wage, and on a wider plane, where personalities disappeared, the 1900 struggle with the committee of the Five was still developing. In those days, a man of adventurous spirit eager to guard the free springs of thought had set himself up against a group of intellectual bureaucrats trying to impose their own doctrine. The same thing happened all over again. Only in different circumstances.

While, in defiance of the forecasts, the *Cahiers* continued to appear, the Five had had a run of bad luck. Their concern, never a prosperous one, finally gave out when an accountant appointed by Herr, who trusted him, went off with the takings. A sardonic letter from New York put an end to the hopes of the Five: cash and cashier had gone for good.

Such was the inglorious end of the *Société Socialiste de Librairie et d'Edition.* Herr and his friends had learnt wisdom: henceforth their work was done under cover of public administration, where private shipwrecks are unobserved among the permanent shipwreck of State finances in the throes of party politics. With no change of face, they proceeded directly to the conquest of the University itself.

At this time the University was liberal. There was a certain degree of inevitable officialdom, but no attempt to regiment the young. There were University teachers of considerable standing, such as the philosopher Bergson, the jurist Hauriou. In the ordinary course of events, Hauriou would have been called from Toulouse to Paris, and Bergson been appointed to the Sorbonne and placed in close contact with the students. But this was ruled out: they were not of the party. Herr and his friends determined to instal militants of their own, to create high offices for them, and to furnish them with a doctrine to propound. The word *socialist*, so proudly displayed by their society, was unsuitable this time. The more prudent word *sociological* was chosen. A keen enthusiast, with limited powers of thought but good organising ability, a man named Durkheim, had started using it ten years ago, and Herr and his friends had at first disapproved,[1] stating that neither the word, nor the theories, nor the man were likely to prove of use. They suddenly changed their minds and decided to make use of the word, the theories and the man.

It all turned out as they had intended: Bergson was appointed to the Collège de France, where University students do not go; a course in pedagogy was made compulsory for candidates for teaching degrees: Durkheim was appointed to the Chair. Durkheim compulsory for the lettered youth of the University of Paris: such was the effect of the decree. Durkheim professor of a branch of study of which he knew precisely nothing. With childlike ease he changed the meaning of the word: 'The object of a training in pedagogy is not to load the teacher-to-be with methods and recipes, but to make him fully conscious of his function.' His aim is the training of the workers of to-morrow, so the teacher-to-be must cease to consider the past, any of the past. 'It is the men of to-day that we must consider; it is of ourselves that we must become conscious; and in ourselves, it is the man of to-morrow that we must seek out and free.' Thus the new kind of pedagogy is a prophetic meditation on the future. Durkheim's lectures were an insolent display of the stranglehold of one group of doctrinaires on State education. Simultaneously with this

[1] 'I cannot consider anything built on that basis and with that material as scientific,' wrote Herr in the *Revue Universitaire*, December 1894, and Andler in the *Revue de Métaphysique et de Morale* (March 1896) pronounced that it was monstrous to attempt 'sociology without psychology and without history.' It is a pseudo-science, he concluded, which, far from resolving, cannot even state, its problems, and the only sane advice for any man engaged on work in such thick darkness is to beg him to desist. This is most judicious. Durkheim's sociology turned out to be a blind alley and a most unfortunate guide for the young students who were encouraged to follow it. Finally, Durkheim concentrated on the study of Australasian primitive peoples, Lévy Bruhl on the mentality of savages, Mauss on the practice of magic. Strange avatarism of a doctrine intended to enlighten the modern world. Durkheim, Lévy Bruhl and Mauss proved Andler's criticism to be correct by their inability to find material for work elsewhere than on the fringes of pre-history and the zones anterior to the evolution of psychology and history.

Chair of sociology, others were being established in all the Universities, and the up-to-date young men who had seen which way the wind was blowing, watched, as Bouglé put it so naively, ' soft carpets unfolding under their feet,' as though by magic.

Standing at the door of his shop in the rue de la Sorbonne, Péguy saw his old fellow-students go by, the successful, clever ones who had made sure of the soft carpets, on their way to the building across the road. They waved at him with kindness and condescension, poor *déclassé* that he was. Even the Ecole Normale has its failures, they thought to themselves; Péguy, poor chap, always bad at managing his life, was one of them. Péguy nodded in reply. Scarred inwardly by the vehemence of his thought, outwardly by money cares, he felt how much he hated these parvenu socialists, these one-time revolutionary dreyfusards living in perfect security, who by standing together and marrying the daughters of distinguished University families had established themselves, self-promoted to the grade of ' permanent civil-servant heroes,' as he put it.

His fury broke out in the three 1907-8 essays. Péguy wouldn't have France divided between dreyfusards and anti-dreyfusards, republicans and conservatives, free-thinkers and Catholics, any more. He would only recognise two parties in France, separated not, as Clémenceau said, by a barricade (where have our barricades gone?) but in mean and modern style, by a ticket-office. On one side, the tape-measures, papers and figures functioned; on the other, production and paying. Those were the two Frances. On either side of the ticket-office there were Catholics, free-thinkers and Jews. Péguy was on the side of the Catholics, free-thinkers and Jews who do the paying, and against the Catholics, free-thinkers and Jews who take the payments. On these, politicians, bureaucrats, young up-to-date University men who invent new sciences in order to provide themselves with Chairs, Péguy declared war, and pounded them with zest. For two thousand years, all of them, Roman financiers, monks, men of law, high and low, marquesses and farmers-general, excisemen, clubmen, jacobins, jesuits, free-masons, delegates, and financiers again, no longer Roman but tarred with the same brush, have lived snug like parasites of the people, vermin they are compelled to carry and feed; doing it bravely, hoping and singing, though always in drudgery. Péguy was against the whole race of parasites, whatever their colour. Though fleeced and fleeced again, the French flock will survive, of this Péguy was convinced. But it must put up its defence and be fought for. Péguy was all in favour of fighting. He turned rhapsodical pamphleteer, nourishing his rhapsody with all the resources of sarcasm, irony, historical analysis and metaphysical meditation at his command. It was an ocean of words, not tumultuous as it seemed at first sight but under masterly control; wave followed wave, the tide surged in, and invisible order ruled these pages, so terrifyingly dense to the eye. If there were moments when the high waves no longer rolled and unfurled with such vigour and the surge slowed down to steady billowing, it meant the wind had dropped, only to rouse the seething waves to renewed fury soon after. Such was Péguy's thought, with an additional element of irritation providing that corrosive, acid quality which puts an edge on the finest pamphlets. Let him speak for himself:

Bit by bit to undermine the quality of a profession by the biased selection of candidates, by family nepotism, by clan nepotism, by the most shameful favouritism of dynasty or party; covertly to eliminate, coldly and inexorably to relegate to the meaner posts, the poor posts, the graceless, despised ones—the only ones to be held with honour to-day—all who are socially weak, all who are poverty-stricken, all who are cultured, all who are free. To bring about a forthright or covert, but always thorough, invasion of politics into the teaching profession. To protest from time to time about this invasion, and thereby to pursue it only the more consistently. To give politicians, parliamentary politicians or university politicians, parliamentary politicians and at the same time university politicians, all the choice posts and places, the sought-after places and posts, consequently the posts and places with controlling powers and influence and authority to some extent. The calculated vilification of the syllabus. And by favouritism, the calculated vilification of the personnel. Moreover, and at the same time, to refuse credits however indispensable, though everywhere else they change hands all too easily. To discredit and starve. To diminish and weaken in every way. This is only a part of the treatment meted out inside the barracks, these are only a few of the activities displayed and exhibited there, this is only a part of the treatment which the State imposes on the University, and can impose on it with impunity since the ancient imperial University became the wife of the French State, and it is a united *ménage*, because the two parties who form this queer *ménage* are unhappily far from living in divorce of board and even less (if possible) of bed.

That is how Péguy fought keenly and bitterly for independence of life and creation, and (to repeat the words in which Péguy states so forcibly what he is and what he likes) for the salvation of *all who are poverty-stricken, all who are cultured, all who are free.*

Under the old governments, honour (*la gloire*) was an almost wholly spiritual power. Under the old governments, there were enough powers to counter-balance the money powers—strong powers, *other* strong powers, or spiritual powers—so that through all these powers, and even throughout their fights and struggles, in fact chiefly here, honour could remain an almost wholly spiritual power. By a curious combination, a curious interplay of events, at the advent of modern times a large number of strong powers, most of them in fact, fell away; but far from their downfall being any sort of service to the spiritual powers, by leaving the way clear, on the contrary the suppression of the other strong powers profited only that one strong power which is money. It served only to leave the place empty for the benefit of the money powers. The counter-poise of force, of the other forces, being suppressed, there was no gain to the spirit though this was supposed to be expected, none to the spiritual powers on whose behalf the revolution of the modern world was supposed to be taking place. Contrarily to all one might have hoped, when one was not well up in things . . . it all went to the only remaining strong powers, the money powers.

So there was a double landslide, to the money powers, and to the State which is itself a big business, the biggest of all and the most implicated in the deadlocks of matter. Péguy attacked it in these terms:

Vilification is of its deepest instinct. By vilifying whatever it comes across, it knows, deep down and with great assurance, that it is on the right road of its destiny.

. . . The modern world is a vilifying world. Other worlds had other things to do. . . . Other worlds were idealising or materialising, building or destroying, performing acts of justice or acts of force, other worlds made cities, communities, men or gods. The modern world vilifies. That is its distinguishing trait. I should say it was its *métier*, but for the respect due above all else to this lovely word. When the modern world sets about vilifying, let us put it that it is then busy at its own business.

So much for anger; Péguy had felt the weight of the oppressors' hand and rose against it. But there is far more in these three essays than a man seeking vengeance. Péguy showed up the true meaning of this new sociology, not a real sociology at all, he said, refusing to allow it any right to the name Auguste Comte had invented; not sociology but sociagogy: he would call it by no name but this. Durkheim and Herr were engaged without subterfuge in destroying in the young what was usually called general culture, or in other terms, the humanities. All the humanities, for there are several kinds: Ancient, Christian Renascent and Classical.

Péguy is one of the first, maybe the first[1] to have shown up the opposition between the modern world on the one hand and on the

[1] Here there is an historical problem which deserves to be cleared up. It is in M. Louis Weber's remarkable work on the rhythm of progress (*Le Rhythme du progrès*) that I found the first and complete analysis of the kinship of the ancient and christian ages. M. Louis Weber holds that the present technical revolution imposes on us the task of revising our historical classifications. In the past, we have pre-history with its technical genius, to which we owe the invention of tools. To-day we have a renaissance of techniques, a revival of tool-making. Between whiles there stretches a closely-knit period of thirty to forty centuries, one of the characteristics of which is stationary technical development. The development of thought has its successive moments, it is true: the ancient, the scholastic, the modern. But 'between these moments there is no hiatus noticeable, nor irreducible differences in the trend of thought. It is a great intellectual movement engaged in the examination of the faculties of the thinking subject, which then opens out into the contemplation of the nature of God . . . henceforth to swing between the two poles of all philosophy: the personal self, the starting point, and the personal God, the aim and end, of all things; to quote Maine de Biran, *Les fins et les aspirations sont les mêmes*.' Op. cit. p. 291.

The bookshop, 8, rue de la Sorbonne *(Collection André Bourgeois)*

other hand the entire ancient cultures, drawn together by this very opposition. Once, men were only conscious of the contrast between them, and now their kinship begins to appear: they had in common their concern with religious values and the bettering of men. Modern civilisation, under the sway of technical development, subordinates every activity to material ends. The new reformers have a confused vision of an idol to which everything must be sacrificed: they call it 'collective consciousness,' but it is merely the degraded consciousness of the bureaucratised citizen and proletarianised man.

Finally, Péguy returned to certain ideas outlined in *Notre Patrie*.

To-day's masters would be in a poor way if, to exercise the power that has fallen into their hands, they had none of the inheritance of the ancient worlds they despise. So many dwelling-places slowly set in order, cottages, middle-class homes, country houses, palaces; so many places to pray, chapels, churches, cathedrals; so much land and flowing water, scrupulously tended by Frenchmen; and Paris, all-embracing, lovely with running water, trees, buildings, and the eternally young people. Children are taught that until the 31st of December 1788, the children of France were born utter idiots, but that since the 1st of January 1789, they are born intelligent and free. To make them believe this piece of nonsense, they get hold of them young, and it's a serious matter, because they do believe it.

The end of the last of the three essays is all lit up: it is a joyful delighted description of France, with its monuments, its people, and the Loire which gathers its waters together. The light comes from outside, leaving the inner landscape still in darkness. Still the curtain was not raised. Here and there, however, a sudden note strikes deeply through the solid prose: an accent to the name of the Eternal, a brief pause at the word prayer. These are allusions to thoughts beyond words, the rays of dawn lighting on distant peaks. The more one reads these pages, the more traces of things untold does one find. For instance, writing of Renan, that antithesis to Péguy on whom Péguy spent so much thought, he raised the question of why Renan, unable to surmount the difficulties of Catholic belief, got himself involved

in much more difficult difficulties . . . in infinitely clumsier metaphysical problems which are in very fact the difficulties, impossibilities, contrarities and metaphysics of history and sociology.

This is a problem that worried Péguy a good deal. Why did Renan do that, instead of. . . . Now pay close attention to the following words:

instead of waiting, living alone, doing something—anything—else, and watching, to see, to bring nearer, to bring about. . . .

Here is the whole secret of the Orsay solitary in a few words, each of which needs listening to carefully and weighing. *Watching to see,* is an attitude. *To bring nearer* is another, and the simple enunciation of an operation which is not simple at all. But we are convinced that what is to come is there already, rising beyond the horizon. Péguy incites us to look into the distance:

> So the first glimpse came to us (in the course of this first *Cahier*) in this form and figure, on the far horizon of our field of research, of the outline, the first traces of the mountain range, the first signs of jagged, chiselled outline and translucent profile announcing to the traveller on the march and to the man of the plains that the immovable mountains are there; so the first lines were drawn of the immense question, of the system as the geographers say, of the powerfully worked and weighted problem which will be the very watershed of our studies.

Here the curtain rises slowly.

•

We know the rest from Lotte. He was teaching at Coutances and his visits were few and far between and all the more welcome to Péguy; this is what Lotte wrote:

> In September of each year I used to go and see him. In 1908, I found him in bed, worn out and ill. All that immense burden borne without faltering for twelve years had got him down at last. I myself had gone through very unhappy days. He told me about his worries and weariness and longing for rest, for a small philosophy class in some secondary school a long way off, somewhere near me, in the heart of the provinces, where, without obstacles or troubles, he would at last be able to produce what he bore within him.... At one moment he raised his head and leaning on his elbow he said, with tears in his eyes: 'I have something more to tell you... I have got back my faith... I am a Catholic.' It was as though a great storm of love swept over me; I felt my heart melt and with warm tears, head in hands, I said, almost in spite of myself: 'Ah well, old man, we are all in the same case.'
>
> We are all in the same case. What made me say that, when a minute before I was still an unbeliever? What slow, dim, deep principle had been at work? At that moment I felt I was a Christian.

That is all that is known, and doubtless there is nothing more to know. Fifteen months later Péguy published his first *Mystère*. It all came to a head together, belief achieved through tears, work achieved through belief. I remember that December afternoon when I met Péguy at the door of his shop in the rue de la Sorbonne. Jean Variot was with him. Mysteriously and without a word, Péguy unbuttoned his long greatcoat and took out of the inner pocket the freshly printed *Cahier* which had appeared that very day; I read the title: *Le Mystère de la Charité de Jeanne d'Arc.*

I read the book that evening, gradually finding my way through the immense poem. There is a prologue, and then the body of the work. The prologue: Jeanne is barely fourteen and we watch the distress of this child in the first throes of her vocation. The body of the work: two solitary meditations, two dialogues, reveal the steady groundbed of her life. By her talk with her friend Hauviette, the peasant child, we learn to know her in her kinship with the people; by her talk with the nun, Madame Gervaise, covering the whole history of Christendom, we know her in the scope and depth of her religion. She has seen men suffering all round her and France become like a foretaste of hell: she knows that Jesus Christ gave Himself even to death to save mankind. That is all she has seen and known.

To give herself and to save; that is her one idea. Always to save: Jesus has not done it all, since nature is still able to stand and resist good. Jeanne, alone in the fields, is praying:

> O God, if only the beginning of your kingdom would come. If only the sunrise of your kingdom would come. But there is nothing, nothing to see, ever. You sent us your Son, whom you loved so much, your Son came, who suffered so much, and He died, and there is nothing, nothing ever. If only we could see the dawn of your kingdom begin to break. And you sent your saints, and you called them each by name, and your saints came, and nothing, nothing ever. Years went by, so many years that I do not know how many there were: centuries of years went by; fourteen centuries of Christendom, alas! since the birth, and the death, and the preaching. And nothing, nothing, nothing, nothing ever. And what reigns on the face of the earth is nothing, nothing, nothing but perdition. . . . God, God, can it be that your Son died in vain? That He came, and it was all for nothing.

The immense prologue, six pages long, with the ceaseless refrain, *nothing, nothing ever*, with which Pèguy opens his work, may be compared to the great choruses at the opening of Bach's oratorios. It attracted practically no attention in 1909; thirty years later, at the Théâtre Français, the audience was swept off its feet by these words.[1]

What is this poor helpless girl to do? She doesn't know, but she does not despair because that is a sin. She thinks about the small village of Bethlehem, no smaller than Domrémy, where a saviour was born. (Bethlehem, Domrémy: the two parishes are then connected and inter-related with exquisite skill and power.) A small Christendom that is the recipient of such great promises, and that has in its own church the precious gift of its God coming to it each day, lives in hope after all. But hope is not enough for Jeanne. She wants to act, but how?

She listens to the nun, Madame Gervaise, a woman of the neighbourhood, and together they ponder over the Passion of Christ; the agony, and death, and that mighty cry that hangs over the world,

[1] This is an allusion to the evenings of June 1st, 2nd and 3rd, 1940. A fourth performance, supposed to take place on the 12th, had to be cancelled.

uttered in anguish and maybe revolt, leaving men's distress still unanswered. Madame Gervaise is a good honest believer who tries to comfort the child with her somewhat professional fervour. Jeanne says very little: long speeches would suit neither her age nor the state of her feelings. But each of her brief interpolations is in itself a cry from afar with far-reaching resonance:

'Jesus himself,' says the nun, 'could not save all living men, nor bring all the damned back from hell; do you want to save better than He did?'

'Well, Madame Gervaise,' says the child, and she stops spinning while she speaks, 'who is to be saved? How are they to be saved?'

'How you do talk, child, how you do talk. We are following Jesus, my child, we are going along behind Him, we are His flock. . . . We have not to go running—we must not go walking ahead of Him. . . .'

'Madame Gervaise, I want to know,' says the child, 'I want to know: Who is to be saved? How are they to be saved?'

'By following Jesus, by listening to Jesus,' says Madame Gervaise.

Then she begins an account of the Passion. Christ on the Mount of Olives. The Temple guards come and seize Him, and *one of them that were with Jesus, stretching forth his hand, drew out his sword. . . .*

Jeanne interrupts with four short words: '*So they had swords?*' 'They had swords,' the nun continued evenly, not understanding what Jeanne means and quite unable to understand the immense bearing of her short remark.

She goes on with her account. But she leaves out a verse: a good Christian cannot say it without trembling, and Jeanne, who knows it by heart of course, says it word for word:

'Then the disciples, all leaving him, fled.'

'Child, child,' says the nun, taken out of depth again by the renewed insistence of the small girl, 'how you do talk, you don't talk like a little girl.'

'I believe . . . I believe . . .' says Jeanne under her breath.

'My child, daughter, what are you daring to say?'

'I believe that if I had been there, I should not have left him.'

The Franciscan nun lectures the child: those first disciples were saints, the first saints; to think one would have done better than they did is sin, it is pride. . . . Jeanne sticks to her point.

Frenchmen would never have left him. People from Lorraine, people from the country of France. . . . I am saying what I really think. I know the sort of people we have round here.

I am saying what we are like, and what our saints were like. They were not afraid of hard knocks.

Saint Francis would never have given him up. Saint Clare would never have given him up.

. . . To have given him up, that is worst of all. Madame Colette would never have given him up.

...I am saying what is a fact.

...I cannot lie about it, I cannot lie about it. I am saying what is a fact.

....Giving up, no. Giving him up. How could they give up the Son of God?

...All I am saying is this: we would never, never have let him go.

...I only said, I am sorry, I am only saying: we would never, never have given him up, it is the truth. I am only saying, the people from hereabouts, we people, the people of Lorraine, would never have given him up, the people of the Meuse valley, never, the people of our parishes round here, never, the people of Vaucouleurs, never, the people of Domrémy, never, the people of Maxey, never, never would we have left him. We are very bad people, we are great sinners. But we would never have done that.

...We would never have let that happen.

...Which is worse.

...Which is worst of all.

...I don't like the English. I say: the English would never have let that happen.

At last this fundamentally unheretical girl yields. But with her peasant astuteness she succeeds in withdrawing her blasphemy without falling into that other blasphemy of disavowing her courage: 'Yet I believe I am not a coward,' she says.

Then the Franciscan nun goes away, and Jeanne stays by herself and starts spinning again. What flash of inspiration, what mystery brings the name of a town to the surface of her mind? Péguy offers no explanation and we do not ask him for one. One line is enough:

Orléans, qui êtes au pays de Loire....

It is the end of the poem. Henceforth, Jeanne's vocation is ripe. She knows her courage, her arm: the sword, and her aim: Orléans.

•

The passage I have used here is an almost verbal transcription of an article published forty years ago in the bulletin *Union pour la Vérité*. 'Congratulations,' a lecturer with a great reputation in the Sorbonne for learning and subtle thought, said to me with kindly irony: 'one would gather from your eulogy that Péguy's *Jeanne d'Arc* is a masterpiece.' I was not unduly elated by this praise. I knew that all I had done was to set out a powerful symphony in simple linear form, as Charles Lamb did in England to put Shakespeare within the reach of children. My account was as much as could be borne. Albert Thierry (a rare soul who died in battle in 1914) amused people by asserting that not since Pascal had anything so powerful been written in French Christian literature. It was a bad beginning and Péguy knew it. 'My first feeling was that it would not come out,' he said in a conversation which Lotte wrote down, 'and that would have been terrible. Ten years in the dark are bearable, but once the time is up, out it must come! A wrong start, a bad throw, can put everything off, and it means ten years more. . . . As in childbirth, until the pains start, all is well, but once they start, the child must come. Fortunately I had some friends, seventeen good fellows who stuck to the job. They made it happen. . . .' The success of the seventeen was very relative. Their valiant counter-attack had no effect on the general public who remained obdurate. But they did reach and touch that imponderable élite which can grant, or refuse, literary existence to a writer.

Before the *Mystère*, Péguy had no existence except between the rue des Ecoles and the rue d'Ulm. After, things were different. A few people read the *Mystère de Jeanne d'Arc*, but it was more than the reputation of a man-about-town was worth not to know that such a book had been written by a man called Péguy. When a writer reaches this stage, he is launched.

The seventeen did not probe very deep, this would no doubt have involved them in difficulties. No one attempted the analysis of Péguy's Christianity and Catholicism. People considered the book from the point of view of style, and this was a good beginning, because the toughest obstacle between Péguy and the public was certainly his style, meaning his own individual means of expression and communication. The first thing we are taught in school is to avoid repetition of words. And Péguy consistently broke this primary rule. All educated Frenchmen were shocked and he was not forgiven his infraction. Péguy's prose was written in a style to which people were not accustomed. The public is a very stern critic of innovations in language. Painters and musicians are permitted all sorts of liberties with their canvasses and orchestras, but the writer is allowed none, or very few. The general public consider that they have rights because they use the language themselves. This does not necessarily follow, however. Language is related to communication, on the practical plane: whence a certain set of conventions which are passed on from one generation to another like tools; but language has other affiliations too, it is related to the inner life and functions on the poetic plane. The whole trend is different and the material is different too. The born writer (or among uncultured people, the born talker, such as Péguy's grandmother, the wonderful story-teller, the unlettered woman who *first taught him the French tongue*) finds in language matter for invention, he has his own rights just as the painter and musician have their rights.

In 1910, François Porché, Michel Arnaud, André Gide and I set ourselves to discover the meaning of repetition in Péguy's prose. Porché saw it as a rhythmic effect, often appearing to correspond to the inner rhythm of Péguy's thought. And that is why it sometimes appears to be merely marking time, to the uninitiated reader. This is very wide of the mark, Péguy never marks time, but he does advance only pace by pace, cautiously, like a good infantry footslogger. The road is hard, the end of the journey a long way ahead, and a man has to keep a look-out on his left-hand side, with his gun under his arm, for the thickets are full of ambushes and evening is coming on.

Porché's picture is valid. It is true that Péguy came of a race of peasants and soldiers used to meeting a life of hardship with that patience and endurance he too requires us to share. But essentially Péguy was a meditative man, and it is in the sequence of meditative acts that André Gide finds his clue. 'What you call repetition,' said Porché, 'is a rhythmic footstep.' 'What you call repetition,' said André Gide, 'is the probing of a man in prayer.'

Péguy's style resembles the style of very old litanies. It is like Arabian songs, like monotonous moorland songs; it is comparable to the desert; grass desert, sand desert, stone desert. . . . Péguy's style is like the stones of the desert, one here, another there resembling it, each like the other, but just a little different; and the difference is underlined, insisted upon, repeated, seeming to be repeated, is emphasised, asserted ever more clearly, and so we progress. What greater variety do I require? Not for me those loquacious landscapes where in a glance and without moving I am offered more things for my consideration than my life can attend to. Deserts and gardens shall be my only loves; very trim gardens, and monotonous deserts where the same flower, or the almost identical one, will repeat the almost similar perfume for leagues on end, and the same stone, the same colour, yet each time slightly different; like the Arabian flute on the same phrase, almost the same, during almost the whole concert; like the believer, the same prayer, during the whole of his orison, or at least almost the same with a slight difference of tone, of which he is almost unaware, and which starts again as it were in spite of himself, while his faith has still not exhausted its ardour. 'Words! I shall not leave you. Same words, I shall not hold you quite so long as you still have something to say. Lord, we shall not leave you until you have blessed us.'

IX

POLITICAL DIFFICULTIES—PÉGUY AND MAURRAS

Freedom is a system based on courage.—CHARLES PÉGUY.

PÉGUY SOON BECAME aware that the partial success of the *Mystère de la Charité de Jeanne d'Arc* had done little or nothing to improve the state of his affairs. On the material plane, things were worse: a number of subscriptions had lapsed. *Jeanne d'Arc* was not to the mind of the old Dreyfus guard formed by Péguy. From the point of view of influence, though this is harder to estimate, the general impression is one of marking time. This man, so highly endowed with the qualities of a leader, was the leader of a very small band; and though so highly endowed as a writer, and a popular writer in the most exalted sense of the word, nourished from roots in such deep soil, he remained quartered between his four walls and aroused no echoing voices.

There were many reasons for this, and we will take those of a political order first.

In that order, facts are stated summarily. Following the rules of the game, we must admit that Péguy had of a sudden taken a position on the right, to judge by the opinions he had just expressed. Whether he liked it or not, he had thus entered heavily occupied territory, just at a time when feeling was running extraordinarily high, lashed by the pre-war storms. Two chiefs, both outstanding men, Barrès and Maurras, shared between them leadership of the nation's youth. Very different in type, in many respects of opposing trends of thought, they were nonetheless linked by a subtle bond. Was there room for a third? This was the tactical question.

After thirty-five years, it is easy to see the affinity between Barrès' inspiration and Péguy's: in both men the political outlook was determined by powerful feelings of a largely traditional character. But there was no sense of affinity between the men themselves. Barrès had known of Péguy for years from Charles-Lucas de Peslouän, a relation of his, and from the Tharaud brothers, his young secretaries, of whom he thought very highly. He was fond of listening to their accounts of their friend's exploits, and felt sure that Péguy had real power of a racy, genial, mediæval kind, or, as he once said to Lucien Corpechot, 'richness.' He was amused by what he heard and took a distant interest in what was going on, with no intention of getting involved himself. The *Cahiers* bookshop was to him merely a haunt of old Normale students more or less de-normalised: protestants, Jews, heretical dreyfusards or out-and-out dreyfusists even, plebeian moralists and pernickety Talmudists. He had no wish to join them. 'Your Péguy,' he said to Tharaud, 'is a sort of Ballard!' Ballard was the peasant visionary, finally heretical and condemned by the Church, whose story Barrès had told in *La Colline Inspirée*. He was wrong: Péguy was not of the heretical kind and would never have become so. But Barrès, having stated his opinion, stuck to it. I remember a talk I had with him after Péguy's death. He spoke of the way Péguy had led his life alone, in the thick of constant bitter quarrels. 'It all seemed to me so silly,' he said. 'Now Péguy is dead, he is a hero, and that is all right.' We may add that on tactical grounds an understanding with Péguy would have put him on an awkward footing with Maurras. He never contemplated such a thing. An excellent article on the *Mystère de la Charité de Jeanne d'Arc*, written at the request of the Tharaud brothers and Peslouän, and not without its reserves, was an act of generosity which did not commit him in any way. It was all he did.

Now we come to Maurras. He was younger than Barrès, a lesser man as regards worldly honours, but nonetheless the leader in battle as far as the younger generation were concerned. In 1909 the *Action Française* became a daily paper and the very instrument he needed to deploy his forces. Barrès was king of the *Echo de Paris* once a week, and Maurras, king of the *Action Française* every day. Every day, and under two names: Maurras on the first page for political doctrine, and Criton on page three for newsprint-policing and criticism. Nor was this all: Maurras was king of the spoken word on the first floor of the *Café Flore* every night. The young people of Paris had got into the habit of turning up and he questioned them in the classical manner, confronting them with posers and indefatigably repeating and illuminating in a thousand ways straight statements about the State, always about the State; as to its continuity, its forms, the ineptitude of Number; monarchic rule, its beneficence proved by comparing what was done in France when it existed, and what was being undone with it lost; such was Maurras' relentless, overwhelming preaching.

Between Maurras and Péguy, what contrasts: one coming of honest middle-class stock, producing men who served the State in the civil service and army and were conditioned by the life they led. The other, of peasant stock, naturally suspicious of the State, avoiding contact or collusion with it, resenting its taxes and impositions. Maurras with his old allegiance to its gods and their laws, civil or State, canonical, written or prescribed. Péguy the complete Bourbonnais, tempered by the young and skipping Loire, the child of green fields and human ways, a clear-sighted Celtic peasant, watching his footholds but far from deaf to the call of adventure. Maurras, whose teachers were priests, faithful to the Church but not as the Body of Christ. Péguy, the child of the faubourg Bourgogne, proudly celebrating July 14th, joyfully celebrating Christmas, sorrowful on Good Friday. How far apart they were. Maurras was a man of the Mediterranean: his mind conceived clear-cut forms to which death would put a term; he was Cassandra, Demosthenes, or Machiavelli, the hard mind which points out where danger lies, even mortal danger. Péguy did not believe in death, he believed in the eternal re-birth of the virtue of nations and men.

This is where the contrast is most marked: Maurras knew what death was, and Péguy would have nothing to do with it. *People must be saved:* both men were convinced of this and both said so. But in one case it was the cry of the believer, an act of faith as well as a call for help; in the other, it was the cry of the man who knew how harsh history was, full of cities destroyed and dead peoples. Péguy's reactions were Christian, Maurras', tragic; he knew how disorder ends in destruction, that disorder and destruction are one and the same, and that the disorder of France, unless some great remedy could be applied, would inevitably end in the destruction of France itself. Maurras would not admit the chaotic state of affairs in which a Péguy consented to live and managed to live.

Despair can be an inspiration and a driving force, as it was in men like Barbès and Mazzini in the nineteenth century. It looks at death and makes it visible. Such a vision as this was behind Maurras' conquering power. He showed France death, like a surgeon trying to overcome a patient's unwillingness to be operated. 'France cannot be perfectly restored,' he said explicitly, 'but by the extirpation of disfigured France,' which he called *Anti-France*. What a gloomy doorway to the future! Maurras was undismayed; he had no fear of bloodshed (perhaps he liked it), and his instruments were all ready for the most drastic operation, the most thorough manipulation a nation could possibly have to endure: the extirpation of two whole centuries. He knew the operation would be no easy one: *The way is steep*. But it was a question of that or death, as he kept saying, and to help the hesitant to make up their minds he unflinchingly showed them death relentlessly. 'Our idea, once it were recognised, understood and obeyed, would save France,' he wrote. 'If Frenchmen reject it, the truth will not be altered or impaired, but it will bring about the downfall and loss of France. The Republicans can choose: the Republic, or the Country?'

Choose is not quite the right word. Under threat of death a man does not choose, he acts as his anxiety dictates. It was an act which Maurras was able to provoke in a great many young Frenchmen, overwhelmed by sheer force of logic and objurgations.

But Péguy, never. He had no time for this mortal vision which Maurras evoked. In the recent past, he could not see the age of inexpungible error to which Maurras pointed. There had been mistakes, human and redeemable mistakes, he held, but honour was safe, the heart was still beating. As he was to write in his last poem:

> *. . . Et l'arbe de la grâce est raciné profond*
> *Et plonge dans le sol et cherche jusqu'au fond*
> *Et l'arbre da la race est lui-même éternel,*[1]

and that is what he already thought. That did not mean he shut his eyes to the possibility of very great trials ahead, I believe myself that he foresaw them. But the prospect of difficult times does not unduly disturb a man of courage, and least of all a man who has faith as well as courage. Péguy's mind had no room for those extirpations and bloody operations which Maurras was proposing. The two men lived on different planes. Maurras had in mind coming events and wanted to act quickly. To act quickly was alien to Péguy's ways.

We have seen how intrinsically he was a man of slow growth, silent ripening and pregnant pauses. The field of his interests lay outside the political field proper, and the Maurras line of controversy was something essentially remote from his experience. What the name, form and coat-of-arms of the State should be were matters of small importance to this harassed man at his work-laden desk. A royal State would not have been a heavier weight to bear than this 'multi-cæsarism of committees,' as he called it, then in power. But to a corrected, rectified, repentant France he preferred old republican France (already so old a France) with its turbulent claims and dissensions. He did not see any point in a change of tools, he had no fear:

> *And the tree of the race is itself eternal.*

It is not difficult to imagine what a controversy between Maurras and Péguy would have been like: they were well-matched. Péguy would have provided memorable proof that Maurras completely misinterpreted the spirit of France. Maurras would have given memorable proof that the process that stood for thinking in Péguy's mind was a tissue of contradictions. But neither of them wanted this controversy. Each was busy, in the way most suited to his peculiar gifts, preparing the French for imminent war; both were able to call the same ardour to life; neither wished to do the other down and, for a time, parallel lines of influence were possible. What they had in common was their sense of crisis, and so real was it that certain phrases of Maurras could be attributed with equal validity to either:

[1] . . . And far down is rooted the tree of grace.
Through deep soil driving, down to the lowest place,
And the tree of the race is itself eternal.

Just as all the lovely inventions of mankind were born of sorrow and dissatisfaction, so the high moments in the history of peoples were prepared, ripened and given birth as it were in pain. A touch of anger and wrath mingled with much generosity and much love are what determine those mysterious compounds and vital ferments which make fecund and bring to fruit.

'Mysterious compounds, vital ferments' are very un-maurrassian terms to describe the movements that were agitating the young men of the day, with their tragic destiny ahead of them. They were to die by hundreds and thousands. They were ready, but not for death as a mere incident in the bloody strife: they intended their death to be a sacrifice alight with the conviction of truth.

•

Péguy was too level-headed not to see the complexities of his position. The part assigned to him by circumstance of free-lance latecomer to the battle, had no substance whatever. It was an illusion due to the fact that no one appreciated the real nature and extent of his battlefield. Ultimately it was no concern of his whether a Barrès or a Maurras were commander-in-chief *in sæculum*. He had the assurance of an altogether different destiny: he knew his field was in the future, not the present, and that one day he would command *in sæcula*. This conviction was an odd one, but not grounded in pride. Undoubtedly pride went with it but it had not produced it. It sprang from that *elsewhere* that worked in him and through him so powerfully. It was so, and he knew it was so; the difficulties would be there all his life long; it was his job to put up with temporal difficulties and to see that everything else took second place till his mysteries were finished. And the small barque of the *Cahiers* was to do it unassisted.

Nonetheless, Péguy came to the point of having to state his position. Here comes a series of events in which I had my part. In 1907, Péguy told me that Joseph Reinach was asking him to write an article on his history of the Dreyfus affair. He was not at all keen. Historical events have their own history, decline, revivals and dead moments. In 1907 the *Affaire Dreyfus* had reached one of these dead moments. It had had its ideological exponents and its political consequences. It had aroused complex passions. Ideologies, consequences and passions had, in fact, in the course of ten years of unrest and violent controversy, coated it over; and so, dismally reduced, it seemed to have no place in memory in a Europe bent on warfare and a France grown national in spirit again. It is a fact that the tenth anniversary of the *Affaire* passed with no celebrations or commentaries. There was just a blank and unbroken silence. I had noticed the turn things were taking with some concern: silence on such occasions is a sign that all is not well. I told Péguy so and suggested trying to do something about it myself. After a lapse of ten years, I thought it should be possible to place the *Affaire* in its historical setting and to attempt to sort out the underlying passions, and to some extent to pass judgment on them. I was aware that such a piece of work, done on the quick, had its perils, but I wanted to try my hand at it. Péguy gave his consent, and I set to work on my *Apologie pour notre passé*. I still believe that the first words of this essay were the right retort to the silence I had observed and wished to break: 'How has it come about that our dreyfusism, which made us so joyful, and more than joyful, so proud, means so little to us to-day?' I queried. 'What can it be, if not the sign of an unavowed regret and the effect of a sense of wrong?' These were the opening words, and after a hundred pages or so, the essay ended like this:

The victim was rescued and the culprits punished. So far so good. Let us keep our memories lively, for they nearly all do us honour, and none of them dishonour us; let us do honour to the actual crisis, harsh but not harmful, which kept us all so busy; *but we should not sing our own praises too loud:* victory was ours but the battle was hard-won.

It is one thing to stop shouting, quite another to let others shout us down: let us hear no more of the word traitor applied to an innocent man whose life was broken; the word scoundrels, to the men who rescued him; we are entitled to ponder on the extent of our wrongs, but no one is entitled to put us on the defensive as to the extent of our rights. And our chief hope is that we may never again find ourselves in the position in which we were in December, 1897. There is no question but that, more careworn and no less resolute, we should start campaigning again. What else could we do?

I am entitled to say, with the text itself before me, that there is no faltering in this stern small document of mine.

I knew my Apology would get me into trouble in some quarters. I had certainly not foreseen that it should bring me up against the man who had been my first and constant guide all through the slow maturing of my work. Yet this is what occurred. Three months after my book had appeared, I was amazed to receive a large *Cahier* entitled *Notre Jeunesse*, bearing on the same subject which I had tackled, a retort, and a downright virulent one, written and published in surprising haste, to what Péguy called my 'penitential' mood. 'When I was reading the proofs of our collaborator's *Cahier*,' he explained, . . . 'I foresaw this misunderstanding and I rebelled inwardly; dumbly, of course, because I have no eloquence.' It is true, Péguy was not a man of words: he was as short-spoken as he was long-winded on paper; but his terseness could be very expressive, and during that fortnight of working side by side, I had seen not a sign of this dumb rebellion. I always thought, and I still think, that my Apology displeased certain supporters of the *Cahiers*. As I set it out, the *Affaire Dreyfus* was no longer anything exceptional, impeccable and sacred, and this reduction of the crisis to ordinary daylight was not acceptable in certain eyes. Jewish susceptibility is acute. Though I measured my words, there were hurt feelings. There had probably been recriminations and complaints. And whenever the *Cahiers* were threatened, Péguy reverted to the born Beauceron-peasant type to which he always conformed, doggedly and aggressively, when his rights were in question.

I have gone into this incident in some detail, because those familiar with Péguy's work would be surprised if I said nothing, and also because it brought about a change in our relations. My admiration was his once and for all, but I no longer appeared at the Thursday gatherings and only saw Péguy from time to time.[1]

Let us say at once that *Notre Jeunesse* is one of Péguy's finest pieces of writing; some hold that it is the finest of all. Péguy took the subject in quite a different way. I had approached it as a psychological historian; he did so as a poet. He called to mind only that generous impulse which had fired him and his friends in 1897. This page must be quoted in full:

And what did we ourselves hold? We held that one single injustice, one single crime, one single illegality, especially if it is officially registered and confirmed, one single injury to justice and right, especially if it is universally, legally, nationally and conveniently accepted, one single crime breaks and is enough to break the whole social pact, one single forfeit, one single dishonour is enough for the loss of honour and to dishonour a whole nation. It is an abscess corrupting the whole body. What we are defending is not only our honour. It is not only the honour of our people, in the present, it is the historic honour of our whole race, the honour of our forebears, the honour of our children. And the more past we have, the longer is our memory, and the greater is (as you say) our responsibility, and so therefore the more we must defend it. The more past we have behind us, the more (precisely) we must defend it and keep it untainted. *Je rendrai mon sang pur comme je l'ai reçu.* For Corneille, that was the rule and honour and driving force, the old Cornelian driving force. It was the rule and honour of the Christian driving force. A single stain stains a whole family. It stains a whole nation, too. A nation cannot sit down submissively under so studied an insult, under so solemnly and thoroughly endorsed a crime. The honour of a nation is all of a piece.

There we have Péguy's glorious memory of the event. That first surge, that spirit of generosity and honour had really existed; that

[1] Tharaud says in *Notre cher Péguy* that I wanted to fight a duel with Péguy. Such an idea never crossed my mind. I should have thought it as absurd as I do now. His mistake is due no doubt to the fact that I had a clash with an *Action Française* writer, Pierre Gilbert, now dead, on this same question. The duel is a convention which on a certain plane has a certain value. But no value and no sense on the plane on which my relationship with Péguy stood.

set-off, as he liked to say; that explosion. As for the consequences, the ground strewn with wreckage, Péguy takes a bird's eye view. The history of peoples, as he tells it, is an unfolding of forces based on two poles, one positive: he calls it *mystique* (the spirit); the other negative: he calls it *politique* (policy).

Tout commence en mystique et tout finit en politique (spirit at the rise, policy at the close, of all things): everyone knows this tag, by which the two words have taken on a fresh meaning which has become part of our language. It is not altogether a good thing; *mystique* has come to mean something so diffuse as to lack all precision, and *politique* has suffered an unwarranted depreciation. Policy, in the classical sense, is not degrading, but entails rights and a dignity of its own. But the phrase does sum up in a striking manner Péguy's idea of the life of nations: only fervour and ardour counted.

The other high-water mark of the book is forty pages on the Jewish people. They come at the right place in his work in this book. We need to remember the lines written in January 1900, in the course of that violent repudiation of Hell: 'What we will never consent to is this: the queer combination of life and death which we name damnation, the queer reinforcement of a presence by an absence and the whole reinforced by eternity.' This was an exact description of the mediæval ghetto, closed for ever on a race existing in every part of the world, yet in each and every one shut out from its normal spiritual atmosphere. 'We don't admit that there should be any men forbidden to cross the threshold of any city.' Such had been the fate of the Jewish people for centuries, and it might happen again. For Péguy, the Jewish people were the standing exponents of that destiny of which Sophocles and Virgil had revealed the modes: the exile begging for his bread and bowed in supplication outside the temples he finds on his way.

In the motionless Jews at the Weeping Wall in Jerusalem, he saw the living heirs of the ancient suppliants, Œdipus blind and without the City. His deep sense of tragedy held him spellbound before this basic historical and spiritual situation. He knew that the Jewish people were not behind others in possessing a *politique* as well as a *mystique*, a political as well as a spiritual attitude to life, but he was only concerned with the *mystique*, and that unique destiny.

Péguy's paramount interest was still in persons: he chose the person of Bernard Lazare to hold and occupy his attention. We are given the portrait of this strange figure who would have been completely forgotten if Péguy had not thrown so powerful a light on it. *Libertaire* in 1892, when the very word was a scandal, Jewish patriot in 1895 when no one else in France dreamt of such a thing, dreyfusard before anyone else, allowed no part in the struggle by the leaders of the *Affaire*, those high counsellors, newspaper directors and publishers, because he was different, Bernard Lazare had become one of those mysterious figures the curious find here and there on the margins of history. Cautious characters considered him a dangerous man. Péguy made a bee-line for him and took him to his heart. Bernard Lazare was one of the very few people he used to go and visit. He would sit at his bedside (Bernard Lazare had fallen ill and was to die young), watching and listening, with a growing sense of veneration for this strange Jew with his impulsive, clear instincts. At number 7, rue de Florence, on the third floor of a Parisian house, a Jew who lived and breathed for the salvation of his people drawn and quartered by the dispersion. A *man of fifty centuries*. This is how Péguy describes him:

I can still picture his short-sighted way of looking at me, so intelligent and kind both at once, with his invincible, enlightened, enlightening, luminous gentleness, his unwearying, understanding, enlightened, unaffected, incurable goodness. Because a man wears a double eyeglass firmly set on a large nose, barring and screening a pair of big, kind, short-sighted eyes, the modern can see no further and misses the look of the man, that gaze lit by a flame fifty centuries old. But I was able to come nearer. . . .

The whole development is admirable, right to the end:

. . . There was not a trace of feeling, not a thought, not a shade of emotion that was not drawn and ordered by an order fifty centuries old, an order established fifty centuries ago; a whole race and a whole world on his bowed shoulders; on his round shoulders, his heavy shoulders; and a heart consumed by fire, the fire of his race, consumed by the fire of his people; the fiery heart, the ardent mind, and *the burning coal on the prophetic lips.*

Elsewhere Péguy wrote of Bernard Lazare as *an atheist radiant with God.*

On the day he was buried, Péguy wanted his friend and secretary André Bourgeois to go with him, so that the whole governing body of the *Cahiers* should be present at the final leavetaking. He has described it for us, it was just a transfer of human remains, with very few present: a handful of friends, a handful of Eastern Jews faithful to their defender. And Péguy and Bourgeois, that is the *Cahiers*, walking with them.

•

To return to the problem of the French people. 'I am an old republican,' said Péguy. Not 'I am a republican.' Now this old republic to which he paid allegiance was certainly not the one we lived under, his carefully chosen epithet made that quite clear, and he never mentioned ours but to revile it. 'It was all right till 1881,' he said. What happened in 1881 was that the great provincial Catholic families were beaten and the republicans began to impose their laws. So Péguy had got his knife into the republican's Republic, had he? It is difficult to follow him through these surprising statements; the republic of the notables, of the good Marshal and of the Duc de Broglie, the one that used to be called the republic without republicans, and which the faubourg Bourgogne must surely have loathed for this very reason, was held up as the model republic. Péguy was obviously improvising and the *Cahier* betrays the haste in which it was written. But let us read on:

The Republic was a restoration until about 1881, when the intrusion of intellectual tyranny and primary school mentality began its reign of chaos.... At this date, the Republic began to be discontinued. It went from republicanism to cæsarism. Radical and radical-socialist rule is, properly speaking, cæsarism, and in particular the multi-cæsarism of electoral committees.

To sum up: the Republic began to be discontinued on the day it began to exist; or to put it more reasonably, the republicans ceased to be republican on the day they came into power. Péguy as a republican was the champion of a certain human way of life, not of a certain kind of government. Péguy was indefatigable in decrying the customs and formalities, and no less the institutions and documents, of our Third Republic. I don't believe he ever voted. A republican who does not use his vote is an anomaly: democracy and the vote stand or fall together. Actually, *Notre Jeunesse*, the most republican of Péguy's *Cahiers*, does sketch a defence of the electoral system. But it was far from being convincing; Péguy addressed himself to Variot, one of the Thursday familiars, a royalist and follower of Maurras, and rather loud of voice for the cramped quarters of the shop. His voice, his blond beard and his sturdy form were all outsize, and in Péguy's view took up too much room:

...My dear Variot, in days gone by, heroic days, the sick and dying were borne in litters to go and deposit their chit in the ballot-box. '*Déposer son bulletin dans l'urne*' is an expression that strikes you as screamingly funny to-day. It took a century of heroism to forge it.... Of the most undeniable, authentic heroism. Of the most French, shall I say. And then there was an election. And that was the great division of the world in two, the great election of the modern world between the *Ancien régime* and the Revolution. And then, Variot, Jean Variot, there was the most colossal going to the polls. There was that little trek that started from the Valmy windmill and reached the heights of Hougoument before it was done.

It is a brilliant piece of work, but underneath there is much confusion of thought. The word 'election' is taken first in its political sense, then without warning in quite a different sense. The electors disappear, the scene is filled with soldiers, and according to the old rite of the Lord of Hosts, arms it is that decide the day. Moreover, the result of the war-election was not the one to which the argument was leading: for the Revolution fizzled out on the slopes of Hougoument.

In fact, though infallibly sure of touch in lyrical improvisation, Péguy improvised very badly when it came to historical debate. He was not a democrat nor ever had been one; he never thought that a sum total of ballot sheets could express the will of a nation; he had too high an idea of freedom to submit it to a numerical count, and too high an idea of authority to believe it could be produced by mere arithmetic. And yet he said: '*I am an old republican, I am a revolutionary. . . .*' The words can have such different meanings: what did he mean? '*What we used to call the Republic . . .*' as Elisée Reclus said sadly towards the end of his life, calling to mind the ideal and the religious impulse which had enchanted his young days. Let us discover what value Péguy himself set on these terms, *Republic, Revolution*, to make them last down to our own times, and claim men's homage still:

The *Republic*, which was the object of an ideal (mystique) and which was a system of *ancien régime* government founded on honour, on a certain honour of its own, and an old-France government, became in their hands [the republicans'] matter for politics (politique), modern ones, and generally of the lowest kind, and a system of government founded on the satisfaction of the lowest appetites and on the appeasement of the lowest interests And all that still stands and all that still properly belongs to the old Republic is what has not yet been contaminated with the Jaurès' outlook.

The *revolutionary force*, which was the honour and greatness of the race, and which consisted essentially in willing that all should go well and in doing more than one's share, the revolutionary spirit, which was essentially a generous one, the revolutionary instinct, became in their day and under their government and in their hands, a low spirit of sabotage and devaluation and spite, which consists essentially in being delighted at the bad turn of things, and in willing and working for things to turn out badly, and in doing less than one's share; and even none of it.

So the Revolution is not the glow of expectation which the prophets of Israel brought the world; nor the proud undertaking of human and rational renovation which for a hundred and fifty years, no longer, has haunted French reformers, and through them worked among the peoples. Péguy was quite clear about the double error, but he wanted to save the initial impulse by an interpretation of the word retaining it intact. The Revolution, *la Révolution aux bras levés*, as a poet put it who attracted attention and devotion in his twenties, Francis Viélé-Griffin, was for Péguy an explosion of ardour and social charity. In a *mystère* in which he made God speak, he extolled this ardour:

Soldier people, said God, there is nothing to equal a Frenchman in battle.
(And so there is nothing to equal a Frenchman in the crusade.)
They are not always asking for orders and they are not always asking for explanations of what has to be done and what is going to happen.
They find things out for themselves, they make things up as they go along.
They know without being told. There is no need to keep sending them orders.
They are good at getting out of a mess. They understand what is going on. In the fray, they act as occasion demands.
They take a look round and they always know what to do without going to ask the general.
Without bothering the general. But the battle is on all the time, said God.
The crusade is on all the time.
And the general is always a long way off.

This inventiveness, this gift for improvisation, was for Péguy the outstanding French virtue and the source of the nation's greatness and power of recovery. But it shrinks to nothing if it is deprived of freedom. So Péguy became a defender of freedom. He was, and remained, a liberal (the word is old-fashioned but still holds good). And God, as Péguy would have us know Him, God first of all is liberal in His Government. To be served the more worthily, He sets man free:

By the mystery of my creature, freedom,
I left him, in my kingdom,
A share in my own government.
A share in my inventiveness.
Not to mince words, a share in my creativeness.

Here we are back on the spiritual plane. It was inevitable, for Péguy was ill at ease on any other, and as he saw it the civil order was related to the divine order. Service to one's country is on the same terms as service to God: in both cases, freedom is essential.

Freedom is not an idol, or an end, but a prerequisite condition of human worth. Man needs a margin to move about in and try himself out and show what he is worth and attract grace. God, Péguy's magnificent, kindly God, made this quite clear:

What prudence is necessary. This freedom must be made and taught
Without exposing their salvation. For if I support them too much they never learn to swim.
But if I do not hold them at the right moment,
They go headlong, they splutter and choke and go under.
And I can't have them go to the bottom,
Not in this sea of turpitude. . . .

So freedom has its limits and must be won by resolve, needing an act and a gift for its accomplishment. That is the condition. When limp and out of action, it is prostitution. *Corruptio optimi, pessima.* Péguy said: 'The Republic was a certain system of *ancien régime* government founded on honour and on a certain honour of its own, and an old-France government. . . .' *A system of government:* men are interdependent, and need a certain kind of rule, there is no anarchy here. *A certain system of ancien régime government founded on honour:* not on the counting and discounting of votes; not on hereditary government; not on administrative regulations or police powers; but on that virtue by which, in a single word, is described all the inner life and worth of a man: the word *honour*.

What is the meaning of this, and how is one to picture this government, all honour, which Péguy called the *Republic?* An incident I remember throws light on the question. In about 1904, Péguy, though no lecturer, gave a lecture entitled, I think, 'A scrutiny of democracy.' It took place in that School of Journalism, fifty yards away, which had for a time housed him and the *Cahiers*. He sat at the lecturer's desk as unconcernedly as he sat at his own writing table in the shop, and spoke in his precise, rather toneless voice, for the usual length of time, one hour; he had brought a dictionary and sat like a good scholar turning over the pages to make sure of his definitions. When he had done, he got up and went out so quietly that there was no applause. The audience got up and went out too, most of them very annoyed because they thought Péguy was making fun of them again and they were past the days for looking things up in dictionaries. With a little good will, they would have realised they had heard a very meaty lecture, which is a rare event. In his examination and comparison of different systems of government, Péguy decided that the best way to test them was to analyse the terms by which they are known: *democracy, autocracy, plutocracy* he put on one side, *monarchy, oligarchy* on the other. And then he deduced that there are low forms of government (submission to the mass, to tyranny, to money) well defined by the final *-cracy*, expressing blind force; and noble forms of government, well defined by the final *-archy*, expressing spiritual force, the source of commandment.

This distinction is not unshakeably supported by the words themselves: we say *aristocracy*, not *aristarchy*, and yet aristocracy is a form of government based on quality from which *oligarchy* (not *olicracy*) is the first step down, according to the Greek. But in a rough and ready way the idea is useful and the resulting classification of governments is fruitful, while the personal statement to which it gives rise makes sense. Péguy is *a-cracy*, he is *archist*. Necessarily, since he believes in man and in the majesty of this being to whom God, his Creator, has entrusted part of His all-powerfulness:

A share in my inventiveness.
Not to mince words, a share in my creativeness.

God the Archon withdrew a little, in order that man should have a spark of *archy* and room to be hero or saint, creator, leader. 'Freedom is a system of courage,' he wrote later. And again: 'Freedom consists in believing.' So freedom is an opportunity given to men: if they miss it, all is lost, nothing is left. If they seize it, then the differences grow manifest, the scale of quality and authority and hierarchy. To try to rule mankind by a count of votes is to mistake its very nature, as though men were worth one, two, or three, according to whether one, two, or three are there. The more exact the count, the more the result is a failure, for men can't be weighed and measured, they tender respect where it is due and worth can't be calculated. 'We, that is, man, the world, humanity; creation. Or again, price, value, hierarchy. Or again, holiness.' Every man is a more or less strong or swift upward-springing flame, shedding more or less light through the darkness:

If there is a spurt of water, if there is a spring, the desert is watered. And if there is genius, the whole gradation reappears, the small and the great, and the small and the great in holiness, and the customers and the shopkeepers, and the sinners and the saints. And grace, watering. *Rorate, coeli, desuper*. Heaven, send down dew from on high. . . .

Now we may be able to form a coherent picture of the world of men and the society of living souls. Freedom first: in freedom, man developing his strength, and through him, the emergence of values (devotion, goodness, audacity, creative power) which will determine the hierachies, that is to say, the authorities. *A-crate*, enemy of laws, or even indifferent to laws: this is Péguy. *Archist:* deferring to order, and to valid authority, to the 'Archons': this is Péguy. Here is the Idea. I write the word platonically: the generating Idea, the Mother, as I might say, after the manner of Goethe; the living idea from which spring the orders of being which characterise real life. All *cracy* is a parody and a lapse of order.

So it is clear, and of course we knew it all the time, that this intrinsically active, personal grouping which Péguy named *Republic* had no connection with our type of government, where the multicæsarism of committees and the anonymity of ministries manipulate the masses. Péguy wanted leaders; on occasion, one leader, a master and a stiff one. 'I don't like a kind man in power. May God give us firm masters, that is all we ask of them. Nothing is so dangerous for the underdog as a good-natured man at the top.' Is Péguy's Republic nearer the Monarchy? To some extent, yes, for all monarchy is personal power in the hands of a single family, surrounded and served by other families devoted to the maintenance in the world of its prestige, which is the prestige of all. The kings and nobles of old France, through all their manifold weaknesses, did preserve in France a high sense of the qualities of command. But suppose the monarch is incapable and the families are mere parasites? Péguy's answer is this: 'Louis XVI was rightly deposed because for the war that was coming and had already begun he was out of place and was replaced by more jacobin, more kingly, more *ancien régime*, more Richelieu men than he was.' Carnot, Saint-Just and Robespierre were kings then, *more kingly kings* was their due title.

Enough of this. There is no point in trying to elucidate a man's idea of the State when that man's every instinct was opposed to the State. True peasant that he was, his concern was with those things that stood foursquare on solid earth: the family, the workshop, the parish. 'The chief thing that needs re-making,' he said to Lotte, 'the most important of all, is the parish.' That is pure Péguy. That is the level of his interests. His lyrical outburst, his moments of insight, and his inexhaustible supply of happy turns of phrase are not the material for a coherent policy and were not supposed to be. Political science is directed towards the maintenance of order, and Péguy is an explosive improviser. So neither the Republic nor the Monarchy will fit his bill:

Republicans and monarchists all speak the same language. All of them . . . believe in a régime, and that it is a régime which makes, or does not make, peace or war, strength and virtue, health and disease, and the disposition, duration and tranquillity of a people. The strength of a race. It is just like believing that the Loire *châteaux* make, or do not make, earthquakes. We believe the opposite (contrary to one and the other side, and to both at once): that there are infinitely more profound forces and realities, and that it is in fact the people who make the strength or weakness of a régime: and much less, the régime those of the people.

So Péguy dismissed both opponents. Let the republicans stay republican, he said, and the royalists royalist. There is no such thing as too much love and service for France, nor too many different ways of offering it.

At this point, he could quite well have developed his ideas in a commentary on current events and have made himself heard. Some passing remarks which Lotte wrote down show what he might have done:

. . . I'm not a man to look at the gloomy side of things. What is bad is parliamentarism; but parliamentarism can only do a certain amount of harm. Some real hard work has been done these last five years. At the present moment, the cabinet is quite admirable. No other country in Europe has so many first-class men as we have. The poor Germans have lost their Biberstein and simply don't know where to turn next. . . .

There is just that faint indication of satirical comment on the courtiers of William II. Then there are these critical remarks on the *Action Française:*

The *Action Française* have set their points very badly. Instead of making for disorder, they could and should back and strengthen whatever is permanent in the Republic, and thereby continue the *Ancien Régime;* I mean the ministries for defence (war, navy, foreign affairs), and the presidency of the Republic, which is a sort of royalty. The odd thing is that the men they attack and disparage most are precisely the *Ancien Régime* types. Take Briand: he is eminently the great courtier; and Millerand, the great accountant; here we have it: Briand-Mazarin, Millerand-Colbert.

What journalist could have equalled this for terseness and lightness of touch, or sketched so clear a portrait in five lines:

. . . I observe the reliable stolidity of a Millerand, the thickset form, square shoulders, square brow, set foursquare like a strong oak table, the keen, almost curt energy and eyes firmly set under that enormous arch of bristling grey stubble, looking out limpidly and powerfully. . . .

What a magnificent journalist he would have made had he wished: he was as telling in brief decisive strokes as in his copious outpourings. But he did not wish it. All his mental activity would have been caught up in the machinery, and he knew he had something else to do. The *Mystère de la Charité de Jeanne d'Arc* ended on a brief word from Jeanne:

Orléans, qui êtes au pays de Loire. . . .

These words, uttered by a small peasant girl in the open fields, listened to by God himself, had reverberations which demanded to be noted and made known; they provide the subject of his second *mystère: Le Mystère de la Porche de la deuxième Vertu.* The second theological virtue is Hope. His job was to write down the live metaphysical implications of Hope, and nothing must disturb him.

For the rest (no small matter), there were domestic duties, the family home to be kept going and the shop in the rue de la Sorbonne to be run. As well as the daily battle for the survival of his precarious little enterprise in despite of buffeting winds and treacherous waters.

X

RELIGIOUS DIFFICULTIES
PÉGUY AND CLAUDEL

My God, you know my secret prayers.—CHARLES PÉGUY.

PÉGUY'S DIFFICULTIES ON the political plane were serious enough but not unduly distressing. Maurras, in a discussion with Péguy, would say: 'You are wrong, your mind is on the wrong track.' He would not say: 'You are sinning, your heart is at fault.' The religious plane makes its own very different demands. Communion is closer, wounds are more deeply felt.

Even on this plane Péguy found someone on the field ahead of him. He had of course the highest possible idea of his mission: 'A Catholic Renaissance is coming about through me,' he said to Lotte. He was sure of this from the very beginning. Now this renaissance which he felt alive within himself had its tradition and some of its origins from that 1890-97 period, a sort of haven between two storms in our contemporary history: abruptly closed by the Dreyfus upheaval. The underlying spirit of it was connected with that youthful socialism which Péguy described so vividly, and with the Encyclicals of Leo XIII and the social disturbance they aroused both within and without the Church. Our socialism, said Péguy, was a sort of Christianity from outside. And it is true that Péguy had found, in the very heart of socialism so intended, that exaltation of souls through love which is the essence of Christianity. Within the Church itself, it is permissible to distinguish a specifically Roman tradition and a specifically Christian one. Péguy's adolescence was strongly impregnated with Christian influences, but the Roman strain as such was far less clear. His chosen term for the complete body of his belief is not Catholicity but Christianity. Catholicity has a Greek root, Christianity has its root in popular French speech and sprang naturally to the lips of Joinville and Jeanne who knew no other.

On the opposite slope of this historical division, Péguy missed the rich ground to which he had grown used in the old days with the *cour rose* friends. There was a Catholic renaissance going on, but unlike the one he had himself so nearly set afoot: the Dreyfus whirlwind had swept both slopes and hardened and steepened the minds of those on the right as much as those on the left; the result was a form of belief remote from Péguy's experience, radically Roman Catholic with emphasis on the *Roman*, and proud to boast of it. The movement was inaugurated by Bourget's *Echo de Paris* and Maurras'

Action Française; at this stage, Maurras was not a leader but an exponent of the movement and its controversialist and paid mouthpiece, and as such was in favour at the Vatican. So much for public action. Behind all this there was that mighty fortress held by the initiate, Saint Thomas Aquinas' doctrine, which, after three or four hundred years of neglect, had been revived and restored to its authoritative position by order from Rome. Some of Bergson's following left him to gather round the Dominicans. The Montagne Sainte-Geneviève has seen many such shifts of opinion in the thousand years of its experience. But Péguy did not like it. He was not in the least interested in the battery of proofs with which his thomistic friends supported their belief. The texts of the sacred liturgy were sufficient nourishment for him (as Sorel said, *Liturgy is diffused theology*), and the attacks on Bergson, after so much high praise, made him furious. He said so to a friend: 'Think of all Bergson has done for us. It is sheer ingratitude to attack him as you are doing.' To the reply, 'God breaks his instruments when he has done with them,' Péguy retorted: 'Are you so God-like . . . ?'

But these academic quarrels could be kept in the background. Péguy had his own field and his own manner of speech, essentially lyrical, admirably adapted to this field. In his *Mystère de la Charité de Jeanne d'Arc* he had developed three scenes from his early work, and there were still a lot of blank pages to fill in. First, there were the two mysteries to come: *Le Mystère du Porche de l'Espérance*, and *Le Mystère des Saints Innocents;* then there were those which remained unwritten, the subjects only mentioned in his last work, *La note conjointe*, written in haste with death imminent: there was to be Jeanne and the king, the mystery of the Human City; Jeanne and the Church: Jeanne's vocation was unique in the annals of sanctity, in that her battle was fought within the bosom of the Church and she died struck down by its own visible lawyers. All that is what Péguy was proposing to do. He was ready to start and on the lookout for a sympathetic audience. And then, just at the time when his so eagerly desired public might have been ready for him, things turned out otherwise: the fame of Paul Claudel, who until then had been known only to a narrow circle of writers, was spread abroad. Paul Claudel was to be the poet of thomistic Catholicity and to draw all homage to his work, while Péguy remained in shadow.

•

We witnessed his encounters with Barrès and Maurras. Now we have Claudel. These are the great men of 1910, the equals undoubtedly of the great men of 1830.

This statement may come as a surprise, however, for it is not a fact we take for granted, the more is the pity. That period, such a high-water mark in French life, is not appreciated by the French themselves, and people are not at all clear about it. The abrupt intervention of war and the disconcerting days that followed do in part explain the oversight, but only in part. The time that has since elapsed (a quarter century) is amply sufficient for judgment to be formed. The 1860 French knew that the great men of 1830 were named Hugo, Lamartine, Balzac, Michelet. Yet a great number would hesitate to name Barrès, Claudel, Péguy, Maurras, if asked who were the great men of 1910, though it is doubtful whether, in any society or any literature, could be found such admirable examples of intellectual and moral energy at work to hold and restore the shaken spirit of a nation in a desperately critical moment. They are never put forward as a group.

Between the two teams, there undoubtedly was a difference of destiny which does partly explain the difference in reputation. There were in fact several differences. The great men of 1830 were the beneficiaries of a surge of national feeling, human feeling, European feeling, which bore their genius on its tide. The whole of the nineteenth century was, of all centuries, the most blessed by hope. But in 1910, the young men of twenty were under the shadow of their fathers' distress and uncertainty. Again, the great men of 1830 found ready at their disposal an admirable language, of sure and supple movement, and with a vocabulary equally acceptable to ordinary people and the élite. But in 1910, the language available for young writers had been thrown out of gear by a score of wilful, almost desperate experiments. Prose, verse and playwriting were all in such a state that each had to work perilously and alone to achieve anything; for French society, that great literary workshop so active over hundreds of years, and still intact in 1830, was by 1890 merely a shell of a house, open to the winds. There was nothing to be done but to start from scratch. And courageous young teams set to work in such workshops as they could find. Instead of the *Comédie Française* and the *Odéon*, there was Antoine's *Théâtre Libre* and Lugné-Poë's *Œuvre*; instead of the Restoration drawing-rooms, there were the café's of the Latin Quarter. So there always remains in the work of our contemporaries some trace of the defiance and despair from which it grew. Nonetheless, their genius took it all in its stride and carried the day. It was a splendid effort, finally crowned by the heroism of 1914-1918, of which the memory must never be tainted by proximity to subsequent, sadder events. If their nineteenth century predecessors command the greater power of language, ours are the more powerful thinkers. Yet the 1830 men stand out in all their glory, while these others still lack favour.

Among the reasons for this, we come first of all on that surge of bloodshed between their heyday and ourselves, and remember all the many choice young souls who went at their bidding to fight for

France and fell almost to a man. The foam from this surge rises in a mist that blinds and chokes us. Then there is the fact that the 1830 men were far from being unanimously acclaimed, they had their adversaries, but these were lettered men who even when not attracted themselves were glad to see and read and pass round the new works, for the pleasure and honour of more lively discussion. The nineteenth century writers lived and worked in a very supple form of society, easily permeated and profoundly cultivated. Whereas twentieth century writers live in a torpid, sluggish society, governed unbeknown by strongly armed political and educational organisations bent on guiding the trend of thought and holding or withholding attention at will. In a word, fully equipped to control judgment. Now the four men we have named had in common the desire to turn the tide of ideas followed by the eighteenth century thinkers and their nineteenth century disciples, and to found the public, private and intimate life of Frenchmen on quite a different basis from that of the Third Republic and its institutions. This accounts for the conspiracy of silence which screens them off, half a century after they first set to work. The word went round that the young men were to boycott them: quite a large staff was set up to carry out the order. Here, for example, is M. Jacques Ancel's *Histoire Contemporaine*: the author was a distinguished University man and the publisher, Delagrave, had a good name. The essential facts for the period 1848-1930 are set down for the information of students. It is a useful piece of work, but the guiding hand is visible. Barrès is mentioned in a paragraph entitled, *Classical dilettantism*. There he is, labelled dilettante; his interest in politics and his nationalism were so much dilettantism. As for Péguy, Claudel and Maurras, they do not appear at all, they are not mentioned once. But the student will learn and will be able to state in his examination that 'the most important work of the younger generation is Romain Rolland's *Jean-Christophe*.' Three writers are honoured with a whole paragraph to themselves: Gide, Proust and Valéry, about whose quality there is no question, of course. But why these three in particular, and no others? The important persons under whose guidance this list of prize-winners was drawn up . . . do of course regret that Valéry's intellectualism is the cover for nihilism, and that Proust's and Gide's humanism has a dubious moral influence on the young. But if Valéry, Gide and Proust were not set up on pedestals, it would be less easy to keep such men as Barrès, Maurras, Péguy and Claudel in the background. What an awkward choice to have to make: on one side, nihilism and the questionable moral influence; on the other, the idealisation of country, Christianity, monarchy and Church. Which is the lesser evil? The official text-books give the answer.

•

Who was Claudel when Péguy came into contact with him: what sort of a man, and what is there to know about him? In about 1910 few people could have answered this. For a long time, Claudel was known privately only to a small group. But he plays an important part at this stage in our story.

In 1883, Renan, presiding at the prizegiving at the Lycée Louis-le-Grand, bestowed his congratulations and the laurel crown on a young prizewinner by name Paul Claudel. 'I started life with Renan's kiss on my forehead,' he said. He accepted it with no feeling of annoyance or revulsion. He was not a believer, nor were his family believers. Romain Rolland was his classmate and friend. So we can imagine the nature of their interests. Now about 1910 he was found to be the most exalted and ardent of Catholic writers.

On leaving the lycée, Claudel had not gone on to University work. He lived with his own set in Paris, a life which Balzac describes so well as it already existed in 1830, and which Claudel's own soaring prose conveys so clearly in a few lines:

> O the long bitter roads of that time and the days when I was one and alone!
>
> The walk through Paris, that long road going down towards Notre-Dame!
>
> Then, like a young athlete making his way to the Oval, surrounded by a pressing crowd of friends and trainers,
>
> One speaking in his ear, dropping his arm which another seizes to fasten on it the band to keep his muscles taut,
>
> I walked among the hurrying footsteps of my gods.

Whither was the young athlete bound? An unbeliever, *one and alone;* what was the nature of his unbelief? He frequently visited Mallarmé and this refined disciple of Hegel was not the man to make a Catholic of him. Was he experimenting with idealism? No: it is impossible to imagine Claudel platonising and plotinising like a Maeterlinck. He was too impulsive and earth-bound to delight in such abstruse exercises. The elucidation of ideas and myths is a pleasant pastime and Claudel was in deadly earnest. Pure thought was not his line at all. 'Kant's conception of duty, as expounded by our philosophy teacher, M. Burdeau, I found quite intolerably indigestible.' He considered the soul, and more especially the heart which is after all just a muscle with blood invading it and making it beat: a handful of palpitating flesh.

Life according to the flesh lured him and held him fast.

> I was living in immorality and I gradually sank into a state of despair. The death of my grandfather, whom I had seen for long months gradually succumbing to cancer of the stomach, filled me with utter terror and I was obsessed with the thought of death. I had forgotten all about religion and knew no more of it than a savage.

Unlike Péguy, who was nourished and supported by the legends and heroic certitudes of his race from his earliest days, Claudel was for a time an out-and-out nihilist. It was a flesh-bound nihilism, dictated by the claims of a violently sensual nature. Claudel would neither consider nor put up with any form of abstraction. To know a thing, he said, is to live it, it is to be born again, '*co-naître*' in it. To be born is always to know: '*Toute naissance est une connaissance.*' It is a play on words and more, for he gets inside the words and loves most passionately these verbal articulations each of which is found to contain an always concrete distant image. 'Let us ruminate this mouthful of intelligibility,' he wrote. He meant the word, for intelligence is a method of absorption, and reflexion is rumination. This is how he ruminated:

There is an unmistakable kinship linking in three different languages ideas of *acquiring in the mind* and of *surging: génoumai* and *gignôsko, nasci, gignere, novi, cognoscere, naître* and *connaître*. . . . Every detail is significant in the anatomy of these verbs.

So all true labour of the mind should bring forth, not so much a thought as an entity, with breath and blood; and should do it like a woman in childbirth:

Thoughts,
Actions still asleep, like new-born babes
With their knees drawn up to their stomachs, curled into the shape in which the womb held them. . . .

Claudel often used terms connected with pregnancy, childbirth and copulation. He said: 'Blue does truly know the colour of orange; the hand does truly know its shadow on a wall! In truth and in fact one angle of a triangle knows the other two, in the same sense in which Isaac knew Rebecca.' We need to be on the alert: the word *connaître*, to know, has a new meaning and a new value; *connaissance* (knowledge) is more and better than just *co-naissance:* it is possession and release through gratification.

Claudel cried out for this release with every pore of his being. He composed extraordinary exercises and rigorous descriptions of objects such as a tree, a river, an idol, a pig. Each object is given such concrete expression and is so firmly possessed and brought so near, almost in contact, damp as it may be, slimy, filthy if it is filthy, that he does not always avoid obscenity. This closeness of Claudel to his object is the close contact of man with woman in the act of love. One of his heroes says in a voice I cannot but take for Claudel's own:

Cébès, I was given power, harsh and ferocious it is! It is the power of the male: there is no woman in me.

So spoke Claudel through the mouth of the hero of his first play, *Tête-d'Or*. Tête-d'Or is a pagan, so was Claudel: both possessed a fury to dominate and create. Listen to Tête-d'Or making his magnificent appeal to the huge tree:

O tree, welcome me home! All alone I went away from your protecting branches, and now, all alone, I come back to you, O motionless father!

Take me back under your shade, O son of the Earth! O wood, at this hour of my distress! Murmur and let me know

The word I am and which I feel straining most horribly within me!

For you are all continual effort, dragging your body out of inanimate matter assiduously.

How you suck the earth, old though you are,

Driving down and about on all sides with your strong supple roots! And how you fill the sky! How you heave whole

To its aspiration in one immense leaf, O Form of Fire!

. . . It takes the whole of earth and sky to keep you upright!

So may I stand upright! May I not lose my soul! That essential sap, that inward moisture of mine, that seething

To which the man I am is subject, may I not lose it in a meaningless tuft of grass and flowers! May I grow in my unity!

May I remain my very self and upright!

Tête-d'Or's wish was fulfilled. He wanted power and he got it, and through it all that goes with power: rapid growth and then catastrophe. Tête-d'Or took control of the energies of a people who had lost their lawful constitution and their kings. With the help of this people he conquered Europe. He bent and broke her. He was all-powerful for destruction but unable to create. Wounded in battle, he died: 'I was nothing!' he said as he fell.

This is the usual end of heathenism. But Claudel refused to be beaten. He had to find something to lean on, some God to whom to pray for the satisfaction of his immense desire. Claudel aspired to know all and to possess all things with absolute knowledge and possession. All: *tout:* the word is formidable and must be understood as such if we would understand the extent of Claudel's longing, involving his whole being. Nature, as his eyes, senses and mind grasped it, did not satisfy him but made him irritable. It could only be seized at a given point for a given moment. Whereas nature exists everywhere all the time. It has depth and entirety, and this entirety which he could not embrace haunted and tormented his mind. Let us hear him on the passing of time, the simultaneous hours passing all together over the face of the earth:

Yet, at every hour on Earth it is all times at once; at every season, it is all the seasons. While the feather-worker observes it is midday by the dial of Pointe-Saint Eustache, the sun is piercing the Virginian leaf with its first level ray, and the schools of whales are playing under the austral moon. It is raining in London, snowing over Pomerania, while Paraguay is all roses and Melbourne is roasting. So it seems that whatever exists can never cease being, and that time, whose function it is to interpret existence as a passing thing, each section having, as we have said, its concrete form and features like a woman, carries with it a permanent, ineluctable need. . . .

The solitary core of nature and the heart are so many clues, to a religious soul, of a whole to be striven for. Imagine a great musician who knew Beethoven only through part of a symphony, say a flute partition, and whose fate it was to hear and attend to this single line constantly; it is incomplete but still lovely, carrying the melody on, only to break off suddenly, pausing. The man will know that this line of melody is insufficient in itself and is a trace and indication of something else; an unknown but real and undoubted whole can alone give the faltering line a meaning. There is that note, and then the following pause: what should it contain? Those twenty even notes, monotonously rhythmical, are an accompaniment to an unknown song. And those other twenty notes, shaping a melodious phrase for the flute to sing, is accompanied and supported by unrevealed harmonies. The flute has paused: where is the answering voice? This is how I imagine Claudel eagerly cross-questioning the world of nature: he must know the entirety, or what he knows means nothing to him. As he said, '*To know is to reconstitute that without which the rest could not be.*'

That is still pagan. Any young disciple of Pythagoras, drunk with the elixir of knowledge, might say and feel the same in his anxiety to grasp the essential qualities of a world perfect and in the round. But Claudel differed in exalting his longing to the scale of the mighty *Octave of creation:*

I who so loved visible things, Oh how I longed to see it all, to possess with appropriation, not only with sight or sense, but with spiritual intelligence.

And to know all, in order to be all known. . . .

None of the ancients would have spoken like that, concluding the idea of conquering with the idea of giving, submitting, and all but offering. The difficulty increases with the vehemence of the claim: what total image can fill and satiate our souls. Image is the most inadequate of words. Call must needs answer to call, person to person, and a divine presence it is that must satiate and transfigure the soul. Soul: again an inadequate word: flesh must needs feed our flesh and incarnation is necessary. Our life will be a misery to us if we do not find it; our deprivation and the hunger of our nature pursue us and we are incapable of satisfying our desire. That is how Claudel knew the inappeasable hunger, not of the thinker, nor the artist, but of the whole man bent to the possession, not of some divine reflection but of absolute being, spirit by spirit, flesh by flesh. He had to have that total mutual possession which is at once conquest and gift. It was a question not of passing need but of vital necessity. A believer is not an idealist but first and foremost a desperately hungry man. Claudel in his youth had worshipped and besought a tree as the incarnation of power and solitude. That time was passed, and it was not to a tree that he would pray now, nor to nature. With his keen mind and vehement heart, Claudel aspired too high to be satisfied with blind, cruel nature. Now she was matter for his gaze to traverse: she signified a supreme whole, perfectly ordered and ruled, innumerably peopled with holy angels, Virtues, Dominations and Archangels. What Claudel demanded was (to use his own magnificent words) *the mighty octave of creation;* and to bring him ease and release, this *mighty octave*, the voice of invisible things over and above the visible order, must whisper and *communicate to him. . . .*

. . . The word I am and which I feel straining most horribly within me.

How was God to be possessed? Only by a miracle, there is no other way. Man cannot find faith alone, his nature won't let him. But if he is looking for faith, it can find him. It can even take him by surprise if he is not looking for it. But man can never take faith by surprise. The miracle of faith brought about by grace, when it happens to whole peoples, generations and ages, works so continuously that there is no sense of constraint. The quiet action of education, ritual and example is all so much nourishment for the maintenance of belief. But in our time of broken tradition in education, neglected ritual, and thinly-spaced example, it must be otherwise. Grace acts suddenly, that is, with vehemence. In revolutionary times it is perforce revolutionary; when it is prevented from mingling with the rising sap, it acts by countercharge and conversion. Such was Claudel's own experience: on December 25th 1886, he attended the Christmas Mass at Notre-Dame; this is what he tells us:

I was standing in the crowd near the second pillar at the choir entrance, on the right, where the sacristy is. Then there occurred the event which has soared over my whole life. In an instant, my heart was touched and I *believed*. I believed with such strength of adhesion, with such a stirring of my whole being, with so powerful a conviction, such certitude, leaving no room for any sort of doubt, that since then none of the books or reasonings or chance encounters of a distracted lifetime have succeeded in shaking my faith, nor even, be it said, in touching it at all. . . . I was sobbing and weeping, and the lovely hymn of the *Adeste fidelis* contributed to my emotion.

It was three years before his mind was able to submit wholly to this Church which puts God into the mouths of the faithful: *satisfaction, as after food; ease and release, as of a man with a woman.* And ten years or so were still to pass before the bright glow of his new-found allegiance was perceptible to the reading public of Paris.

puisqu'il traduit le courant spirituel, qui unit les poètes à Dieu. Voila pourquoi il faut lire ces livres et les méditer. Ils ont place sur notre bureau auprès de nos mystiques préférés. On les ouvre n'importe où ; on en lit vingt pages ; c'est un bain de spiritualité. Dans l'aridité de notre civilisation ils sont une source fraîche, jaillissant des couches les plus profondes et les plus chrétiennes de notre race paysanne et française.

Fils des maçons et des vitriers de Notre-Dame, Péguy est l'homme dans la paroisse ; et la profonde unité de tous ses mystères, c'est qu'ils sont le christianisme dans la paroisse.

Péguy a bien su son catéchisme quand il était petit. Il ne l'a pas oublié, et, maintenant qu'il est grand, c'est son paroissien romain qu'il lit chaque matin à l'office du jour. Il ne doit guère fréquenter les Docteurs. Il est, je crois bien, de ces chrétiens qui donneraient toutes les sommes pour le *Magnificat*, le *Salve Regina* et les litanies de la Vierge. Dans tout ce qu'il écrit ou perçoit comme une résonnance des psaumes, des proses, des hymnes de notre liturgie.

Et c'est sans doute là le secret de sa grâce et de son rayonnement.

J.-A. DUREL.

A proof corrected by Péguy (Collection C.-Th. Quoniam)

EDINBURGH UNIVERSITY LIBRARY
WITHDRAWN

Five plays were published, of which the public knew nothing, then came the Five Great Odes, a triumphant shout uttered at the outcome of an extremely perilous emotional crisis:

Hail, O world, new to my eyes, world now entire!
O total credo *of visible and invisible things, I accept you with a Catholic heart!*
Wherever I look,
I am faced with the mighty octave of Creation!

Péguy's *Mystère de la Charité de Jeanne d'Arc* had just been published. The two works appeared more or less simultaneously and both made an impression on the minds of certain sets of people. But it was soon clear that Claudel's soaring utterance was getting a better welcome than Péguy's level prose. Readers were able to recognise some of the traditional sources of great French style (the breadth of Church Latin, the sumptuous language of Bossuet and Hugo). Even the peculiarities were somehow traditional, as they could be traced to Rimbaud, and the *Nouvelle Revue Française*, arbiter of a new orthodoxy in letters, claimed all respect for them. But Péguy's meditative scrutinies reminded them of nothing at all, so they shut the book. Hope was centred on Claudel.

I mentioned the *Nouvelle Revue Française:* there the expectation aroused was chiefly of a literary nature; but it was of a very different kind, far more ardent and intense, in such groups as the one *l'Occident* had brought together around André Mithouard, where a real and zealous effort was made towards an order and hierarchy both Catholic and French. The question was, whether Claudel would be the poet of this effort and this zeal, and whether he was to be, to use his own expression, the man *to gather together the land of God.* He chose for epigraph for his *Art Poétique* these magnificent lines from Saint Augustine: *Sicut creator, ita moderator. Donec universi seculi pulchritudo . . . velut magnum carmen ineffabilis modulatoris.* Would Claudel's work, dredged and grown limpid, moderating at the same time as creating, be the reflection of that Catholic truth: *magnum carmen ineffabilis modulatoris,* and become the French equivalent to Dante? 'It is the dog-star of truth,' said young Jacques Rivière, writing about the Odes in the *Nouvelle Revue Française.* 'Perhaps we may now expect Claudel to give us work strained of all traces of suffering, made of the very brightness of his faith. I imagine plays springing from short rays of light sparkling like crossed swords, and poetry as warm and brief as summer.'

That was the general tone and the hope in the air. It is very understandable. There is so much good and lovely stuff in Claudel. His work (which is all of a piece with himself) is made of perfectly sound material: a vigorous mind, a brave heart, and an unfaltering tongue. Some of his heroines (Marthe in *L'Echange*, for instance) bring him near to Balzac, so ample and solid in conception are they. One hesitates to say more. For there are signs of some disturbance in his nature, seen as a whole. It may not come from very deep; it may be due more to the difficulties of the century he was born in, and to the crises of sensual nihilism which shook him on two occasions and which he had to stifle twice. A conversion is in a man's private life the equivalent of a revolution. It is not for nothing that Péguy never let himself be called a convert: he knew his whole life was borne forward on a single surge, and though he erred in thought, he never ran amok. Claudel is the essential convert. All Péguy's life unfolded under the sign of his unsullied childhood which remained clear and effective all through the storms and ashes of life. Whereas Claudel's whole life was marked by the crises he endured and disclosed itself as the life of a man who had twice escaped from himself in terror. The second time was certainly the worst. It is the subject of the play called *Partage de Midi* which Claudel himself withdrew from circulation. Claudel could never believe that he believed enough, he was always longing to believe more and to be more urgent and strong in belief: all because of that crisis. And still in the Odes, which are songs of healing and health, his mind kept reverting to the sad and troubled side of his belief, and his entreaty grew correspondingly intense:

Stay with me, Lord, for evening is coming and do not leave me!
Let me not be lost with Voltaire, Renan, Michelet, Hugo and all other infamous men!
Their souls are with dead dogs, their lips held in dung.
They are dead, and even after their death their name is poison and corruption.

Péguy was a mediæval Catholic, a Pre-Reformation Christian. Claudel was a modern, a Counter-Reformation Catholic.

In response to the hopes he had aroused, Claudel published a play, *L'Otage*. It was an outstanding success, but the hurt in Claudel's inspiration was all the more apparent. It had already shown itself in an earlier work, *La Jeune Fille Violaine*; there the intrusion of Grace had destroyed a home; everything was redeemed and emerged shining, but the miraculous radiance could not blot out all trace of the ruin that had preceded it. Claudel returned to the same theme in *L'Otage*, underlining it with a masterly hand. The total effect is very strange. On foundations worthy of Sophocles rose a structure for which the elder Dumas might have been responsible, composed in a flamboyant style straight from Barbey d'Aurévilly. Everyone is familiar with the subject: the Coûfontaine family was scattered and decimated by the blast of the Revolution. Sygne de Coûfontaine alone remained attached to the neighbourhood and the land. Years went by, and Sygne quietly, stubbornly built up again what men had torn to pieces: *I am the one who remains and who is always there.* At last, one day, her cousin Coûfontaine came, the only surviving bearer of the name. She gave him a great welcome and at her business-woman's desk she showed him her diaries and account books: everything was in order, nothing was lost; such had been her task, and now she wanted to know what was to become of it. Her cousin was an adventurer and a hunted man. He was not interested, and said, 'Keep it. You will marry and this shall be your dowry. . . .' Sygne refused: 'It is Coûfontaine land and Coûfontaine it must remain; Georges, let me be your wife. . . .'

Let me be sworn in like a new knight! My lord, my love, let me place my hands in your hands.
And take my oath like a nun being professed!
. . . Land is lacking, strength has receded from us, but faith between man and man
Remains, and the unsullied heart discovering its lord and saluting the colours!
. . . May God hear our prayers!
He Who gives Himself in the host for good and all,
He has given us, too, this sacrament of the giving of ourselves for good and all. . . .

There we have the imposing and sure foundation for the play. Claudel then plotted the destruction of the foundation itself as the theme of his play. The unexpected return of the emigrant was cover for another high plot: he had brought with him and hidden in the house at night an old man of humble appearance, unbeknown to his cousin; there was a priest in the house. Hence the catastrophe, for the priest was the Pope himself whom Coûfontaine had rescued from the prison where Napoleon had put him, in the hope of getting him out of France. But the secret was known. M. Turelure, the prefect, an old valet of the Coûfontaine's who had had them guillotined, a one-time jacobin turned bonapartiste, a Talleyrand minus the manners, a crawling sort of Fouché, appeared at the door:

You have got the Pope here, he said bluntly to Sygne. You are in my hands. But everything can be arranged. Like the Emperor, I, too, want to make a fine marriage. Marry me.

Sygne was furious.

Think it over, the creature continued. It is you or the Pope, I shall have one or other of you. So however it turns out, I am the winner.

He went off chuckling and met the village priest, M. Badilon, on the doorstep. Sygne told M. Badilon the whole story: the Pope's danger, the disgusting proposal and her own fury. The curé listened, he was a very holy and wise priest; he listened attentively and quietened the poor woman's fears; then, having comforted her, he showed her where her sacrifice lay: the Pope is God's representative on earth, God helpless and delivered over to men. . . . But Sygne was not, after all, free; she explained this: I became engaged this very morning.

He who gives himself in the host for good and all

He has given us, too, the sacrament of the giving of ourselves for good and all. . . .

But was she really engaged, commented the priest. She only gave her human word. There had been no consecration, it did not count. An oath given at night, said the priest, was merely a promise, and neither an act nor a sacrament.

Sygne had never contemplated a situation where her faith and her honour could be on opposite sides. She was willing to admit she had been mistaken, and that man left to himself was nothing and had nothing to give, not even his word of honour. His childish honour had no value. Sygne was ready for whatever sacrifice was necessary: Have you any order for me? she asked the priest impatiently. No, it is not a command; in strict right, you have no obligation. You are free, that is all I have to tell you.

You are free: what a cruel phrase for a casuist dramatist to put on the lips of a country priest. Sygne had been used to obedience all her life and to certainty. And when she heard the words *you are free* she lost control of herself. With tears and sobs she saw that she was done for. The Pope would be set free and she would become Turelure's. The rest of the play is about Turelure's brilliant career: Napoleon fell, Louis XVIII came to the throne; Turelure was received at court on account of his alliance with the Coûfontaine's. And we end with Sygne sullied, the king made ridiculous, and Turelure the strong man.

What an odd piece of work. Bossuet would have been up in arms at the idea of such a case of conscience. Take it for a moment to Calvary: a glance from Mary Magdalen to Pilate or the High Priest, and everything settled: two crosses instead of three erected that Friday evening, and no Christendom. But Bossuet is not of our times. There was the Church of the Fathers, then the Church of the Bishops, who pronounced judgment. In the nineteenth century, there were writers and no one to judge them at all. So they judged one another. *L'Otage* caused quite a sensation: the *Nouvelle Revue Française* public and the Catholic public together made it a great success.

Péguy, who read less than anyone, made an exception of Claudel. He had recognised the power of his inspiration from the very first. It would be rash to go so far as to say he took him for his equal. But he did admire the *Grandes Odes*. But he reacted very strongly to *L'Otage*. The sullying of the woman involved in this pious plot roused his disgust. Claudel's success added bitterness to his distaste, and scorn for the sort of clericalism then in vogue.

Péguy must have been all the more hurt because of the fact that his own life was in a state of crisis not unlike the one Claudel described in *L'Otage*. I am only considering it from the point of view of the basic themes, of course. But Claudel had staged in his baroque style one of those cases when the family order and the clerical order may find themselves on opposite sides. Now Péguy's own return to the faith had produced a similar situation in his own household. His wife, who was just as forceful a person as he was, had not taken the same line, and refused to have their marriage consecrated in church; she also refused to let her children be baptised. Mme Beaudouin, Mme Péguy's mother and a member of the household, was on her daughter's side; the Beaudouin's had been republican free-thinkers since 1848, they did not intend to give in now. And the children, of course, listened to the women. One must picture this Lozère home, almost a cottage, a long, low building under a few high trees: at this time Péguy had his room and work-table on one side and the women and children lived on the other; Péguy claimed absolute quiet for his work and the atmosphere was strained and painful. So there was nothing but disorder all around him, crowding right in on his soul, where songs destined to be heard a long time ahead ripened under more than difficult conditions.

The whole situation was intensely paradoxical. According to Church law, Péguy was living in concubinage with a pagan and was the father of a family of little pagans who were his children by the flesh alone; the whole atmosphere had become intolerable to him. A similar case arose at this very time in the rather high-brow little world he shared with his friends. A young woman married to a free-thinking university man, the mother of unbaptised children, had suddenly given up the revolutionary creed which she had previously accepted in complete accord with her husband. There had seemed to be no solution to the problem but for her to make a complete break, leaving her husband and children and going home to her own mother. In Péguy's circle there was some dismay at this cruel story. But Péguy had no intention of following the fugitive's example. The thought of breaking up the home he had founded in his twenties, and had bravely supported through so many difficulties, never entered his mind. This inspired, stubborn creature who made a point of honour of never renouncing a particle of his past, honoured his own youthful intention and living past in the persons of his family: he also honoured their intention, to impose anything on anyone was not in his nature. He was the man of the short, sharp retort: his own retort to the crisis was to accept it in all its cruelty without flinching. He was faced with a problem, well, that problem should become his life. His life would be the sadder, but never broken by it. He was in a false position as regards the Church; his meditations had brought him to it as well as the graces he had received (he had no doubt about this), and from the point of view of his soul he was living in sin. The written law forbade him to come further than the threshold and there he stayed, submitting to the equivocal situation without undue restiveness. Meditation on tragic themes had, through long acquaintance and practice, taught him respect for insoluble problems. As a Catholic poet, and great among the very great (he had no more doubt of this than of the graces he had been granted), he would live in whatever conditions he was given. Maybe, by accepting the trial and drinking it to the dregs, he would find in it a source of greatness.

There is no evidence that even his most intimate friends (such as Peslouän and Lotte) presumed to come forward with advice in such closely personal difficulties. But Maritain felt no such reticence. He had been the confidant and almost daily witness of the re-birth of Christ in Péguy's life; it was without question one of the most powerfully moving experiences of his own life. And what he had seen begun he ardently wished to see full-grown. He was distressed and shocked to see his friend stop at the door of the Church. With the support of his wife who was also an intimate friend of Péguy's, he implored him to convert his good dispositions into deeds: 'You owe your children baptism,' they said; 'you should insist.' Maritain at that time was a different man from the personalistic, pluralistic Catholic we know to-day, so charitably disposed to other men's vacillations. A neophyte of the doctrine of St. Thomas, at that stage he ardently embraced it in its most rigorous definitions and most exacting requirements.

One day, won by his insistence or merely in a fit of impatience, Péguy gave him a free hand and sent him off to talk to the women: Mme Péguy, and her mother, Mme Beaudouin. 'Go and see for yourself,' he said. The only thing we know for certain is that the interview was wordy and without result. According to the women, Maritain said: 'Baptised children are more Péguy's children than his own.' According to Maritain, the women answered: 'If the children are baptised, we shall commit suicide.' Or according to other reports: '. . . we shall drown them.' None of the protagonists admit having used any of these words, but it remains true that all three kept the most terrifying memory of this encounter.

Maritain continued to plead with his friend. Nothing had been gained by laying down the law, but there were other means. The Church has its own way of resolving apparently inextricable cases of conscience; Péguy should take consultation and pay heed, he should ask a priest to advise him. Péguy himself did not agree: M. Badilon's remarks were of no interest to him. A way out of the difficulty might have been found to give him access to worship and the sacraments. But Péguy was not a man for makeshift arrangements.

His suffering was very real, nonetheless. One day Maritain's sister met him, pale and worn out, in the back-shop of the *Cahiers*. 'Go and see Baillet,' he said. Baillet was the *cour rose* friend, now a Dominican. For a moment, Péguy seemed ready, but only for a moment. Baillet was not called in after all.

The Maritains say that they saw Péguy on the verge of making up his mind on several other occasions. But Tharaud says they are mistaken; Péguy never hesitated about making up his mind all his life. If he paid attention to what Maritain and his wife and sister said, it was in order to satisfy his liking for confession and pathos which increased as the years went by; the princesses of tragedy, endlessly discussing the situation with their attendants, listen and reply, turn and turn about, but never change in love or hate. So it was with Péguy; he might seem about to yield, it was not so. At bottom there was no hesitation. We agree: Péguy wished neither to use his authority nor to fall back on a makeshift. It suited him to linger at the heart of his problem. A day came when he begged Maritain not to concern himself any more with his affairs. It was through Maritain that he was corresponding with Baillet; this, too, he brought to an end. 'From to-day's date, April 25, 1910,' he wrote to Baillet, 'the spiritual mandate which I had given Maritain ends. When an ambassador so persists in deliberately acquitting himself of his mandate in the wrong way, there is nothing left but to withdraw his powers.'

•

There was a good deal of talk about all this in the bookshop circles. Some saw in Péguy's conduct a proof of insincerity. 'Péguy treats us like dirt,' said a free-thinking subscriber when he called to withdraw his subscription. Sorel, who immensely admired Claudel, put in an occasional bantering remark: 'What is a Catholic who doesn't go to Mass,' he said to Tharaud. 'Péguy is just floundering, poor lad.' Other observers took a more subtle line: 'An exceptional situation, one out of the ordinary, is what suits Péguy. He is getting a certain amount of pleasure out of it.' L'Abbé Battifol, whom Péguy still went to see from time to time, declared that Péguy had immense pride.

Pride may not be quite the right word. A cursory judgment admits it, but on second thoughts it needs altering and correcting. As Max Scheler observed with his customary insight, 'Genius is immediately aware of its own value and riches and its deep rooting in the universe, without the intermediary of thought or elucidation; this awareness is brimming to the surface of his conscious mind all the time, but it cannot be called pride . . .'[1] Max Scheler brings us very near the truth. But the first impressions are not without point: there undoubtedly was some satisfaction in the situation, and there was pride, too. But to stop there and judge by that alone would be to base one's final judgment on merely accessory elements. The fact is that we are here faced with one of those injunctions which from time to time came to the surface in Péguy's life and took command. Just as he was impelled to leave the Ecole Normale, first to write his *Jeanne d'Arc*, then to marry, found an independent business and launch out, without support, with wife and children on his hands, on the wholly unreasonable venture of the *Cahiers*, so now he was impelled to take his stand and work and believe and hope, clinging as best he might to his perilous high ledge between a household where he was no longer really at home and a Church he remained outside.

Neither dizziness nor doubt afflicted him. This was not his first risky adventure, the new one was on the spiritual plane and might lead anywhere: all he knew was that he would hold on tight. 'One should never know in the morning where one will spend the night,' he said to me once. It is a picture of a man travelling on foot; so went the pilgrims in the olden days. The mediæval believer setting out for Jerusalem could not always count on meeting a priest to say Mass for him at the right time. But he set out just the same, with his wallet on his hip and his prayer on his lips. Such a pilgrim was Péguy.

•

Prayer: that was all this Christian had, shut out as he was from the communion of saints; Péguy spoke of it to Lotte, his favourite confidant:

> What is so tiresome is that one has to be careful of the priests. . . . They administer the sacraments, so they like it to be thought there is nothing but the sacraments. They forget to say there is prayer as well and that prayer is at least half. Sacraments and prayer are two different things. They control the first, but the second is at our disposal.

Only prayer: Péguy knew of someone else who had had to manage with prayer alone. Jeanne d'Arc with her coming mission on her mind, had, as Péguy was fond of remembering, taken refuge in solitary prayer for a time. No doubt it was to avoid being told to be more reasonable, not to get so excited, and to keep quiet. That was not Jeanne's idea at all, she wanted to dare and take risks, to carry on regardless as Péguy put it. He admired this trait in her, he too wanted to carry on regardless: risk was the breath of life to him

[1] *L'homme du ressentiment*, by Max Scheler, p. 28, Gallimard. I have curtailed the quotation. The whole of this fine analysis is worth reading.

and one of the forms of his vocation. Every soul has its distinctive sign which qualifies its life, and qualifies its holiness if it is holy. One man has charity and is ever ready to give; another has poverty, and goes from deprivation to deprivation; the mark of Péguy's soul, his genius, was risk: life could not be too insecure for him. He was only so attached to poverty because risk was a constant element of it.

Complacency and pride may well have had their place, let us repeat, but we have no right to stop at that: by following Péguy we shall see how his adventure broadened out. Though cut off from all religious rites, he was far from being cut off from his fellow men, and he stepped out to meet the peril ahead neither lightly nor alone. The first risk that faced him was the risk of a division: he was told that if he did not baptise his children, insist on having them baptised, they were lost. Such barefaced dogmatism only served to anger him. He had had his own reasons for leaving the Church at the age of sixteen: he could not admit that souls were damned, implying an eternal victory for evil. He pondered on this refusal for years, and traces of it are found on the lips of Jeanne in Péguy's early work. Jeanne, wholly believing, accepted the dogma but gave free rein to her heart's revolt:

O s'il faut, pour sauver de la flamme éternelle
Les corps des morts damnés s'affolant de souffrance,
Abandonner mon corps à la flamme éternelle,
Mon Dieu, damnez mon corps à la flamme éternelle.

Et s'il faut pour sauver de l'Absence éternelle
Les âmes des damnés s'affolant de l'Absence,
Abandonner mon âme à l'Absence éternelle,
Que mon âme s'en aille en l'Absence éternelle.

Péguy returning to the faith remained that sort of a believer, not arguing at all but protesting at heart. *We are one with the eternally damned*, he said in his young and angry days. Obstinate peasant that he was, he stuck to his juvenile declaration. And now people were telling him his own children were among the damned. Well then, their destiny and his were one and the same. Any threat to them roused him to fury. He was never the man to ensure his own salvation by keeping away from suspect friends. Such poor prudent salvation was but mediocrity to him. Risk was better any day, made fruitful by solitary valour and hope.

Péguy never renounced hope; at the end of all his queer excursions there was always a gleam of dawn in the sky. People said to him: You owe your children baptism. He knew it perfectly well; it was simply a matter of finding out how the obligation was to be carried out. To impose it was against all his instincts; his pride would not let him beg for it. What other expedient was left him? The very

F

simple one of asking nothing, precisely nothing, and waiting. We have already seen something of his capacity for waiting, for 'long-term deals,' and for slow maturing. Here we have the finest example of all, and one crowned by outstanding success: the day was to come when the almoner of Sainte-Barbe, become Monsignor Battifol, was to welcome into that same study where Péguy had once come to tell him of his registry office marriage, two young people, brother and sister, asking to be baptised; and a few days later, Madame Péguy came too, bringing her youngest child, born in 1915; coming to kneel herself, after all these young ones. So all who played their part in the Lozère story, with one exception (Marcel, the eldest son), came of their own accord to carry out the wish of the man who never asked but knew how to wait.

We can push forward still further: Péguy's waiting and hoping are apt for wider bounds. The narrow hypothesis never works with a man like that, the broader one is always more likely to be the true one. In that dim region of his mind that underlay his work there were always terms still to run and open vistas.

We have caught a glimpse of the one that led to his children's baptism. There were others, with the eventuality of a more widespread and problematical baptism. If his children's lack of belief had separated them from their father, there was no knowing what chain of separations would not have been started, for he had more brothers than those born of his flesh; there was that family of *cour rose* friends; the *Cahiers* family, with its thousand subscribers who provided his livelihood; André Bourgeois, his secretary; Payen, his printer; and the typographers who worked for him, whom he knew individually, never asking them how many years ago it was they last made their Easter communion. Is that all? Not yet. There was, unknown to his Paris friends, but ever near to him, and ever dear, the family of the faubourg Bourgogne, that vanguard of working, peasant France, venerable and traditional too, by now, which neglected to practise its religion, but could never be accused of sin through lack of ardour or elevation. With all these Péguy had affiliations of blood, heart and memory. The parable tells us not to tear the cockle from the wheat for fear of hurting the wheat. Péguy was all against things being torn up by the roots. If his children were to be damned, so was he; if his people were lost, then so was he; if the authorities blamed him, he would put up with it. Besides, on the plane of invisible things, who is to see what is cockle and what is wheat? That the authorities do not tell us. 'What one has to realise,' said Péguy to Lotte, 'is that the geography, the map of Catholicism, of the Church, and the map of those saved by grace, do not exactly correspond. I know Jews who are given astonishing graces. . . .'

His children, his friends and his fellow countrymen suffered a common fate: they had been 'dechristianised.' (*Dechristianised*, *re-christianised* are ugly words which Péguy wrote once only, with an apology.) Fellow countrymen, friends, children were all living deprived of the dignity of religious rites, deprived of God, with neither voice nor words to pray. Men past masters in the art of undermining souls (Péguy knew them well from personal experience) had taken much pains to reduce them to this state and to breed on their impoverishment. It was a very serious situation for children and more serious still for the French people, weighed down by its own mass.

The enemy of all forms of pessimism, in fact congenitally disinclined to entertain any thought with a pessimistic tinge, Péguy never let his mind dwell on such subjects and would not allow others to do so in his presence. But the darker view was not unknown to him, and it may even have held in the bottom of his secret soul an immense and decisive place.

Even the mysteries, carefully read, discover it. Each of them (there are three, to which we may add the poem called *Eve*) first soars into supernatural regions, then, by slow transitions, bends gradually down to solid earth, a certain particular tract of earth, Péguy's native land, France, and there it finishes, sowing seeds, wrapping disquietude in the illumination of hope.

This tendency can easily be traced in the second and third mysteries (we shall come back to it). The first is a more complex case. First, because the allusion to modern France occurs on every page and can be read by implication between the lines, in the 'extra-text' of which Péguy was so fond. Jeanne, as he interprets her, is haunted less by external peril, in the shape of the English enemy, than by internal peril, which is the spread of impiety. Now history gives no clue to this second peril; fourteenth century Christendom was torn by the great schism, but wide awake and kept so by its great mystics such as Catherine of Siena and Vincent Ferrier, the wandering preacher of the Western peoples. It was deeply devotional. Péguy's personal situation and his vocation are what explain the double sense of inner and outer peril, of the decline of power, in war on one hand, in Christianity on the other. Péguy, not Jeanne, was the one to feel constrained by this. The final return to earth, to France, is briefly traced, or rather merely indicated. It is all given in one short sentence, the very last. Jeanne breaks off her meditation and turning her mind to her native land, she exclaims: *Orléans, qui êtes au pays de Loire. . .* And that is all. On these few slight words the mystery, as we usually read it, ends.

But brevity is only apparent here: it appears that the *Mystère de la Charité de Jeanne d'Arc* is an abridged work. On sending it to the printers, Péguy cut out the last pages containing a long passage which his son, Marcel Péguy, published in 1924. The *Mystère de la Charité* de *Jeanne d'Arc* is not complete unless we add the text of this second part to the first edition. Instead of seven words there are a hundred pages, containing much food for thought. The essential was given in pages which the public were not allowed to see.

Péguy gave no reason for his cut, so we must guess it. According to his son, Péguy considered the *Mystère* was too long as it stood. We must admit that the abrupt ending is very effective, and that the seven words, *Orléans qui êtes au pays de Loire*, come like the flash of a sword to light up the whole play. But Marcel Péguy's surmise is pure hypothesis, and Péguy had so often shown his predilection for 'lengthiness,' and so often flouted the would-be hurried reader, that we should not accept any simple explanation offered. A careful scrutiny of the pages he sacrificed suggests another possible reason: Péguy may have cut them out, not because they were too lengthy, but because they were too revealing on intentions it did not suit him to lay bare. Several of these pages deserve consideration: they are connected with Péguy's most intimate preoccupations and with the very heart of his praying.

In reading them we must never lose sight of the fact that Péguy practised the imitation of Jeanne d'Arc as St. Francis did that of Jesus Christ, and made no distinction between the words he attributed to her and his own. Now let us hear what Jeanne has to say about that Communion which Péguy allowed circumstances to withhold from him:

> When I think that now while I am talking, all the time you are busy damning souls, forgive me, O my God, it makes my head go round and round. When I think of that, I can't pray any more. The words are frozen on my lips. The words of prayer itself seem to me bloody with cursed blood. My God, what poisoning, what poisoning of the blood. The words of prayer are as it were eaten up with maggots and hollow. Communion itself, O God, is as it were maggotty and hollow. . . .
> The Communion of Your Son's Body no longer has all its grace.

He was obsessed with the idea and with his stubborn refusal to leave the fate of the damned to God. Jeanne saw the threatening shadow of Hell reaching out over the earth and darkening it. She shuddered for the living, so soon, she feared, to be snapped up by the fiery fangs.

> *And the world of exile, and the hell of an eternal exile,*
> *Those two worlds of exile. . . .*

Those two worlds: here they are evoked together. For Jeanne, the line of demarcation between them is not clear, nor was it clear to Péguy; Antigone's fate seemed to him to be hell on earth; Jean Coste's too. To return to Jeanne, to whom thinking about France is as natural as breathing or the beating of her heart: a long war had worn France to shreds till it was, as Jeanne says, 'an anticipation of

Hell.' Always Hell, the inadmissible thing. Fallen as though for good under the blows of the English, already half lost (and maybe for-ever), the Eldest Daughter of the Church lets the Church's Feast days go by without her. She no longer belongs to Christendom, she keeps away from it.

And Christianity and the Church both suffer from her absence, and worship is not what it was. Jeanne was aware of it, and Péguy was too. For him and for Jeanne, Communion was more than a solitary repeated act, it did in fact set out afresh each time the Supper which all the companions of our Lord shared, not excepting the traitor, and which would not have been as it has so often been shown in art, and re-lived by living men, if one had been missing of the thirteen taking part. Péguy was convinced (and Jeanne too, doubtless) that peoples, nations, are members of the Church, and that each one has its own importance and each its contribution to make. He once said to me: 'With the Reformation a half of Europe left the Church. It undoubtedly took a certain amount away with it.' And then the French people, throwing itself so passionately into the fray of the Revolution, left too. Or at least, that is the impression it gave the rest of the world and itself. And Christendom was shaken and thrown off its balance; and left imperfect in practice. If the Church is to bear all its fruit again, its unity must be restored. There must be no more absentees at the supper-table of the nations.

To return to the cut pages. Jeanne's brooding over France deepens, and certain words occur which help to explain why the cut was made. They come in a dialogue between Jeanne adolescent and Madame Gervaise, the nun:

God, forgive me, you know one cannot help loving the land of one's fathers above all other lands, all the other lands in the world. It is a weakness. One cannot help loving this kingdom among all the kingdoms of Christendom. One cannot help loving this land of France.

This kingdom of France.

To pray. To pray that a whole people be spared from falling among the dead souls, the dead peoples, the dead nations. Be spared from fall-ing down dead. Be spared from becoming a dead people, a dead nation. Be spared from mildew. Be spared from going rotten in spiritual death, in eternal death; in the earth, in hell.

These are the nun's words, be it said. Jeanne would never have said, 'Loving the land of one's fathers above all others is a weak-ness'; nor linked in a single sentence the thought of France and the thought of death. The words would have stuck in her throat. But her ears heard tell this terrible coupling, and the vision of death affronted her eyes. And that was more than enough. Péguy wiped both the idea and the vision off the slate, and for ever; he never wrote like that again. The nun goes on:

This people, our people. This France, our France.

Jeannette.—She is the Eldest Daughter.

Mme Gervaise.—She is the Daughter and the scandals that come through her are the most hurtful of all.

Jeannette.—She is the Eldest Daughter. She has to give an example, a good example to the others. She is the one who helps her mother. She sees to the house and looks after the others and teaches them, she teaches the others and sets them a good example.

Mme Gervaise.—She provides the example and all the teaching for all her sisters in Christendom.

And when scandal occurs in her, it is most hurtful to all her sisters in Christendom.

It is most grave.

Madame Gervaise withdraws, and Jeanne converses no longer with her but with God, alone, speaking words to which no clue is given:

There is a secret between the two of us. We've got a secret.
I dare to have a secret with You.
There is a secret between us.

It was Jeanne's secret, it was Péguy's secret: it is all one. Péguy never said what it was, and for very good reason: to announce that you have a secret to keep is one way of spreading it abroad. Jeanne said: 'God, you know I have secret prayers.' This must be the same secret, linked to a prayer.

The prayer must have been for France. But why was it a secret? To pray for one's country and one's king is permissible. The secret must be connected with some peculiarity of the prayer itself. In Jeanne's case, it is clear: all in authority over her, parents, parish priest, Mme Gervaise the nun, did not approve of her zeal; Mme Gervaise scolded her and lectured her. She said, 'Why want to save better than Jesus himself? God rules the event, the faithful must learn how to accept in all humility.' And Jeanne refused. Her resolve, made in secret, was to throw herself, sword in hand, into the thick of battle. Risking everything, even her salvation, she would fight on, and if France were to lose, she too, body and soul, would be lost.

This brings us very close to Péguy: everything pointed to the end of the Faith in France, at the time he was pondering on his *Mystère de la Charité de Jeanne d'Arc*. It was against this menace that Péguy took up arms, and his own personal experience and his inner voices all told him to stay by his threatened friends, and to stick to them as closely as possible to keep their confidence and their friendly ear. He knew them so well and the sort of things they said: 'It's jolly handy, being a Catholic; you go to confession, and you get forgiven; you go to communion, and you get saved . . .' Péguy went without these aids, and without them submitted to the trials which the practising Christian takes upon himself willingly, in addition to sharing the risks run by non-believers.

The French people were to be re-established in all their native nobility, of this Péguy had no doubt. As for delays and means, time alone would show. One thing is quite certain, and that is that Péguy hated the very idea of any authoritarian restoration of belief. In the nineteenth century the attempt had been made and the results were worse than useless. No more of that, thank you. Perhaps he foresaw, the other side of still unknown troubles to come, a new Church, as different from the Counter-Reformation Church as that was from the Church of St. Louis, or as St. Louis' from St. Gregory VIIth's.

Perhaps. We do not know. Péguy was no historian and did not speculate on the vicissitudes of the centuries; he never attempted clear outlines of the unforeseeable. His method was a constant sifting and re-sifting (his prose shows it) mingled with half-visions. For example, there is this page from *Clio*, written in 1914; between now and then, there was no change:

> Grace is insidious, it twists and is full of surprises. . . . Men that God wants He gets. When Grace doesn't come straight at a man it comes askew. When it doesn't come from the right it comes from the left. When it doesn't come straight it comes bent, and when it doesn't come bent it comes broken. . . . When it doesn't come from above it comes from below; and when it doesn't come from the centre it comes from the circumference. . . . When it doesn't come like a bubbling spring, it can if it likes come like a trickle of water oozing out from under a Loire dyke. . . . Certainly the modern world has done all it can to proscribe Christianity, to rid itself of all substance, every atom and every trace of Christianity. But if I catch sight of an invincible, insubmersible, incomprehensible Christianity creeping out again from below, creeping in from the surroundings, creeping in from all around, am I to miss my chance of hailing it just because I was not up to calculating where it would come from? . . . Where is it written that God will abandon man in sin? . . . This people will finish a way they never began. This age, this world, this people will get there along a road they never set out on. And many moreover and thus will take upon themselves and find themselves together in the sacramental forms.

We already know how it turned out in the family circle. The nation's destiny is still in suspense. What can be stated in all certainty is that there is no more active agent of a Catholic renaissance to be seen in France to-day than this man who chose to remain alone, at the point of danger, *in periculo maris* as he was fond of saying. Like those holy figureheads which Basque and Breton sailors hang over the outermost, most sea-swept headlands.

XI

SHADOWS AND LIGHT

THERE WAS A steady intensification apparent in all aspects of Péguy's life: troubles, temperament, and faith; he was living through harrowing days. Under the threat of forced solitude, he built around himself voluntary solitude. His irritability cost him faithful and good friends; he deliberately broke off relationships which he valued and ceased to be a visitor at homes where he was always welcome. He stopped going to see the friendly Goyau's, and Lorrain, so kind and generous, of whom he was very fond. He no longer saw anything of his important Church friends. Ever since 1910 this effort towards withdrawal and separation had been in his mind:

What I am, anyone who sees me, anyone who looks at me for an instant, can tell. A child would not be taken in. I cannot help it, I did what I could about it. In me, around me, over my head, there is a general conspiracy in which I have no part, over and above my head everything contributes to make of me a peasant and not a Danube peasant, which would still be literature, but simply a Loire-valley peasant, a winegrower of the banks and sandy flats of Loire. And already I'm struck mum and don't know where to put myself at all in the drawing rooms of those friends of mine whom I used sometimes to visit. I never could sit properly in an armchair, not for fear of making myself too comfortable, but just because I couldn't. I sit there as stiff as a poker. What I need is an ordinary chair, or a good stool. The chair is better for one's back; the stool was good enough when I was young. The old folk, how they do know, how tenacious they are: they will win all right. . . . I feel my shoulders growing rounder; and I see what is up: I see I shall not end like these city gentlemen, who go upright to the last day, in fact more upright when they are old than when they were young.

I shall be an old man bent in two, bowed and knotty. I shall be a twisted old fellow, perhaps a beaten old fellow (beaten by the events of this hussy of a life) . . . a cramped, hoary old fellow. People will say: 'There goes old man Péguy.' That's all right, good souls. I'll be going all right. Dreams of my young days, what has become of you? . . I shall be a shrunk old fellow with a wrinkled skin, with skin like bark, an old fellow at the end of his tether, a foreshortened old *pésan*. Precisely, *païsan*, emphasising *paï*, the voice pushing *paï* out in one wide open sound. . . . There are too many old men behind me who spent all their life bowed, bending down to tie up the vine shoots. . . .

So he foresaw what he would be, and so he might well have become: thickened and shortened by weight of years, hardened like the heart of an old oak, forcibly rammed back into his native peasantry.

As a young militant socialist, he had not been particularly aware of being a man of the people; he drew neither material for argument nor pride from the fact; he just did not mention it. In fact he would have condemned any such pride of caste and blood as out of place. He was particularly anxious that socialism should not be restricted to a class movement or become the tool of a class. But Péguy was now neither young nor a socialist; he no longer believed in the advent of that united city which he had described in his first work; he knew himself for the man he was born, marked out for a certain kind of life by a certain destiny; and he accepted to be so marked out and made no secret of it. Things are as they are: he was a peasant, a *pésan*, quite incapable of rubbing shoulders with the bourgeoisie. Acting upon this knowledge, he withdrew. But not without pain. The friendships he was giving up had meant a good deal to him. And Péguy would not consent to suffer himself without making others suffer too, without striking a blow and executing vengeance. He had no sense of proportion: the least obstacle was intolerable to him.

It was from the French Academy that he got his hardest knock. The circumstances are worth recalling. The Academicians were put out at the success of the Goncourt Prize in comparison with their own out-moded prizes, and they decided to offer an annual grand prize for literature, starting in 1911. Two candidates were proposed, Romain Rolland and Péguy. This was before the time that Rolland took sides. He was neither revolutionary nor anti-patriotic, but a sort of romantic liberal. For the *Cahiers*, which had published the work of both candidates, the occasion was an honour and a piece of good luck. Of the Academicians the same could be said: whichever they chose, the choice would be a good one. So Lavisse, Bourget and Barrès settled down to discuss the matter. Lavisse had considerable influence in State affairs at the time, as well as in society and letters. He was Lord High Steward of the University. A one-time tutor of the Imperial Prince, and a faithful bonapartiste for many years, he had strong conservative instincts. But his mind lacked focus, and as in the case of many not over-strong characters, he liked to dabble in so-called new ideas, 'advanced' ideas, as some people said, or 'ideas of the future.' As though the still unsettled future were specially apt for guaranteeing the value of ideas. So disposed, he allowed Herr to influence him, and word was passed to him that Péguy was not to have the prize. He co-operated magnificently: not only did he offer Romain Rolland high praise, he went on to attack Péguy. He was not without wit and found some happy turns of phrase: 'Péguy,' he said, 'is a Catholic anarchist who has put holy water in his petrol.' The phrase caught on and passed from mouth to mouth in different forms, but always with the three recurring words: anarchist, holy water, petrol.

With his ready flow of language and over-famous lightness of touch, Emile Ollivier made his contribution to the discussion with the statement that Péguy was a Latin Quarter Bohemian. Faguet remained silent. As a Sorbonne Professor he did not allow himself to forget the respect due to his colleagues. A literary critic, an indefatigable reader, and a writer of fabulous output, he none the less succeeded in summing up French literature between 1900 and 1914 without once writing Péguy's name.[1] Barrès and Bourget spoke up for Péguy, so the defence was a good one, but academicians don't like quarrels. The permanent Secretary, René Doumic, acted prudently and the final decision was that there should be no award. Bourget and Barrès did however persuade their colleagues to do something on Péguy's behalf: he was given a grant of eight thousand francs. Barrès went to the rue de la Sorbonne (was this the only time? I think so) with the not very exciting news. Péguy realised at once that it was a matter of courteously-disguised defeat. The illustrious company of the Academy hoped that a handsome gift would compensate for the recognition they withheld, but it was mistaken.

The blow was all the heavier in that, through Lavisse, it came from Lucien Herr. Péguy was quite sure of this. *We shall fight you with all our might*: he had not forgotten how those words rang in his ears, all that time ago. After thirteen years the threat still held good, and in the most illustrious gathering in France, Péguy was caught on the quick with Lavisse's broadside: *Péguy is a Catholic anarchist who has put holy water in his petrol.* Barrès had not refrained from repeating it to him, and Péguy was too good a pamphleteer himself, and too good a jouster too, not to savour to the full this venomous piece of wit. He went about repeating it with delectation, and this was anything but a good sign. He brooded over his retort and gave some hints of what it was to be: 'You will put yourself in the wrong,' some wise friends warned him. 'You allowed yourself to stand as a candidate for the prize and adjudication; you have no right to object.' Péguy took no notice and went on fuming, biding his time. The opportunity was provided by an article by young François Le Grix in the *Revue Hebdomadaire* which Péguy did not find to his liking. It said: '. . . M. Péguy tried to get along without rites or ceremonies; he said the office was all wrong, like the eccentric and argumentative cleric that he was. . . .'

The *Revue Hebdomadaire* was a very right-thinking paper, so

[1] Silence is a most effective weapon. M. René Johannet observes in his essay on Péguy: "M. Lavisse succeeded in writing a long article on the grand prize for literature in the Revue de Paris, without mentioning Péguy's name once."

Péguy was jeered at from both sides. Lavisse and the left were on one side, Le Grix and the *Revue Hebdomadaire* on the other. So much for the favour of the powers of the day. Eccentric cleric, vitriolic Catholic were what they dared to call him. Insolent men were insulting in him that greatness and genius with which he knew he was invested and which it was his duty to have respected. Le Grix gave him the pretext needed, and with no loss of time, in three months, he produced a large volume seething with vengeance and all his accumulated rage.

It was summer time. July to October was the *Cahiers'* vacation, so he had time to work. Shut up in his house at Lozère, he let his fury seethe unabated and rid himself of it by covering page after page with his unflinching handwriting, zebra-striping as he put it. It was anything but a mere retort to Le Grix. He was giving his answer to all the important people whom the young critic represented in his eyes, through his collaboration with the review they sponsored. Sorel had once uttered this piece of advice: 'If ever you have a review to complain of, don't answer the author of the article, but strike at the head and attack the editor: then you will win respect.' Now the *Revue Hebdomadaire's* editor was an old diplomatist, a well-known man-about-town, soon to be a member of the Institute, M. Fernand Laudet. Just the sort of man Péguy wanted to bait. He took no notice of Le Grix and went straight for Laudet, not only holding him responsible for the other man's article but even (in a wild flight of combative fancy) treating him as the author of every word of it. Imagine this man's dismay on receiving a large volume entitled: *Un nouveau théologien, M. Fernand Laudet.* Sorel's piece of advice had not come amiss. Just as Joseph Prudhomme will stand out for a long time as the incarnation of a certain type of nineteenth century bourgeoisism, M. Fernand Laudet, for so long as there are readers of Péguy, will stand for a certain conservatism of our day, a certain diplomatic manner, at once courteous and cautious, of remaining Catholic without any qualms about making a successful career in a society which has ceased to be anything of the sort.

Péguy came to grips with his opponent, the cultivated Catholic who pays all due respect to Church ritual but privately reserves almost infinite liberties as far as criticism, judgment and social contacts are concerned. Péguy was in fact and by deliberate choice the very opposite of such a man. The *Revue Hebdomadaire* critic distinguished between the Jeanne d'Arc of history and the Jeanne d'Arc of legend: 'the Jeanne d'Arc of our popular French history,' 'the Jeanne d'Arc of our childhood.' What does this imply, if not that there is a Jeanne d'Arc for simple folk, who is a legend and a saint, and a Jeanne d'Arc for cultured people, who is the real one and no saint? Does M. Fernand Laudet (addressed in person) believe, like Voltaire, that religion is good for the people? The *Revue Hebdomadaire* critic went out of his way to be polite to the great names of the world of art, not great in Christendom at all. 'M. Gabriel d'Annunzio,' he wrote, 'capable of miracles. . . .' Now we know what sort of miracles a cultured Catholic may let himself believe. 'M. Anatole France, in his saintly lay exegeses. . . .' What a way of using words, what impropriety, what indecency! Péguy's comment follows:

Væ tepidis; woe to the lukewarm. Shame to the shameful. Woe and shame to him who is ashamed. It is not so much a matter of believing or not believing . . . as of knowing the deep source of manifest disbelief, the true depth of the omission, and where incredulity comes from when it comes to the surface. No source is so shameful as shame. And fear. And of all fears the most shameful is the fear of ridicule, of being ridiculous, of appearing ridiculous, of being taken for a fool. A man may believe or not believe (at least here we agree). But shame to the man who would deny his God in order not to make clever men smile. Shame to the man who would deny his faith in order not to look absurd, not to make people smile, not to be taken for a fool. All this refers to the man who doesn't enquire of himself whether he believes or does not believe. To the man who has but one care, which is not to make M. Anatole France smile. To the man who would sell his God in order not to look silly. To the man who fears, to the man who is afraid, to the poor creature shuddering in his skin at the thought of being afraid, at the thought of looking like a dupe, at the thought of raising a smile on the lips of one of the auguries of the intellectual party. It all refers to that man, poor fearful creature, on the alert all the time, fearfully throwing circumventing glances to make quite sure that none of the honourable audience has been seen to smile at him, at his faith, at his God. It is the man who casts preventive glances all around him. On Society. Conniving glances. The man who is all of a tremble. The man whose glance begs pardon for God beforehand: in the drawing rooms.

Péguy swept on and in the ardour of striking hard made profession of that same radical faith on which he questions his opponent's hold. 'The Catholic Faith is one,' he said, 'and can only be whole and clear-cut; it is all in the catechism, which tells us word for word what we are to believe. . . .' Up till now Péguy had not made such an outspoken affirmation of his belief. Experiences on the spiritual plane and his own yearning had drawn him to Christianity; trials, works and prayers had bound him to it. He had been given Grace, of that he was sure: but is faith essential to this? Do people without faith not receive graces? Now, on the full tide of his disgust at the flabby adhesion to the faith of the cultivated believer, shall we say his inadherent adhesion, and of his own violent opposition to such an attitude, he spoke right out and made these downright radical affirmations, doubtless at some cost to himself. To know whether it was the declaration that was painful, or the affirmation itself, we must stop once more at the threshold of that region of the spirit where once before our enquiry halted. Here analysis has reached its term. We must trust to observation and now two facts emerge: one is the particular moment of this profession of faith; the other (which concerns the future) is the growing precision and force of Péguy's belief.

Such progress in his efforts would be no surprise to Péguy. He wrote: 'Our fidelities, our modern credits, isolated in their world, assailed, beaten by storms and seas, still standing alone in a whole world, alone in a whole sea set inexhaustibly seething, intact, entire, unshaken, unbreached, unaffected, do in the long run make, constitute, raise a lovely monument to the face of God, to the glory of God.' *Isolated, assailed,* is the condition of their existence, and it inevitably leaves its mark on them. *In the long run they make* . . .: the effort is all part of it and contributes to their final form. How right Péguy is: the Faith carried forward so energetically in these modern days does constitute a marvellous spiritual epic, and it is from the effort itself that it gets its 'own great tragic beauty' as Péguy discovered it.

Our fidelities are citadels. Those crusades which transported the peoples and threw whole continents one against the other, are carried on into our day, and they have swept over to us and come back to our very homes. Like a wave, in the form of a wave of incredulity, they have flowed all the way back to us. We no longer go fighting among the infidels. It is the infidels, and still more the infidelities, which have brought the struggle right here. The least of us is a soldier. The least of us is literally a crusader. Our forefathers, like a wave of nations, like a wave of armies, invaded infidel continents. Now, on the contrary, it is the wave of infidelity which commands the high seas and breaks upon us on all sides. All our homes are fortresses *in periculo maris,* in peril of the sea. The holy war is everywhere at once.

Péguy was right: the holy war is everywhere. It goes on in the heart of the believer himself and raises the smoke of battle there too. It leaves its mark and its wounds which are sometimes bitter ones. Péguy knew all about this: this book of his, *Un nouveau théologien, M. Fernand Laudet,* was born of his despite and ends on that note. Péguy said his say to M. Fernand Laudet and passed on to other matters, settling a handful of short outstanding quarrels: first of all a short bout with Salomon Reinach with no bloodshed, Péguy using a light stick as weapon. Then he set upon the editor of a university review in which he had been mentioned with levity. It was still Sorel's method striking at the head. There was not much more, a few passing thrusts: Péguy knew what he was about and soon came to the point. He came to his greatest bugbear, Levisse.

As far as I am concerned, let it be known that I personally would not endure that a man like Lavisse, swollen with incomes and pensions and salaries and honours (all very much in the plural, please) stuffed with stipends for having sown disasters all around him, in the Republic and in the University, I would not endure that a man like Lavisse, were he member of twenty academies, should come forward to shed his gratuitous facetiousness and vulgarity upon this life of care and trouble, labour and distresses of all kinds which we have been leading for the last twenty years. This year he has said quite enough. This year he has done quite enough. This year he has paid me quite enough attention. Let him get back to Louis XIV. Let this plump gravedigger lay his papal hand on some less recalcitrant corpse. . . . If he were to turn his attention on me again, I warn him that the most earnest entreaties would be of no avail to stop me from demanding an account of him: the only form of account, be it said, which anyone would ever dream of asking of him.

Péguy was quite capable of passing judgment on such raw, frowning pages himself: 'I realise how mean it is to stoop to gather all this meanness and hatred and envy and filth and shame. . . .' To Lotte he opened his heart still further: 'Would you believe that for eighteen months I could not say *Our Father*. *Thy will be done* was quite impossible to say. Can you understand it? I could not accept His will. It is terrifying. Praying isn't a matter of trickling off a few prayers, you have really to mean what you say. I could not really mean: *Thy will be done*.' It was an impossibility. It was still more impossible to say: 'Forgive me my trespasses as I forgive. . . .' He could not forgive. The words for forgiving Lavisse would have stuck in his throat; he would have had a liver attack he declared. 'So I prayed to Mary. Prayers to Mary are reserve prayers. There is not one, in the whole liturgy, not one, you see, not one single one, that the most miserable sinner cannot say and really mean. In the machinery of salvation, the *Ave Maria* is our last resource. With that, you can't be lost.' Not with those humble words to the rescue, less a prayer than a plea and entreaty, the cry of a speechless child to its mother.

He had not, however, stopped writing, 'zebra-lining' the pages: 'There is a fullness of work which is a satisfactory substitute for happiness,' as he wrote to Charles-Lucas de Peslouän. He throve on this fullness which was also the full play of his art and craftsmanship. He hit about him and hurled his insults and enjoyed himself thoroughly. He said as much in this same virulent pamphlet. He invented a new word to show up his sad case more nobly. He had spoken of hate: this is a mean, displeasing word. The hate-ridden man (*le haineux*) grows rotten and putrid. This was not Péguy's case at all. So he chose *haïssant* as his word, instead of *haineux*. *Haïssement* is a swift, active form of hatred and *le haïssant*, the hater, achieves his own release by the very violence of his thrusts.

I don't mind being a jack-of-all-trades,' he concluded. 'I'm used to it. All I ask is that the whole of my bile shall burst upon these foul creatures so that soon I can get back to work with a pure heart.'

What work of his was ever done but in purity of heart. A remarkable thing occurred at this time. *Un nouveau théologien, M. Fernand Laudet* came out in September 1912, precisely on the 19th of the month. One mouth later, on the 17th of October, Péguy put his name to the first copies of another book, entitled *Le Mystère du Porche de la deuxième Vertu,* the most hope-inspired of all his works, and on certain pages the most gracious and profoundly metaphysical, a theogony, a fairyland of hope. The *mystère* had probably been conceived during the winter and spring, and as soon as he had finished it Péguy set to work on the murderous pages of the *Nouveau théologien.* But those winter and spring months had been terribly harsh ones: they were part of that eighteen-month prayerless period, as Péguy was to tell Lotte on another occasion: 'My second mystery was an anticipation; when I wrote it, I did not believe in hope.'

If he did not believe in it, what force was driving him, or what hidden soul in him? What unknown Péguy guided the hand of Péguy-the-furious? We always come back to these two same planes on which his life had unfolded from the beginning. In this case the phenomenon is most remarkable. Everyone knows that the soul of man is not a simple thing, but one cannot be too much aware of it. The French language has only one word for this complexity. Latin, more subtle in this case (and Greek too), had two. *Animus,* the breath of life θυμὸς in Greek, temperament; *anima,* the Greek ψυχὴ We need not hesitate to make use of these precious words and to say that *Animus,* reared in the thick of the fiery life common to mankind, wrote the *Nouveau Théologien,* while *Anima,* living in secret, guided the hand which wrote the *Mystère du Porche de la deuxième Vertu.*

Péguy had a very high idea of the value of the titles he gave his books. *Le Mystère du Porche de la deuxième Vertu* has one great quality: it is rigorously accurate. We need not pretend it has any others. It is indeed a Porch which Péguy built and fitted with diverse figures: at the top, over the arch, God the Father; on ground level, a labourer, a woodcutter, a shepherd girl; between, kings, dukes and soldiers. Praying saints, angel presences in the air. Such is the scene. A single voice: *Orléans, qui êtes au pays de Loire.* It is the voice of the shepherd girl, Jeanne. The first line of the second mystery picks up the last line of the first. Then all heaven is astir. Jeanne is still unknown in France, she is the lonely child of Domrémy. But God already gives her His ear.

Péguy makes God speak. In his picture, God is an ancient patriarch seated in front of His farmstead. His servants and herds have gone in. He is resting and watching the sky bright with stars that are all His worlds. And word from one of them reaches Him: *Orléans, qui êtes au pays de Loire. . . .*

What assurance that girl's voice has! What strength of hope! The call came from the earth. God looks through space to find it. The earth, which His Son loved, where His Son went! God is still astonished, still in pain at the thought of that immense adventure: incarnation, passion, death; enduring passion, and the Body left to men as a hostage; then incredible disorder, hope surging against the law, and the creation of a new order named grace. And all this through Jesus. What father ever understood his son's undertakings? Péguy's God is a father, with all the affection of a father. To put it as clearly as it appears: Péguy's God is a Jewish patriarch who cannot understand Christianity, and everything that happens on earth simply amazes His old heart.

He bends down to her; He hears the sounds that rise from our land, and we hear them too. A woodcutter in the forest, striking the wood with his axe; cold congealing his breath in his beard and welding his hands to his tool. How the man goes on hitting away at the wood. Meanwhile he is talking to himself and we overhear what he says; he is thinking of his children, his love, his cares. He is kept prisoner in his forest and sees very little of his family, which worries him. What is happening to them, what are they doing? All of a sudden, he thinks of Our Lady Mary, kind as she is, and in one swift joyful lift of the heart, he hands his little family over to her and puts them all in her arms.

. . . So quietly he put them there.
By prayer he put them there.
So quietly in the arms of her whose part it is
to bear all the sorrows of the world.
And whose arms are already so laden.
For the Son took all the sins.
But the Mother took all the sorrows.

The woodcutter goes on striking the wood and the strokes go ringing to heaven. But the cry that astonished the skies did not come from him. God lets his gaze wander from place to place of the earthly landscape, and at last he finds what he wants: it is in Lorraine; fire is burning down the cottages, the herds are scattered. A child it was who spoke, and there she is.

Orléans, qui êtes au pays de Loire. . . .

What courage in distress; what a strength of hope. God feels for the entreating child and for all those brave unhappy creatures whom His Son loved. He feels for them and with them, and their touching virtue suddenly awakens in Him: O wonder of wonders! All-powerful God opens His heart to hope.

The immense adventure: and this was the result. Men so intimately mingled with God that nothing can ever separate them again. Jesus, forever crucified, suffers when they give in, and rejoices at their fidelities. He made Himself their slave, and by this bond has bound God too. If man hopes, God hopes; man hopes in God, God hopes in man; each can only be saved with the help of the other. What incredible act is this which submits the Creator to the creature, sharing sorrow and joy. Jesus, the Man of hope: that is Péguy's name for Him. By taking the way of man's heart, Jesus transforms God's heart. What a revolution! Heaving up from the depths of humanity, lifting it with it. The men who won, that is, the saints, bear it to the skies, where they carry it on in the presence of God Himself, all in league against Him, so that

Bit by bit, Justice,
Step by step, may yield to Mercy.

The old patriarch would like to stand up to the suppliants His Son has faced Him with. But the Christian multitude supports the claims of the saints with its prayers and makes the bells of all the parishes ring. That is hope's tocsin, and that assault of Christianity breaches the walls of Heaven.

The angels watch the struggle from on high, it is not their strife. As pure spirits they can take only a small part in it. To be Christian is to be carnal and to bear in your veins the heavy blood that ran down over the Cross. The angels, non-carnal beings, children of another divine generation, are amazed, as God their Master is.

Péguy speaks his mind to them:

That, my child, is what the angels don't know, I mean what they have never undergone.
The sins of the flesh and the unique remissions of the flesh.
The sins which are of the flesh and only of the flesh.
And which no creature can know who is not carnal.
The sins of Earth, of Earthy earth which the angels only know by hearsay.
Like a story about another world.
And, so to speak, about another creation.
They know nothing of anxiety or despair, or pride, that old human pride which rises in the heart of man like sap in the tree. They had their pride, too, those who were lost with Lucifer;
But it was proud thinking; a poor pride of mind.
A pale pride, a vain pride all in the head.
Smoke.
Not at all a gross and greasy pride nourished with fat and blood.
Bursting with health.
With a bloom on the skin.
And which could only be redeemed by flesh and blood.
Pride swollen with blood

Booming in the ears
With the thud of blood.
Pride in bloodshot eyes,
Beating like a drum on the brow.
That is what they never knew.
So they don't know there is Easter,
An Easter Day, an Easter Sunday,
An Easter week.
An Easter month.
For the rising and tautening of carnal hope.
As there is for the sap of oak and birch.
A month of April, a month of May.

. . . .

They don't know the old royal pride, so they don't know the ancient pride,
The pride of blood, bursting of its own accord, pride bursting its skin, so they don't know
How young, carnal, shy hope
Marches at the head of the procession,
Steps out in all innocence.
It is to us, the stricken, that a gift was given,
It is on us, stricken and carnal as we are, that depends
The living and nourishing and keeping alive in time
Of those words spoken living in time.

So the axis of the activity of souls is no longer the Throne on high but the Cross on earth. Round it is waged the decisive struggle. The believers of the Old Law wondered in desperate anguish: What is it that God wants? And now God, Father of Jesus, is asking: What is it that men want? For His Son gave Himself up to them, and the glory of heaven awaits their answer.

Orléans, qui êtes au pays de Loire. . . . What is the child wanting? Her cry comes from Lorraine, Lorraine in France. God knows the French, who were good servants to His Son on more than one occasion:

Christendom, Lorraine must remain.

The call of the child is a sign of expectation and hope. And God is pleased because of this virtue, now His favourite one:

I am, said God, the Lord of virtues.
Faith is the sanctuary lamp
Eternally burning.
Charity is the lovely great wood fire
You light on your hearth
So that my poor children can come and get warm on winter evenings.
And around Charity I saw all my poor
Sitting round the fire
Holding out their hands to the warmth of the hearth.
But My hope is the flower and the fruit and the leaf and the bough.

And the spray and the sprout and the seed and the bud.
And it is the sprout and the flowerbud
Of eternity itself.

Each moment is a drop of eternity, said a metaphysician. A drop of hope is what Péguy would say. That is the whole story: this articulation of the here-and-now which constantly brings to every man an occasion for risk and the chance of success.[1]

There lies the origin, the spring of man's greatness and of the events of history. There, too, lies the secret of his revolutions. The rationalistic and optimistic ideologies of the French eighteenth century are something quite unknown to Péguy. But the French revolutions bore, through all their errors of thought (mere errors), a force of courage and hope which touches the essence of human nature: that is why he loves them and will always do so. They went off, he said characteristically; a traveller goes off, and a gun goes off: this notion of the explosiveness of the human soul and of the history of mankind keeps on cropping up.

For this courage and hope, Péguy pays honour to the whole French nation, and looks forward to further exploits similarly inspired, but this time markedly Christian. Hope is there to urge on and shape these revolutionary creations-to-be. 'There are five kingdoms,' said Péguy, 'the mineral kingdom, the vegetable kingdom, the animal kingdom, the human kingdom, and the Christian kingdom. . . . And there is no less of a gap and no less of a progression and no less discontinuity between the third and the fourth, and between the fourth and the fifth, than between any of the other three.' There is no need to suppose that Péguy was indulging in some form of illuminism as he used to do; here it is rather a matter of theogony, arian palingenesy, and those divine generations which Hesiod sings and to which we have drawn so near. Hope stands at the threshold of that heroic tale enacted in the heart of man.

Péguy's soul was stirred by many forms of human greatness: Greek, Roman, Jewish.

He was aware, however, that for him they were all growing dim in

[1] This may be the place to point out how much Péguy's mystical realism owes to Bergson. One of the writers who have studied him most thoroughly M. René Johannet, has made some very pertinent remarks: 'It is to the Bergson of *Matière et Mémoire* and still more to the Bergson of the *Données immédiates de la métaphysique* that he owes his intellectual formation. . . . Péguy went further than his initiator . . . on the practical ground of points of view and conclusions in art. Péguy stood out against the bergsonian stream of long noisy discussions and insipid chatter. He "bergsonised," but without going into ecstacies about it. But he did it so thoroughly that his work, and especially from the religious point of view, may be considered as the crowning achievement which should have belonged to the bergsonian philosophy and did not.' *Péguy et ses Cahiers*, p. 154-55. Bergsonian philosophy could, in fact, lead either to humanist realism or to mystical realism. Péguy came through the first and opted for the second. In any case M. René Johannet's remark has lost some of its force since Henri Bergson published his *Les Deux Sources de la Morale* in 1932.

the face of the humble greatness of the Christian which he found again in middlelife. The Christian follows a master who bore a heavy burden; he has no ambition for the vain exercise of power and temporal eminence; he is the burden-bearer of creation. Providence set him in his place and the burden fell to him: he takes it on as best he may and claims no special merit for doing so. On the day of battle, the brigades awaken and equip themselves in the morning mist; each is at its post and awaits what the day may bring. Their only job is to wait in readiness. Then one is picked out to fight at the heart of the battle. It was not a matter of deserts: the honour fell to it. And the other brigades, its fellows, fighting themselves too, are nonetheless aware that elsewhere the struggle is keener, death more exacting, sacrifice more valuable and the issue decisive. They may relax their efforts from time to time, but not so those at the centre; those have a pretty good idea they are well and truly engaged; they guess what glances and shouts are thrown them and feel the chief's mind with them. With such encouragement, their wounded, decimated troop fights on with courage greater than its own courage, and stays the course with strength greater than its own strength. In the morning, it was like all the others, neither more brave nor less; and by nightfall it has changed. It has survived the trial, it has come through the fire. So it is, and will remain, different, marked in the sight of all by the august grace of battle. It was no cause of it: heroism descended upon it. Such is the Christian, one man among others, and like the humblest of them all. But his fight is for the whole of nature, and the powers on high pin their hope on his effort. He was picked out, and that is where his extra strength comes from.

We say: such is the Christian. We may follow Péguy still further, follow him through this poem we are studying: he is carried on almost imperceptibly, on and over to the people of France. The tendency is constant, we pointed it out only a while ago, it is an underlying principle of each of the long poems and of the whole of Péguy's work and life, this perfect curve which brings them back to earth, to the land of France; inevitably they return to it, as Péguy himself was soon to return to it. For Péguy, his is a good land, as for every child his is a good mother, the best of mothers. It is a belief that will admit of no shadow of doubt. Over and beyond his own land, there is nothing on earth as far as Péguy is concerned. There is an authentic link in his mind between Christian greatness and French greatness: he thinks of them continually. France never made a determined bid for her destiny, it is just that she *is* great, and great even down to her weaknesses and down to her failures. A Frenchman is not hard like a Roman, nor puritanical like an Englishman. He follows his own inventive nature; slips and falters; falters more often than most, maybe; but he picks himself up and goes on, and what he does is great. His exquisite sense of life and his tireless, ardent humanity are what save him in rough times. And whatever he does, whether he goes astray or longs for rest, there he is, at the heart of the fray, destiny has set him there as everyone knows. The honour came to him and he must get on with it.

Listening to Jeanne speaking and observing the Lorraine landscape, so strongly marked with the devastation of wars and the courage of hearts, God comes to consider the people of the land, the French people.

There must have been some secret understanding between our Frenchmen and young Hope.
They are so marvellously good at it. . . .
The art of faltering and picking themselves up at once, clean, is what God admires in them:
That is what moves me, that.
That is what gets me.
I can't get over it.
And my grace must be so immense.
And that they instantly forget the bad days.
At the time. At once.
Almost before. Almost beforehand.
. . . And they mop up the bad days so to say faster than the bad days rain down on them.
Sooner.
The bad days that rain down like rain in autumn.
Like sheer, grey, unceasing rain,
Pitiless
Like slanting unceasing rain.
. . . But contrariwise to all that comes down and the numberless rains and numberless bad days,
At once, instantly, almost before, they go and make running water of it,
Quick, clear, soft water,
Lovely transparent water,
Pure water, springing and trickling through those meadows
On the banks of the Meuse.
Lovely Lorraine water, a soul of lovely water and the very source of hope.
That it should be from such stuff as this, from these innumerable bad days raining down and down,
That they bring out fresh and springing the very source of hope—
That innumerable source and innumerable river—
That river the greatest of all my rivers—
The only great one—
. . . That is what amazes me. And yet I am not easily taken by surprise.
I am so old. I have done so much. I have seen so much.
And my grace must be so immense.

•

The second mystery ends with the hymn to night which everyone knows. Nightfall on Golgotha, told by God Himself, is one of Péguy's great pages:

> *. . . Every man has the right to bury his son.*
> *Every man on earth, if the great sorrow befalls him*
> *Of not dying before his son. And I alone, I, God,*
> *Bound by the conditions of this venture,*
> *I alone, at this moment, a father, after so many fathers,*
> *I alone could not bury my son.*
> *Then it was you came, O night. . . .*

Let us break off the quotation and dwell on the meaning of the theme.

At first sight this seems to be a sort of final scene with no necessary connection with what went before. The tempestuous *Nouveau Théologien* may have affected the finishing of the work. The connection is indeed a slight one. To perceive it at all we need to remember that this mystery of the *Porche* (at once a poem and a metaphysical treatise on hope) was written at a very bitter time for Péguy, when he was near despair. As he told Lotte, 'When I wrote my *Porche*, I did not believe in hope.' This is a half-truth, for the poet of the *Porche*, that inspired soul which we called *Anima* on an earlier page, most certainly believed in hope. In a sort of hypnotic state that protected it from that furious creature *Animus*, it went steadily on with the job. Hope alive was singing and the song, transcribed by Péguy's hand, was the mystery of the *Porche*.

Now as Péguy lost hope he lost his sleep. Hope and sleep belong together. Anger kept him from sleeping and spoilt his night's rest. So we begin to see the connection, a good night is good sleep, good sleep is a source of hope. God knows it well. 'I am told there are men who don't sleep,' He mutters at the beginning of the lyrical phrase which carries us on to the final hymn; it is Péguy who is being scolded, he is the man who doesn't sleep:

> *I don't like a man who doesn't sleep.*
> *Sleep is a man's friend.*
> *Sleep is God's friend.*
> *Sleep may be my loveliest creation . . .*

Loveliest, because it guards the springing of hope in us. It is at night, and through sleep, that the soul comes into contact with its sources and is renewed. When Péguy wrote his hymn to night, he was a mystical poet in the precise meaning of the word. Elsewhere (in the *Charité de Jeanne d'Arc*, in the *Saints Innocents* and *Eve*, two forthcoming works) the sources may be mystical, the application is not: Péguy was looking towards concrete forms of reality, towards men and nations. In the final hymn of the mystery of the *Porche*, he was considering the springs themselves. 'What is the day worth,' he asked, 'what is the consciousness of a man awake worth?' Very little:

a man awake wears himself out in the effort of coping with the agonising incoherence of the world; he grows sad and weary. His source of greatness is all in that *reserve of being* into which hope dips him at night. There alone is found something which does not change or deceive or dry up. Obsessed as we are with the busy-ness of daily life, we see night as an interruption. Externally, of course, night does interrupt day and intercept its clarity; the fighter ceases to fight, the labourer to labour. Inwardly, the whole process is reversed:

It is night which is continuous. Night which is the stuff
Of time and the preserves of life
And day only opens on to it through miserable windows and sky-lights.
It is day that breaks in and day only opens on to it through poor days
Of suffering. It is the day that intrudes and days are like isles in the sea
Like broken isles that break up the sea.
But the sea is continuous and it is the isles which are the offenders.
So it is the days which are the offenders and broken and breaking into night.
But they can't do much about it and they themselves
Are steeped in night.

The invisible current whose presence we suspected all along Péguy now discloses himself:

Night, I love you and salute you and glorify you, and you are my big daughter and my creature.
O lovely night, night of the great cloak, my daughter with the starry cloak,
You bring to mind, you bring to my own mind the great silence there was
Before I opened the sluice-gates of ingratitude.
And you foretell, to me you foretell the great silence that shall fall,
When I close them again.
O sweet, great, lovely night, the most holy of my daughters maybe, wide-robed night, starry-robed night,
You bring to my mind the great silence there was in the world
Before the beginning of man's reign.
You foretell the great silence that will fall
After the end of man's reign, when I take up my sceptre again.
And sometimes I look forward and think of it, for man is really a very noisy creature.

Animus did not sleep but was busy night and day, and things would go very badly indeed if silent *Anima* did not see to it all without ever waking up. From and through *Anima* Péguy's injunctions came to him, as those forebodings were soon to come which shed over his last days so strange a glow. Monsignor Battifol tells how Péguy, when he paid him a visit, kept on answering him with 'God told me,' upon which Monsignor Battifol remarked: 'I had no wish to break in on this one-sided conversation.' It was well said, but easily said too. Events were occurring in Péguy's inner life which present difficulties to the observer which no mere piece of trenchant wit can solve or sound. Very few souls seem so surely marked as his does with the sign of *belonging elsewhere*, to use Péguy's own expression.

XII

TOWARDS CHARTRES

To be a poet at twenty is to be twenty; to be a poet at forty is to be a real poet.—
CHARLES PÉGUY.

IN HIS FIRST *Jeanne d'Arc* Péguy had written regular verse very beautifully. After a time he ceased to do so. There is nothing very surprising in this, it often happens. Poetry is often a mark of youth. We need not count, except for fun, the *Roi Dagobert* couplets (1902); but we should take as a generally unobserved sign some passages from the 1909 *Jeanne d'Arc:*

Vous avez aimé tout et fait tout pour le mieux.
Dans la bataille et dans la paix des cieux,
Tout pour le mieux, hélas, dans l'infernale flamme,
Et vous avez raison quand vous sauvez une âme,
Et vous avez raison quand vous la condamnez;
Oui, nos blés sont à vous pour la moisson des blés
Et nos âmes à vous pour la moisson des âmes.[1]

Apart from a few irregularities, we have here Péguy's whole prosody, as plain and flat as his native Beauce. If a critical mind had come across these lines, the conclusion would have been that they were traces of the past rather than signs of the future. And in actual fact, prose, that rhythmical prose of Péguy's invention, sweeps over everything. But poetic inspiration was only suspended, ripening unbeknown to Péguy himself.

Early in July 1911, Péguy packed the two scripts of the *Nouveau Théologien* and the *Porche* off to the printer and found himself with time on his hands. Time which he spent in a surprising way: he wrote a sonnet. This, the most strict of all poetic forms, was the last one would have expected him to adopt. Behind it was a private upheaval which we can barely indicate here. He is not the only man

[1] These lines are not in the *Mystère de la Charité* but in the sequel to the *Mystère*, printed with the title: *La vocation de Jeanne d'Arc*, p. 54, 2nd Cahier, Series XVI (1925).

You loved all things and did all for the best,
Whether in battle or in heaven's rest,
All for the best, alas, in flaming hell,
And you can be but right to save a soul,
Equally right to let it go forlorn:
Our corn is yours for the harvest-time of corn,
Our souls are yours for the harvest-time of souls.

whom the heart's concerns have caused to seek outlet in song.[1] Surprised at himself and anxious about the event, he went to Charles-Lucas Peslouän for advice and showed him what he had written. He read it at once.

Un regret plus mouvant que la vague marine
A roulé sur ce cœur envahi jusqu'au bord.
Un limon plus ancré que la cendre d'un mort
Est scellé dans cette urne et dans cette poitrine. . . .[2]

Peslouän praised it as a whole, but observed that the two last lines of this first quatrain had a different ring. The general tonality of the images was of the sea, and Péguy should follow Hugo's example (especially in a short piece) and keep within that one range. Next day, Péguy wrote to him:

Paris, 17 July 1912.

. . . I feel very much reassured by your reception of that sonnet, yesterday. I was so nervous about rhymed couplets. Suppose we start off like this:

Un regret plus mouvant que la vague marine
A roulé sur ce cœur envahi jusqu'au bord.
Un jour plus solennel que le jour de la mort
S'est levé sur le foc et sur la brigantine.
Un espoir plus étroit que la voile latine. . .[3]

The rest as it stands.

We may add that Péguy found a use for the discarded lines: he put them into a second sonnet, *L'Urne.* A peasant never wastes anything.

An invisible dyke had given way, and the flood of rhymed couplets set in. On a September morning of this same year, I paid Péguy a visit at Lozère. He saw me back to the station and while we stood on the platform waiting for the train, he told me what he was doing: writing sonnets. I was amazed. Péguy, the boundless, suddenly caged in the strictest framework of all.

[1] On this delicate subject, I will merely quote some lines from Mme Favre's memoirs (*Europe* 1938, p. 324): 'It was a terrible storm in his life; he stood his ground; it was the most searching test of all. A precious, harmonious young friendship, full of exalted admiration, had flowered in his life; there was perfect understanding: and for "this great stormy love-devoured creature," to use Maurice Reclus' description, it was a thing of absolute value . . .'—and four lines from a letter to Mme Favre: '. . . I am working solidly to keep straight. It made me a bit ill. But I'd rather be a bit ill than fail my vocation on account of a *dérèglement du cœur.*' (September 4th, 1910.)

[2] Regret more searching than the wave's unrest
Has swelled about this heart now full to overflow.
More still than dead man's ash, its silting lies below,
Sealed in this living urn, sealed in this breast. . . .

[3] Daylight more solemn than the day of death
Rose on jibsail and small brigantine.
Hope more skimpy than the lateen sail. . . .

'Perhaps I have got time to say one to you,' he suggested. I agreed. There is always time to hear a sonnet.

Then I listened to fourteen very fine lines. Then ten, twenty, forty more.... My surprise got the better of my attention; I broke in: 'But, Péguy, didn't you say something about a sonnet?'

'So I did,' he answered, with a half-contrite, half-mischievous look. 'But instead of one sextain, I wrote several.'

'How many?'

'Fifty or so.'

He went on with his recitation, and the train came in before he had finished.

It was just like him. The paradox amused and pleased him: a sonnet three hundred lines long is a high event worthy of his invention. One day he boasted to an Ecole Normale friend named Roustan, that on a single theme he had managed to use up all the finals in his rhyming dictionary. So verbal delirium was not far away. But the master hand was there ready to pick up the reins whenever necessary.

The emotional crisis we mentioned which was at the beginning of all this, ended in a voluntary separation,[1] which he commemorated in a magnificent poem:

Quand il fallut s'asseoir à la croix des deux routes
Et choisir le regret d'avec que le remords,
Quand il fallut s'asseoir au coin des doubles sorts
Et fixer le regard sur la clef des deux voûtes,

Vous seule vous savez, maîtresse du secret,
Que l'un des deux chemins allait en contre bas,
Vous connaissez celui que choisirent nos pas,
Comme on choisit un cèdre et le bois d'un coffret.

Et non point par vertu car nous n'en avons guère,
Et non point par devoir car nous ne l'aimons pas,
Mais comme un charpentier s'arme de son compas,
Par besoin de nous mettre au centre de misère,

Et pour bien nous placer dans l'axe de détresse,
Et par ce besoin sourd d'être plus malheureux,
Et d'aller au plus dur et de souffrir plus creux,
Et de prendre le mal dans sa pleine justesse.

[1] I turn once more to Mme Favre for light on this event: 'Péguy wished to assume, all alone, all the suffering of which no one near him had the slightest suspicion; his friend married and had a family in all peace and affection, he wished to remain alone to face the disturbing mystery of sorrow.' (*loc. cit.*, p. 324.)

Par ce vieux tour de main, par cette même adresse,
Qui ne servira plus à courir le bonheur,
Puissions-nous, ô régente, au moins tenir l'honneur,
Et lui garder lui seul notre pauvre tendresse.[1]

Meanwhile, Péguy's thought was still running along the lines of his mysteries. 'I could go on writing of Jeanne d'Arc for twenty years,' he said. He saw everything through her eyes: the State, the French people, the Sorbonne. He had some fun in allotting parts, in Jeanne's trial scene, to well-known Sorbonne figureheads, placing them among their predecessors and colleagues, the Doctors of the fifteenth century, and dressing them in their robes. Lanson and Durkheim in cassocks would be unanimous in condemning the recalcitrant girl.

But Péguy was never in a hurry and enjoyed a certain amount of beating about the bushes. His imagination was suddenly set on the alert by a hymn in the Missal. Lettered men take no notice of this lovely sequence of the poet Prudentius, or else treat it as of little worth, because it does not belong to the right period. It is nonetheless an antique of the finest quality, of exquisite latinity. Péguy knew it by heart, and repeated it to all and sundry, mingling his French version with the original as he was to do later in print.

Salvete flores Martyrum,
Salut fleurs des martyrs
Quos, lucis ipso in limine,
Christi insecutor sustulit,

Ceu turbo nascentes rosas.

Que, sur le seuil même de la lumière,
Le persécuteur du Christ enleva,
(emporta).

[1] When the time came to sit at the crossways,
There to choose regret and not refuse remorse,
To sit at the corner of this double course,
Gazing at either vault where the pillar splays.

You alone, O Queen, heart's secret keeping,
Knew how downward one of the two ways went,
Knew which one we chose, all to the effort bent,
Like choosing a tree or wood for carving.

Not out of virtue, we are not that way bent,
Not out of duty, we have no love of it,
But like a carpenter's respect for measurement,
Our need was to find the middle of the pit.

The axis of distress, for there we do belong,
Our hidden need to know yet more unhappiness,
Take on the stiffer lot, suffer more grievous wrong,
Encounter evil fully in all its righteousness.

With the same skill, the same old sleight of hand,
No longer valid now in happiness' pursuit,
Let us hold honour safe beyond dispute
As best we may, O Queen, with heart and hand.

Ceu turbo nascentes rosas.

Comme la tempête de naissantes roses.

Vos prima Christi victima,
Grex immolatorum tener,
Aram sub ipsam simplices
Palma et coronis luditis.

Vous, première victime du Christ,
Troupeau tendre des immolés,
Au pied de l'autel même simples,
Simplices, âmes simples, simples enfants,
Palma et coronis luditis. Vous jouez avec la palme
et les couronnes. Avec votre palme et vos couronnes.

The Missal gives this explanation:

The children massacred by Herod on account of the God-child deserve their place of honour at Jesus' crib. The Church, true Mother that she is, weeps to-day over their death as over a cruel bereavement and wears the colours of penance; but at the Octave, leaving aside what appertains to time to consider only the eternal triumph of heaven, she will wear red vestments and honour these innocent victims as true martyrs.

It is not hard to guess what was going on in Péguy's mind: beyond the formal beauty there is deep meaning; beyond the Jewish children cut off in their flower, unbaptised yet held as saints and martyrs, flowers of the Martyrs, *flores Martyrum*, there were his own children, in the flower of their youth, unbaptised, whom people had declared to be growing up under the threatening hand of *Dies Irae*. Who can tell to whom shall fall as his lot the red vestments of glory?

That was the starting point. The inspired walker was seen once more pacing over the Saclay heights, and the *Mystère des Saints Innocents* was on the way.

God speaks in person again, but He is no longer the surprised, unyielding old patriarch whom we met in the first pages of the *Porche*. He is no longer the defender of the Old Law, He has embraced the New Law: He has been won by prayer. Péguy evokes the vision of these prayers. Like fleets sailing to the assault, they fill the sky with their sails:

All the immense fleet of prayers laden with the sins of the world.
All the immense fleet of prayers and penances comes to assault me.
Each Pater is like a high timbered vessel with the head you know.
Those words that go in front of every prayer like the hands of the suppliant in front of his face. . . .
Those three or four words which strike forward like a fine head on a poor ship.

After the *Pater's*, the major vessels, there come the *Ave's*, the light fleet; after the *Ave's*, the lesser prayers. Then at last comes a fourth fleet, a voiceless, shameful one with broken masts and torn sails; bearing dim good intentions among so much else spoilt by evil, which God alone will notice and gather up. Bearing, as well, all undeserved misfortune, all tragic destinies. Péguy was far from forgetting the suppliants of old, Œdipus and Antigone have their stricken barge in this fleet. How wide the horizons of salvation stretch: Péguy gladly pursues them to their farthest bounds.

I am their father, said God. Our Father who art in heaven.
My son was telling them that I am their Father. . . .
And now I have got to judge them like a Father. In so far as a father is any good at judging. . . .
It's an old story, how the father judged the son who went off and came back again.
Of the two it was the father who shed most tears.

The son who went off and came back again: the words are set as a landmark and a guide to travellers. If we were listening to a symphony, the whole atmosphere would be changed with a change of modulation. John Sebastian Bach is a master of this art (there are so many analogies between Bach's *Passions* and Péguy's *Mystères*). Péguy knows where he is taking us and what his poem will soon make of the Prodigal Son seen in a flash at this point. More like lightning still was the mention of the parable at the end of the *Mystère du Porche de l'Espérance*. Then, Péguy went on to speak of the French people. *A man had two sons* . . . a mere passing allusion, deliberately unstressed. We know neither his look nor his name from the Gospels, so everyone can interpret the story in his own way. With no undue haste and with lightness and sureness of touch he leads us on and shows us the people of France. Here is the Prodigal Son.

God considers the wanderer and utters words which may be counted among the great pages of our literature. Great, and yet so simple and familiar: is this why no one noticed them at first? 'If there were no Frenchmen,' said God, 'some of the things I do no one would understand.' His best recruits are French and He keeps an eye on the nation that provides them. Hence these famous lines:

People, the peoples of the earth call you light
Because you are quick.
The pharisee peoples call you light
Because you are a rapid people.
But I have weighed you, said God, and I have not found you light.
You who invented the cathedrals, I did not find you light in faith.
You who invented the crusades, I did not find you light in charity.
As for hope, the less said the better: there is none, but for them.

The Mystery of the Holy Innocents appeared at the end of March and received the sort of welcome to which Péguy was unfortunately accustomed. Most of the subscribers did not even trouble to cut the pages of a new *Cahier*. The *Cahiers* with his name to them were a chronic bore which had to be put up with for the sake of getting the first edition of Romain Rolland's *Jean-Christophe*, or Benda's essays.

Outside *Cahiers* circles, there was complete silence. Six weeks later, on the 7th of May, Péguy wrote to Lotte:

Old friend, I must tell you that the *Cahier* has fallen on a complete blank, and has not sold seven copies in a fortnight.

Affectionate greetings—Péguy.

•

During that same February when the *Mystère des Saints Innocents* came out, Péguy was in the throes of family trouble: it had its effect on the book. One of his children was ill, they feared meningitis. On February 29th, it was found to be typhoid, which was very serious.

Our minds turn to the father in his distress, with the added torture of knowing his unbaptised child would be swallowed up in the limbo of those who are gathered under no communal rite, a state of affairs for which he felt himself partly responsible. He had first thought of calling on Our Lady for help some time before. Maritain's sister had asked him, probably about 1910, what he would do if one of his children fell seriously ill. 'I should go on foot to Chartres to put him in Our Lady's charge,' was his answer. That is the first indication. The idea reappears in a veiled form in the episode of the second *mystère*, where the woodcutter lays down his tools in the icy forest to beg Our Lady to take charge of his children. The connection is slight, it may be just a piece of poetic invention. But Péguy had no use for poetry that was merely symbolic. In his own anxious days, he remembered the woodcutter. Could it be that this figment of his imagination, this creature of his fancy, had more faith than he had himself; could his pen have run away with him to the extent of giving him what he had no right to give, not possessing it himself? The woodcutter's action suddenly appeared to him as the very one he himself was meant to perform. As he said to Lotte at a later date: 'My *Porche* was an anticipation: I had never put into practice what I wrote in it.' He decided to make the Chartres pilgrimage on foot, it was a promise.

The child got better and was cured. The promise remained. Péguy was in no hurry, he never was. It was a promise and go to Chartres he would, but the day and the time were dependent on disposition and inspiration. On June 10th, Charles-Lucas de Peslouän received a note which said, 'I am going to Chartres between Thursday the 13th and Thursday the 20th.' So the date was fixed. A week later, Peslouän was asked by Péguy to go and see him at the rue de la Sorbonne. He struck him as being worn out and very quiet. Three months later, he wrote and told Lotte all about it:

My boy Pierre has been ill. . . . Well, old chap, I felt it was pretty serious. I had to make a vow, yes I did. I made a pilgrimage to Chartres. I'm a Beauce man. Chartres is my cathedral. I was quite out of training. I did 144 kilometres in three days. Old chap, the crusades were child's play! It is quite clear that we should have been the first to set out for Jerusalem, and that we should have died on the road. To die in a ditch is nothing; I really felt it was nothing. We are doing something much harder than that. You see the spire of Chartres 17 kilometres away across the plain. Occasionally it disappears behind a fold in the ground or a line of wood. As soon as I saw it, it was absolute ecstasy. I stopped feeling, neither my tiredness nor my feet troubled me any more.

Such were the hasty impressions which were to be focussed in a poem, *La Présentation de la Beauce à Notre-Dame de Chartres.*

Nous sommes nés pour vous au bord de ce plateau.
Dans le recourbement de notre blonde Loire,
Et ce fleuve de sable et ce fleuve de gloire
N'est là que pour baiser votre auguste manteau.

Nous sommes nés au bord de ce vaste plateau,
Dans l'antique Orléans sévère et sérieuse,
Et la Loire coulante et souvent limoneuse
N'est là que pour laver le pied de ce coteau.[1]

The lines are well known. But there is an interesting fact which is more important than a mere biographical curiosity. Péguy at the age of thirty-eight had never been to Chartres. I suppose the case is unique. In the shop where his friends gathered round him, only one man could have said in 1912, I have never seen Chartres, and that was Péguy himself.

Once more, Péguy appears as the man who never hurried. The day will come: this might be his slogan. The day for Chartres did come, and the challenge was answered promptly, powerfully and with much freshness. As soon as he stood in need of Chartres Cathedral, he discovered it. Its poet will now forever be this Frenchman who remained so long in ignorance of it, Péguy himself.

[1] We were born on the edge of this plain for you,
Here in the curve of our Loire so bland,
This river of glory, this river of sand
Is there but to kiss your robe so solemn-blue.

We were born on the edge of this plain so wide,
In ancient Orléans, a city stern and true,
And the running Loire, sometimes muddy too,
Is there but to bathe the foot of the hillside.

Mais vous apparaissez, reine mystérieuse,
Cette pointe là-bas dans le moutonnement
Des moissons et des bois et dans le flottement
De l'extrême horizon ce n'est point une yeuse.

Ni le profil connu d'un arbre interchangeable,
C'est déjà plus distante, et plus basse, et plus haute,
Ferme comme un espoir sur la dernière côte,
Sur le dernier coteau la flèche inimitable.

Un homme de chez nous, de la glèbe féconde
A fait jaillir ici d'un seul enlèvement,
Et d'une seule source et d'un seul portement,
Vers votre assomption la flèche unique au monde.

Tour de David, voici votre tour beauceronne,
C'est l'épi le plus dur qui soit jamais monté
Vers un ciel de clémence et de sérénité,
Et le plus beau fleuron dedans votre couronne.

Un homme de chez nous a fait ici jaillir,
Depuis le ras du sol jusqu'au pied de la croix,
Plus haut que tous les saints, plus haut que tous les rois,
La flèche irréprochable et qui ne peut faiblir.[1]

So all is said. Péguy's foot-slogging lines have gloriously attained one of the peaks to which they were destined. His level prosody seems made to sustain the footsteps of a man walking across a plain.

Péguy went back to Chartres with young Alain Fournier as his

[1] At last you have appeared, mysterious queen,
The tip seen yonder in the creamy surge
Of harvest fields and woods and on the verge
Of trembling distance is no evergreen,

Nor the outline of another tree,
It is too distant, lower, and yet higher,
Firm as hope beyond the furthest lee,
Above the rise the one and only spire

A man of the land it was who so hurled,
From fruitful soil soaring, straight as a die,
With but one spring, one yearning to the sky,
Assumptions-wards, the wonder of the world.

Mary, Tower of David, here is your Beauce tower,
It is the hardest head of corn that ever grew
Upwards towards a sky all clement and blue,
In all your crown it is the finest flower.

A man of the land it was who set it soaring
Here from level earth to the foot of the Cross,
Higher than any saint, higher than any king,
The flawless spire that shall not suffer loss.

companion, doubtless in December 1912. The poem, written at an unknown date, gathers together impressions from both pilgrimages.[1]

---

[1] There are certain complications of detail in the story outlined so briefly here. The date of the first pilgrimage is fixed beyond doubt by written notes. But there was this second pilgrimage of which the date is more uncertain. Lotte, and doubtless through him, J.-J. Tharaud, puts it in August, when the child's health gave fresh cause for anxiety. This time it was diphtheria, but it was caught at an early stage and on August 4th, Péguy wrote to Peslouän: 'The news is wholly good. Needless to say, I am bound for Chartres again. I have an idea I shall go there every year.' On the date of the second pilgrimage Charles-Lucas de Peslouän has let me have the following note: 'I haven't got the date of the second pilgrimage, nor any note mentioning it. I can only guess: the poem *La Présentation de la Beauce* appeared on May 6th 1913. The death of a young man is mentioned in it (*Nous venons vous prier pour ce pauvre garçon . . .*)—a friend of Alain Fournier's who died in December 1912. So the second pilgrimage must be between December 1912, and May 1913. And if it is true, as has been said, that Alain Fournier accompanied Péguy on one of the two pilgrimages, it must have been the second.'

XIII

LAST PAMPHLET

LAST MYSTERY

Ah, I did not know this was what life was like.—CHARLES PÉGUY.

A FRESH STORM broke on the *Cahiers*. The Goncourt Prize was the cause of it. Some people wished it to be awarded to Benda's *Ordination*, which the *Cahiers* had published. Péguy took a lively interest in the business, hoping some material advantage would accrue to him. Good peasant that he was, always eager to get the highest yield out of his concern, he had laid down the rule that a certain fraction of the prizes awarded to books he had published was his due. There was very lively discussion at the Académie Goncourt: *Ordination* was much disliked in many quarters, and so was the author of it. Benda was a Jew and the anti-semitic virus was rife. Léon Daudet opposed the idea. Léon Daudet was *Action Française* in all its young virulence. Elémir Bourges opposed it equally violently; Bourges was the friend of Sorel and Variot, both of the *Cahiers* bookshop's inner circle. These ramifications did not help to sort things out. Finally, *Ordination* was turned down. Péguy's retort came at once. He wired a break of relations with the man he had called 'our master, M. Sorel.'[1]

I recognise your hand in all that is being done against the Cahiers, he wrote. *I beg you in future not to come on Thursdays.* With old Sorel went good, faithful Edouard Berth, and Jean Variot, who had had his share of favour and confidence. Always, all through his life, this sound of broken glass, to use Tharaud's expression.

I will quote a few lines from the diary I was keeping at the time:

December 12th 1912.—I went to Péguy's at about three o'clock. Sorel was not there. I remarked upon it, and Bourgeois murmured a few evasive words. Then he turned to Péguy:

'Halévy has observed that Sorel is not here.'

'I had to break with him,' said Péguy. 'Because of the prize he made Benda lose. Variot and he conducted a fierce campaign against it. I am more and more against anti-semitism. . . . If people want to start the

[1] In actual fact Péguy kept his sense of respect and the use of the title. In the note on *Eve* published by the *Bulletin des Professeurs catholiques*, unsigned, drawn up by Péguy himself, we read: 'In an article published soon after the *Mystère de la Charité de Jeanne d'Arc* appeared, our master, M. Georges Sorel, made it quite clear that the liturgy is diffused theology.'

Affaire Dreyfus again, we will set to work. As for me, as I told ——[1] I'm on the side of the Jews, because with the Jews I can be the sort of Catholic I want to be, with the Catholics I couldn't.'

Granted that the beginning of this outbreak is rather spoilt by the end. In actual fact, Péguy's pro-semitism had two sources: one, a very pure one, expressed with utter sincerity in the pages of Bernard Lazare. The Jewish tragedy and its undying idealism were for Péguy among the grander characteristics of human history. The other source was wholly practical: without his Jewish subscribers, the *Cahiers*, his life and livelihood, would have crashed.

The next day, I went to the rue de l'Ecole de Médecine bookseller, Delesalle. Delesalle was an ex-metal worker, an ex-militant trade unionist of great independence, a sensitive and learned person who had been greatly mellowed by his long sojourn among his books. He rather confused the proletarian revolution with his bibliography, but he would not have cared to hear it said. The proletarian revolution was his youth and most men stay happily in love with their youth. Péguy's excommunication meant for Sorel merely a change of bookshops; instead of going to Péguy's he went to Delesalle's. Old Socrates that he was, he needed a corner of his own to sit and talk somewhere in the Latin Quarter. If there were books to turn over and two or three people to listen to him, it was a satisfactory afternoon. Here are my notes:

Delesalle talked about Sorel, who was, it seemed, much amused at his excommunication.

It is true that Benda attacked Sorel first. It is also true that Sorel had no right to go on going to Péguy's bookshop as he had been going for the last two years, while he spoke and allowed others to speak as poisonously about him as he did.

Berth gave up his subscription, it appears. He wrote to Péguy: 'Since you choose between Sorel and Benda, keep your Benda and keep my copies, too. . . .'

So there is Péguy, high and dry; he has quarrelled with the Academy, he is out of favour with the Catholics, he has quarrelled with the antisemitics. He is beaten and alone. Powerful as he is, he could not avoid his shipwreck. He has quarrelled with Desjardins because he attacks the University. He has quarrelled with André Gide because he hates his dilettante attitude. He stands alone, with his band of a thousand subscribers who provide his livelihood. May he keep them. Romain Rolland's *Jean-Christophe* has come to an end, so a good many will give up. And then there is that queer friendship with Benda. It is a terrible burden for the man. But there he is, like a green and growing oak tree.

In the deserted bookshop, odd as it may seem, Benda inherited Sorel's chair. Benda was one of the few men, perhaps the only one, with whom Péguy never quarrelled. And he is the only one of all who

[1] I did not catch the name at the time.

knew Péguy who has not paid tribute to his memory. Ten years after his death he disclosed a hatred long concealed under apparent scepticism, and placed Péguy among the betrayers of the spirit because he never betrayed his land and his own folk. How curiously blind Péguy was in this case, usually so far-seeing. He probably liked Benda for being something so utterly different from himself. He belonged to another order of man altogether, and the only possible intercourse between the two was on the intellectual plane. There was no sign of that bond which was Péguy's idea of friendship. Péguy's many quarrels always bore upon some deep-lying difference. 'I believe,' he wrote, 'that friendship worthy of the name should put all its energy into discussion, however violent it may become, and to rescuing a friend from what one knows is mistaken or criminal.' There were no such deeps to plumb between Péguy and Benda. Péguy appreciated wit, Benda was very witty. Péguy liked a good laugh, Benda was past master in the art of punning, and Péguy is far from being the only professional manipulator of words to enjoy a good pun. He loved words even to play with. How it did amuse him to tell Tharaud of Benda's latest: 'You're a bore, Péguy, with all your talk about the purity of the *Cahiers*. If you go on, I shall write a book called *Critique de la maison pure*, and if you still go on, I shall write another called *Critique de la maison pratique*.'[1] Such metaphysical skittishness gave Péguy real joy, and joy was not so common in the bookshop these days. Perhaps I should say, too, that there existed, singularly enough, a sort of complicity of bitterness between these two men. In his early twenties, Péguy could not have stood Benda. But life is corrosive. Suspicion and rancour had rusted his soul a little, and Benda's caustic manner suited the rust.

And there was something else, another link: Benda took Péguy to see his cousin Simone, the actress, married to Claude Casimir-Périer, the son of the President of the Republic and great-great-grandson of Casimir Périer, Louis-Philippe's famous minister. Péguy already knew Claude Casimir-Périer; they were reserve officers in the same regiment and met at those huge manœuvres they both attended assiduously. Péguy enjoyed Claude and Simone's company, through them he was in contact with the stage as a pastime, with makers of history, with an atmosphere of breeding and culture, and with charming homes, while a very attractive informality was the key-note of it all. It is conceivable that this son of the faubourg Bourgogne was a bit dazzled by the famous name and the wit and comfort. Snobbery can turn up anywhere. Simone had the quicker, more incisive mind and made no pretence of being his disciple. It was sheer relaxation to have a chat with her and to listen to her. Nothing annoyed Péguy more

[1] Kant's famous books are called in French, *Critique de la raison pure* and *Critique de la raison pratique* (translator's note).

than the well-to-do subscriber descending from his Rolls-Royce to call on him in his bookshop and tell him that he was a fervent admirer of his. In the summer he was often a guest at the château de Try, and he enjoyed going and meeting young Alain Fournier who was then at the height of radiant young manhood, so soon to be cut short by the war. At twenty-two he was within two years of his death. Alain Fournier was a passionate admirer of Péguy's, *that man of God* as he called him. Without Simone and Claude to visit, there would have been a lack in Péguy's life. If it was not worldly glory, it was at least a pleasing and stimulating sample of it. 'For me, you stand for present glory and the taste of glory itself,' he wrote to his hosts. 'There are none to touch you in those dark hours when the assurance of having established one's authority for the centuries *apud posteros* is poor comfort for fifteen or twenty years of semi-starvation *apud equales*.' Try and its friendly host and hostess were the loveliest playthings that came his way. Real life was harsh and exacting.

The other home where he was always welcome and which became a regular home-from-home for him as time went by, was Mme Favre's. She was the daughter of Jules Favre, the 1848 republican, and was republican herself and with more romantic fervour than her father even had shown: daughters tend to exaggerate. Her son, Jacques Maritain, had brought Péguy home, and they had formed the habit of lunching together on Thursdays. Mme Favre was soft-hearted and kind and became a second mother to Péguy, his Parisian mother. But discord broke in on this once intimate little gathering. The same trouble arose as in Péguy's own home: Mme Favre was a humanitarian of the old school, a believer of the George Sand and Pierre Leroux type, and her children (a son and a daughter), who had followed her at first, had then turned aside. Jacques Maritain was brought up a Protestant, and then became a Catholic convert. The daughter did likewise, with unavoidable results in the way of heart-rending scenes and distressing breaks at home. The man responsible for these conversions was Léon Bloy, an eccentric believer given to much violence and abuse. Mme Favre was greatly distressed by all these events which seemed to her unnecessary and incomprehensible. Then the friends of the house became involved: the breath of spiritual regeneration was in the air. Péguy was the first; the second was Ernest Psichari, Renan's grandson, also a guest at the Thursday lunches. Republican Mme Favre was amazed at the table-talk of these ducklings she had hatched and who now swam in strange waters and discussed the nature of angels. Psichari was a soldier of the African cavalry who had galloped into the Faith sword in hand, and loved to display his native truculence even within its bounds. One day he exclaimed at Mme Favre's lunch-table: 'I should love to have cancer, so as to go and be cured at Lourdes.' Mme Favre's motherly heart went out to Ernest Psichari's mother, Henriette Renan, with distress at the thought of the suffering her son's illness would have caused her, and she demurred at the cruel wish so light-heartedly propounded: 'My boy, you must think of your mother!' Péguy came to her rescue: 'I am waiting for the day when someone will go to Lourdes to ask to be made ill,' he said to Psichari.

Péguy left those who did not agree with him in complete peace and had no other feeling but one of great devotion to this woman old enough to be his mother. They disagreed at times, but on other subjects. Mme Favre loathed the idea of war, she refused to think of it and intended to fight it by her very refusal as well as by general disarmament. So she hated the nationalist policy which became prevalent about 1910 and at once won the support of many of the younger generation. That was the subject of many discussions and disagreements. One day Péguy said: 'I've had enough, I'm going,' and left the table. Mme Favre's daughter ran after him and persuaded him to stay. He always did stay, for love of 'that blessed little Republican with her big heart but not tuppence worth of brains,' as he wrote her, as he said to her face, for he loved teasing her.

•

Romain Rolland has recently published an old note relating a conversation he had with Péguy at that time.

February 1913. Saw Péguy at the *Cahiers*, in the back of his shop, all alone and much saddened. He is eating his heart out. In spite of his unquestioned fame, his livelihood is at a very low ebb. The *Cahiers de la Quinzaine* have lost a hundred and fifty subscribers since October. Péguy can't get anything accepted. *The Revue des Deux Mondes* rejected three sonnets from his *Sainte-Geneviève*. The *Correspondant*, after publishing three or four, refuses to take anything longer. The *Nouvelle Revue Française*, which paid the Tharauds a thousand francs for their *Fête Arabe*, offers him four hundred francs for a much more considerable work. Of his last book of verse about *Sainte-Geneviève* he has not sold four copies. He says, pitifully: 'Yet in our time we used to buy Sully Prudhomme's *Justice*! My verse is no more boring than *Justice*.' And he has other troubles . . . which I won't mention here . . .[1]

That back-shop was a dreary spot, looking out on to a narrow yard. Its walls were sadly lined with unsold copies of the *Cahiers*. The door was open, anyone could come in. But there were different kinds of welcome for different people. When Péguy considered that a visit had lasted long enough (and he decided quickly), he got up and gazed at the caller who had outstayed his welcome with that same glassy look that Laurent has given him in his portrait. His meaning was all too clear: the caller went off with his tail between his legs.

[1] The reader is referred to the poem quoted on p. 163-4 and to the brief explanation given there.

'Bores just don't take,' he wrote to Lotte. He knew exactly what to do about them. To Lotte again he said: 'I can only do with Jews of the praying sort.' They can be counted on the fingers of the hand.

From time to time some young people would come to the shop: they got a better welcome. Guéguen, or Krakowski, younger still and as bold as a page-boy, would venture in on his way back from a lecture at the Sorbonne. Péguy did not discourage him. 'Come in,' he said, 'you're not disturbing me, sit down; give me a hand with this sorting, or with these parcels. We'll talk while we do it.' Then they all went out together, and Guéguen still knows by heart lines that Péguy recited to him in those days. So the high spirits and kindliness were still alive, but veiled. Once Péguy greatly entertained his friend René Johannet with his account of some cheerful trifle he had made up. 'Write it down,' said Johannet.—'No, not to-day.' 'Well, but when?'—'One day when I am happy.' Which was as good as saying, never. He said to me once: 'Ah, I did not know this was what life was like.' I can still hear the tone of his voice, surprise was the dominating note: the surprise of a child amazed that life should, after the first enchantment, be so harsh. How far away were the days when standing up in his place in the classroom, Charles repeated in clear ringing tones:

Mes sœurs, l'onde est plus fraîche aux premiers feux du jour.

•

Péguy knew he had reached the age when things are as they are: a man knows by then what he is capable of, what he is worth, and what he must put up with. Péguy's destiny was that of a solitary man with an increasing number of enemies to fight.

And his poverty was unabated, rather the contrary, on account of the increasing number of enemies and the increasing needs of the three growing children at home. 'My wife is always buried in her butcher's account,' he wrote.

Now it was about this time that those nearest to Péguy first noticed the signs of a foreboding—signs which were to become more and more frequent:

Waiting for a death more living than life.

Mme Favre had already observed, though without being able to say exactly when, 'a strange attraction to death.' It grew, it was part of his consciousness of destiny. In 1912 or so, he wrote to Peslouän: 'I seem to be taking the turning which men who died at forty-five take.' Yet his health was good, weariness was only weariness, there was no danger there. There was evidently something else, some sense of being spurred on. Now overhanging fate at that time meant war. Its cloud had moved from Morocco to Tripoli, from Tripoli to the Balkans, and the whole Mediterranean basin was smouldering; by the end of 1912, guns were booming at Tchachaldja, at the gates of Constantinople. And looming above these other distant wars Péguy foresaw ours, his war. He spoke of it incessantly; he wearied his friends, at times he longed for it with fierce ardour, at others he welcomed it in his dreams as an occasion for rejoicing, a treat, perhaps even a deliverance. On the 3rd of January 1912, he wrote to Claude Casimir-Périer:

I had a lovely night. I was at Coulommiers (the place for the mobilisation of the 276th Infantry which was their regiment), on the other side of the small stores. There was some difficulty about the sizes of boots, but we were determined to cover ourselves with glory.

Surely no other note like this was written in all Europe: Péguy had dreamed the mobilisation.

With this forewarning and foreseeing and urging onwards, Péguy doubled his zeal for work. He had just started a *Dialogue de l'histoire et de l'âme charnelle* which enchanted Alain Fournier, the first reader of the first pages. The dialogue was but a sign, the first sprout of a season of immense productivity: mysteries, poems, reminiscences, essays, pamphlets were all buzzing in his head. First he had to finish and publish his recent works, his poems. The *Tapisserie de Sainte-Geneviève et de Jeanne d'Arc* appeared as a slender *Cahier* in January and had no success at all. We already know through Romain Rolland's note the amount of the sales: four copies. I believe that very few people realised that this exercise in prosody was in fact the prelude to a magnificent output. In May, the *Tapisserie de Notre-Dame* appeared and had a much better reception: Péguy had included in it his *Présentation de la Beauce à Notre-Dame de Chartres* and it was noticed. In fact it was an event, it was a real event in the order of things we are considering for a poem to appear which was destined to last. 'People who had read nothing else of Péguy's have read the *Présentation de la Beauce à Notre-Dame de Chartres,*' as M. Paul Archambault wrote in 1939. And the poem somehow became known from the very first, though it is not easy to say how, for the press took as little notice as ever.[1] The sales were not high, for two thousand copies were printed of which one thousand were for the subscribers, and the *Cahier* was not sold out in 1914. Yet there was a certain wave of opinion which, without making a great stir, did rouse a lively and lasting response. Péguy the prose-writer was also a poet: the *Présentation de la Beauce* made this quite clear. The response was personal and propagating and the imponderable

[1] Péguy was partly responsible for this boycott. Sorel's fine piece of tactical advice had borne fruit: 'If a review treats you disrespectfully, your reply should strike at the head, the editor.' All the review editors had suffered Fernand Laudet's fate and concluded that Péguy was a dangerous character, never to be mentioned.

banner of fame was borne aloft. One more great page had been added to the heritage of French poetry, and it was hailed at once.

After this, Péguy left the *Dialogue de l'historie et de l'âme charnelle* to finish later and buried himself in a fourth mystery, to follow the *Porche. The Porche du Mystère de la deuxième Vertu* (the second virtue was Hope, of course), was, as one would guess, an introduction, standing alone. Hope is an aspiration which finds its realisation and its end in the bringing about of the facts for which it aspires. Once the *Porche* was fairly standing, there was the door to be gone through, and the other side, the inside, to be seen. So after the *Mystère du Porche,* Péguy wrote a second mystery, *Le Propre de l'Espérance.*

How clumsy his titles are, so naïvely pedantesque. What on earth does *The Proper of Hope* mean? Dante was less scholastic: when he wrote a poem about Paradise, he called it *Paradise.* And that is the whole point. Péguy set out to describe that same Paradise which he used as a child to wish his grandmother each New Year's day. It was not a new idea. As early as 1911 Péguy was sending Lotte series of verses, or perhaps merely notes, on the theme of Paradise. He wrote: 'Old man, here are the plans for the middle of the third.' He meant the third mystery.

Paradise is the shore of glory is one of these lines. Others are:

Paradise is more secret than closed garden.
Paradise is more open than battle-field.
Paradise is more populous than Paris.
Paradise is more deserted than December heath.
Paradise is public and all may come and drink.
Paradise is more calm than evening.
Paradise is cooler than cool dawn.
Paradise is more scorching than noon.

In Paradisal plenitude all the contrasts which Péguy so much loved were resolved: his hidden garden at Lozère, the open heath at Saclay; his own heart, so kind, yet so given to starting fires; himself, so fresh, so ardent.

Towards the end of 1912 he read Dante's *Paradise* and was not at all disconcerted. 'Dante's gift is to invent, mine is to discover,' he wrote to Lotte. He must have meant that the ideas were too consciously construed in Dante's *Paradise,* and the conceptual scaffolding of Thomism was too apparent around his lyrics. Indeed, factual as he is in the *Inferno* and the *Purgatory,* Dante is often less so in the *Paradise.* Péguy talked to me about this:

What I see is something quite different. In my Paradise, there won't only be souls, there will be things too. . . . Everything in existence that has really come off, the cathedrals, for instance . . . Notre Dame, Chartres, I shall put them in. . . .

His hands performed the action of firmly planting them both on the ink-stained deal table at which he was sitting in his back-shop.

Notre-Dame and Chartres, I shall put them in. . . .

Those familiar with his work may try (I am trying myself) to imagine what the evocation, the transfiguration of these two cathedrals would have been, in his steady, careful prose. Notre-Dame, the Cathedral of Paris, Chartres, the Cathedral of Beauce: the two he was familiar with. And in addition, *everything in existence that has really come off*. What a lot of things, what listed salvage you would have let your lyrical genius and your numerative amplitude discover, Péguy! The tools our workmen used to use for building: trowels, hammers, well-worn ironware, ashwood handles shaped to the human hand, you would not have forgotten these, you would not have separated them from the work done with them; you would have admitted to honour (in the singular, of course) all hard-worked things; you would have set them inside the Cathedral, as Jeanne set her flag there. And the other tools, whether for work or war, and all that man's energy uses and produces (the fireside chair, the cast-iron fire-dogs, the hearthstone). Just as he boasted to his friend Roustan that on a single theme he had used up all the words in his rhyming dictionary, we imagine him working right through the Bazar de l'Hôtel-de-Ville catalogue (household goods, workshop tools, garden tools).

What a lot of things! But not too many: the least has its worth and must be named. Péguy's faith was so human, so earth-loving. Péguy would not have it that God could have come down among men, that Jesus could have lived among them, only to do half a job. It had been saved! The poor old world had been saved! All of it, not in its erring, bleeding shape, but in its very being where Grace has penetrated. *Paradise is the shore of glory:* to this shore and to this glory belong all the things that have their place and meaning in the world.

But the project lapsed. Péguy's mind was occupied with other things. He received a manuscript entitled *Mémoire sur l'enseignement primaire et ce qu'il devrait être* (Memorandum on primary education and what it ought to be), by M. Naudy, one-time principal of the primary training-college school where Péguy had his early lessons. It was he who had first picked the boy out, and it was he who said, 'Péguy must learn Latin,' thereby setting the course for his life. Thanks to him, Péguy had read Homer, Sophocles and Virgil. And for this immense benefit he remained deeply thankful. He replied at once, saying: 'I will publish it.' Here was the poor man gladly handing out magnanimous gifts at which wealthier men might draw the line. The document was straightforward but a bit unsophisticated and needed some filling out. So Péguy filled it out with a preface. At his age and in his circumstances, he welcomed anything that recalled his childhood and he set to work with a good will. Here we find those pages on the faubourg Bourgogne which we quoted in the first chapter, with the portrait of the old people of France, 'where there was such rightness of mind, where everything was a lesson, everything was a legacy, everything was consecrated custom.' Péguy observes that this people has disappeared, and it disappeared very quickly, in about 1880; he insists on this date, just as he did in talk. One day I heard him say: 'The break in our history is not in 1789, but in 1880.' 'What on earth do you mean?' I asked him in great surprise. '1880 is the primary school,' said Péguy. My historical work owes a lot to those few words uttered on the pavement of the rue de Rennes.

But there was no undue pessimism. France was going through one of the most serious crises of her history and he knew it. But he knew it was only a crisis. The problems of work and of the human soul will be solved, though we cannot see how, and a young people will take the place of the young people of old who have disappeared from under our very eyes. 'It is no good having a gloomy view of things,' he said in a conversation of which Lotte kept some notes. 'Our nation has inexhaustible resources. When idiots like old Léon Bloy pronounce that Paris is to crumble under a rain of fire for the punishment of her crimes, one can only shrug one's shoulders. As though Geneviève, Saint-Louis, Jeanne d'Arc were going to cease watching over their city. Poor fellow, he simply doesn't understand about patrons.'

Péguy's essay still lacked a title. It was about a people who had lived a human life on its work as peasants and craftsmen in its own small, home-made workshops. The village smith gave his services in return for his customers' wine, milk and corn; and so it went on. Such was France, gay with laughter and songs that are no longer heard. Money hadn't got the hold it has to-day, driving our French brothers and sons to crowd at office doors, offices of big concerns and offices of the State too, which is itself a big concern. What should the title be? Péguy wrote a single word: *l'Argent*, money. That is the seamy side of the book and an admission of unceasing worry which his mother, the mender of chairs, had never experienced; she had worked and earned enough to bring up her son, she was now growing old and was making ready for a good death, as they used to say, after a good life. That is the true condition of man, and that was the condition of Frenchmen of the past, *always poor, always cultured, always free*.

Having finished his preface, one would have expected Péguy to return to the *Mystère du Porche de l'Espérance*, but the prose-writer in him was on the war-path and was not to be stopped. Something else occurred which gave him his cue. All his life, that was how things happened: his poetry came from within, his prose was a retort to outside events. Each of Péguy's essays had its specific occasion and was provoked by circumstances. The particular circumstance in this case is transparently evident.

L'Argent came out on February 13th. Just as Péguy was busy with his mail copies, a University festivity set the Schools' Quarter buzzing. Paris was very lively in those days: Raymond Poincaré had just been elected President of the Republic, and his election amid the acclamations of the Paris crowds was evidently of national importance. But the University festivity was not connected with that excitemen. The Sorbonne had not seen fit to associate its voice with the acclamations of the city or to contribute to the welcome to the new chief. Far from it. In a general way, it liked neither the policy nor the person of President Poincaré; in a general way, its learned members were socialising and pacifists.

I have said, repeated, and underlined that this was general. To everybody its own group and centre of control, and the group in control at the Sorbonne in 1913 had the bias we mention. As the philosopher Gabriel Scéailles put it, the campaign in favour of a three-year term of military service was merely a ramp of dealers in army boots. Such was the view of the learned of the land. President Poincaré made an appearance at the University festivity in question, but not as a recipient of good wishes and homage but rather to bestow them himself. The Sorbonne had had the idea of doing itself honour in the person of Lavisse, the historian mentioned on a previous occasion. The celebration, complete with State representatives and held in its own great amphitheatre, was in honour of the jubilee of Lavisse's appointment to the rue d'Ulm. One is at liberty to detect some lack of proportion as between the actual occasion and the general to-do of the commemoration.

This sort of festivity roused Péguy's deep and bitter resentment. While the ceremony and the speech-making proceeded, the fine mounted guards and cuirassiers crowded about his doorstep, ready to escort the procession. Péguy admired the fine horsemen but it annoyed him to have them there officially filling his street, in order that pomp and circumstance should crown the successful careers of the anti-militarist University men, his sworn enemies. It was of course an added vexation that the hero of the occasion was Lavisse who had lost him his Grand Prix de Litérature, and had made the academy smile with his catch-phrase about holy water and petrol. This accumulation of honours (in the plural please) was for that man: a man with no personality, who put his ability, not inconsiderable, and his administrative influence, no less so, at the disposal of men who knew how to make the most of them; and chiefly and constantly at the disposal of Herr, with his bushy eyebrows and booming voice, cursing and swearing, 'the name of God being the least of the forms of punctuation he used,' said Péguy. Herr's ambition had been to make Durkheim supreme in the Sorbonne, and Lavisse had helped him carry it out. Herr's ambition was for the French to learn no Greek and very little Latin; Lavisse had helped him carry it out. And all the fine soldiers, and the honour of President Poincaré's presence, were all for him. Péguy's pen still raced on, but in a different strain. *L'Argent* had a mellow quality. The new piece of work, which Péguy called *L'Argent suite* without more ado, was venomous with his exasperation and more virulent than ever. President Poincaré paying homage to the Sorbonne! What nonsense! Péguy told how it was in fact received:

> Besides, M. Poincaré was quickly rewarded for what he had done for the Sorbonne in going to the Sorbonne to be present and in spite of himself preside at M. Lavisse's jubilee. Less than four weeks later, this same Sorbonne was as usual producing the first and most dangerous move directed not only against the presidency of M. Poincaré but also against the three-year term of military service, and therefore, as usual, against France, and also, as usual, against the Republic.

Péguy was well away, and in terse, curt, weighty sentences, like a boxer's well-placed blows, he struck at these detested personages:

¶ — For thirty years, they have been ruining everything that stood in France and France herself. And now we have no right to ruin the ruin. We have no right to corrode the corrosion or to erode the erosion.

¶ — For thirty years they have enjoyed undermining God, France, the army, customs and laws; and now we have no right to undermine M. Lavisse.

¶ — For thirty years, for the last thirty years, their one concern was to de-bunk all the true greatness of France. And their small-mindedness is supposed to be no concern of ours.

¶ — They will allow anyone to talk of God, or the Gospels, or the faith, or France. Anyone may talk (and how) of the saints and heroes, of men of genius. But say a word about M. Lavisse, and the fat is in the fire.

¶ — They are happy to decry any form of honour. But possessed as they are of all temporal honours, they won't have them decried.

¶ — Anarchy, has a right. I mean this absolutely. But where there is no right, and what we will not have, is for anarchy to elect to govern us vested with the authority of the State.

¶ — . . . If Herr's virus was kept for external use only, it would do no harm. But M. Lavisse is the syringe which pumps the virus into the very flesh of the State educational system.

There is vengeance indeed. But Péguy's horizon is always a far-reaching one. *L'Argent suite* is in fact the text-book on that pre-war period, so conscious and sourly, of life in France a quarter of a century ago.

Pre-war: the term did not exist then, but the fact did, and Péguy's analysis of it is brief and deeply illuminating:

War is war and peace is peace. But what are we to call this present situation which has been made for us, where we are always being asked for both at once, where we are always being asked to pile up and bear endlessly all the flat miseries of peace-time and at the same time to be in a constant state of tension, constantly ready for the overhanging miseries of war-time. . . . We have got all the burdens of peace and so to say all the burdens of war. . . . It is perfectly clear that things are happening which never happened before and that our impression is that we are about to launch into happenings of unheard-of intensity.

Loaded with peace-time responsibilities in the sense in which a donkey is loaded, loaded for war in the sense in which a gun is loaded. . . .

For a great many young men to-day, these lines tell of their own stern waiting period in 1939.

After that, Péguy's anger got the better of his head and heart. For there are responsible men, and blind men, and profiteering men, and weak men. An item of gossip which caused some amusement at the time set him off. Charles Seignobos, the historian and Sorbonne doctor, one of those government anarchists whom Péguy had attacked in the mass, had, while lunching with M. Marcel Prévost, flatly contradicted his friend's forecasts. 'I bet you a lunch,' he said, with a great explosion of mirth, 'that there will be no war.' This maker of sinister jokes was an authority on historical studies in France. M. Marcel Prévost did not deprive himself of the pleasure of repeating the astonishing proposition. It caused amusement, as I said; Paris is easily amused. But as Péguy saw it, it was no laughing matter. He wrote: 'I must confess that I am a good deal put out by M. Seignobos' idea of betting M. Marcel Prévost a lunch that there will be no war. . . . M. Seignobos ought to know enough history to suspect that it won't all end in a lunch and will in any case not be settled by a lunch.'

Péguy was in a belabouring frame of mind. He showed up precedents: Robespierre, Richelieu; Richelieu with the block, Robespierre with the scaffold. In these cases, 'the bet is not on a lunch but on one's own head. . . . It is not a matter of lunch or no lunch, it is a matter of life and death.'

Then Péguy left the professor and described the threat of war in terribly precise terms. At that time a certain man was predicting peace in copious speeches, was opposing all forms of armament, was priding himself on withholding his vote from the war budget, and was assuring the French people that the friendship of the German socialists was the guarantee of its security. Péguy struck at that man:

I am a good republican, I am an old revolutionary. In war time, there is only one policy, and that is the policy of the National Convention.

But we must realise that the policy of the National Convention means Jaurès in a tumbril and that great voice drowned in the beating of drums.

All through the sombre pages of *L'Argent suite* may be discerned this sensitiveness to events and the ruminating of a man pondering on future days when he will be gone:

We want so cruel an experience at least to be of some use. . . . When a man's life has been a failure, his one idea is that the same thing shall not happen to his children . . . We were constantly betrayed by our masters and chiefs. Not at any price will we suffer our children to be betrayed by these same masters and chiefs . . . We shall show more courage for our children than we showed for ourselves.

L'Argent appeared on February 13th; *L'Argent suite* appeared on April 22nd. The two hundred and thirty-eight packed pages of the *Cahier* were drawn up, printed and published all within a space of two months and a few days over. To a man of the trade, it is a great feat. But to appreciate it at its true worth, one should be a man of several trades and several workshops, from the writer's study to the room where the sewing and binding is done. They were all kept hard at work: the chief insisted on it in a case like this. At home, in his small house, absolute silence was fiercely imposed, and everywhere the work went forward scrupulously, rapidly, unfailingly. And it was done in that same good child's handwriting, which Professor Lanson held up to scorn sixteen years before, in an Ecole Normale class room: 'M. Péguy's work would doubtless be better if he had not spent so much time on the calligraphy.' In his forties, he still wrote in the same way, forming his letters perfectly however rapidly the words tumbled from his pen in furious assault.

•

L'Argent was an act of gratitude, *L'Argent suite* an angry outburst. Now we get back to what matters most, the Mysteries. Between pamphlet and mystery there was not a pause. Péguy's immediate friends never saw him so tense and hard-pressed. The tension lasted to the end. 'I must not die,' he kept saying. And he cut the hours he spent in Paris shorter and shorter.

It was not the Paradise he had talked about that he was busy on now. A new idea had cropped up in its stead. Quite new, and as though it had made a sudden appearance and demanded immediate attention. Instead of writing his *Paradise*, Péguy wrote his *Eve*. Everyone was taken by surprise. '*Eve*, what does it mean, another mystery?' people asked. 'No, something else, a new *tapestry*. He had used that term in the title of his two first verse *Cahiers*, the *Tapisserie de Sainte-Geneviève et de Jeanne d'Arc*, and the *Tapisserie de Notre-Dame*. The word was the right one for these great dimly-coloured compositions, set out line by line as stitch by stitch in a tapestry. Or rush by rush in the mending of chairs. *Eve* was to be a poem, all in alexandrines in four-line verses. 'Long?—Very long . . . What about?—Eve, the first wife, the first mother. That is what the Fall is: work, motherhood, home life; fading daylight, the lamp brought in, the table laid . . .'[1]

So Péguy came down to earth again. Eternity all alone[2] up there had not detained him, and his genius brought him back as close as possible to man and his troubles. He had said as much in his first *Jeanne d'Arc*:

O mon Dieu j'aime à tout jamais la voix humaine,
La voix de la partance et la voix douloureuse,
La voix dont la prière a souvent semblé vaine
Et qui marche quand même en la route peineuse.[3]

The substance of *Eve* is contained in these four lines written by Péguy at the age of twenty. We see that his vision of Paradise, as far as he let us see it, was from the first strongly inclined to the things of earth. 'I will put Notre-Dame and Chartres there, and *everything that has really come off. . . .*' Eve's table and her bowl, no doubt. But what is the good of a bowl that is not steaming, or a table that is not used? Neither Notre-Dame nor Chartres would be what they are if there was no care-stricken man or woman in some dark corner. But in Paradise there is neither darkness nor care, so neither Notre-Dame nor Chartres. On the threshold of Paradise, Péguy found Eve, the long-haired mother of us all, and he lingered there with her.

O mère ensevelie hors du premier jardin . . .

O Mother, buried outside the first garden . . . This is the starting point, the distance opens out and with Eve the slow, steep return to glory is initiated. The glory is man's and God's interwoven, one of Péguy's main preoccupations.

Paradise, share of glory, as he said. To those who had reached this

[1] In the description of the customs of the faubourg Bourgogne (*Argent*, p. 19) are found these words, so like those I had noted: 'It was all a legacy, all consecrated custom . . . sleep and watching, work and brief rest, bed and table, soup and beef, house and garden, the door and the street, the yard and the doorstep, and plates on the table.'

[2] *Eternity all alone*: these words come from a fine letter of Albert Thierry's addressed to me on July 19th 1914, after reading Quelques nouveaux maîtres, the first sketch for the present book. Two months later, Albert Thierry, a man of admirable character and talent, fell a victim of the war. I will quote these few lines from his letter: '. . . I should not dare state, as you have done, that the *Porche* is finer than the *Mystère de la Charité*. There is more eternity in the *Porche*, but eternity is all alone, as in Dante's *Paradise*. But that besieged and beaten charity, how brave it is! Of such good heart! Jeanne among the English, is it not, all due proportion kept, Péguy among the moderns?'

[3] O God, I love the voice of man always,
The voice of leave-taking, the voice of pain,
The voice whose prayer has often seemed in vain
Yet plods and plods along laborious ways. . . .

shore he preferred those who had set out to look for it. Eve had fallen so low only in order to begin the long climb back again, and Péguy joined her in this climb.

That spring and summer were immensely laborious. He worked at his desk in the complete silence he imposed on the household, and he continued to work pacing across the heath. 'I've worked like a galley slave,' he told Bourgeois when he went to the rue de la Sorbonne. 'Fifty lines every morning, sometimes a hundred,' he wrote to Lotte. It was accurate computation: in six months two thousand four-lined verses were written, eight thousand lines, it comes to about fifty a day. Cut out the days he went to Paris, at least twice a week, and it comes to more than fifty. At the end of his letter to Lotte come the words: 'I must not die.' It was essential to get *Eve* finished.

•

Eve appeared in the last days of December 1913. What a gift for the subscribers, what a challenge! Tharaud writes: 'When one morning I got this enormous *Cahier* with the bare title *Eve*, opened and saw, as though lined up for parade, five quatrains to the page, for four hundred pages . . . and that in the first line Jesus Christ was speaking to the first woman, our common mother, and that in the last line he was still speaking to her, I confess it gave me a shock, and in spite of my devotion to our great ancestress and to Péguy, I was horrified.' I remember my own first impression, which was exactly the same.

Let us put ourselves in the place of the well-intentioned subscriber turning over the pages of the enormous *Cahier*. We need not be more in the know than he was, we can share his dismay and recoil. On the first page:

Jesus is speaking:

O mère ensevelie hors du premier jardin
Vous n'avez plus connu le climat de la grâce,
Et la vasque et la source et la haute terrasse,
Et le premier soleil sur le premier jardin.[1]

The first stroke of the bow has a firmness which we hope will have impressed the subscriber. But here comes the challenge: the second line, *Vous n'avez plus connu* . . . opens a litany which fills a hundred and twenty-two verses, each variation of which fills the four lines of a verse:

[1] O Mother buried outside the first garden,
You never again found the climate of grace,
And the well, and the spring, and the high terrace,
And the first sunlight on the first garden.

Péguy in his bookshop (*Photo Dornac, 'Nos Contemporains chez eux', Collection A. Martin*)

Vous n'avez plus connu la terre maternelle . . .

Vous n'avez plus connu ni la glèbe facile . . .

Vous n'avez plus connu ni cette plaine grasse . . .

Vous n'avez plus connu ce limon qui s'encrasse . . .[1]

Beethoven wrote thirty-two variations on a given theme; Péguy wrote a hundred and twenty-two, that is, five hundred lines, half a Racine tragedy. Later, he exceeded even this.

The *Vous n'avez plus connu* Litany dies away at last, in the half-light of a dozen transitional verses. Then another one begins, of which the theme is the last of these three lines:

Et moi je vous connais seule silencieuse,
Et seule naufragée aux rives de mémoire,
Et seule préposée aux rayons de l'armoire . . .[2]

This is the theme. Cupboard shelves are part of a woman's kingdom; women have a passion for putting things away, and Eve, at the beginning of all things, of this as well as of all the rest, set her daughters a good example. It all comes out in two picturesque lines:

Femmes, je vous le dis, vous rangeriez Dieu même,
S'il descendait un jour dedans votre maison . . .[3]

The theme once given now runs riot for thirty-five pages:

. . . . *Vous rangez la victoire autant que la défaite.*

. . . . *Et tout vous est égal dans un même labeur.*

. . . . *Vous rangez l'énergie autant que la stupeur.*

. . . . *Et tout vous est égal dans une paix mal faite.*[4]

To return to the subscriber: beyond all shadow of doubt he is simply indignant with Péguy for sending him eight thousand tum-ti-tum lines on an incredibly boring subject. *Vers de mirliton;* the phrase caught on. So a strange piece of work utterly beyond the ordinary man's scope was satisfactorily disposed of in three words.

[1] You never found your land of birth again.

You never found that easy tilth again.

You never found the lush pasture again.

You never knew that sticky sod again.

[2] And I only know you grown silent,
Ship wrecked on the shores of mem'ry,
Addicted to the shelves of cupboards.

[3] Women, you would tidy God Himself away,
If He came down to your house one day.

[4] You put victory away as well as defeat.

You take what comes, all in the day's work.

You put away energy as well as numbness.

You take what comes in a badly-made peace.

But it is really not very surprising that the vast majority of Péguy's humble readers did not welcome Péguy's *Eve* with acclamations. One subscriber, patience exhausted, slammed the book shut, and nothing would induce him to open it again. It is a pity, because after the last *rangerez-vous*, a new movement begins:

Femme, vous m'entendez: quand les âmes des morts
S'en viendront chercher, dans les vieilles paroisses,
Après tant de batailles et parmi tant d'angoisses,
Le peu qui restera de leurs malheureux corps . . .[1]

There are fine things in this evocation of the dead and the subscriber will miss them, he has already had more than enough of this impossible *Cahier*. On page 120, there is a new theme, very short, only two pages long. Very few people discovered them in 1913, and they are very fine. Even now they are all too little known. Here Péguy shows us, not the busy housewife, but woman as guardian of the dead, Eve the giver of burial:

Et moi je vous salue, ô première mortelle,
Vous avez tant baisé les fronts silencieux . . .

Vous en avez tant mis dans de pauvres linceuls,
Couchés sur vos genoux comme aux jours de l'enfance . . .
. . . . On vous en a tant pris de ces grêles garçons
Qui marchaient à la mort téméraires et seuls.

Vous en avez tant mis dans de lourdes entraves,
Les seules qui jamais ne seront déliées,
De ces pauvres enfants qui marchaient nus et graves
Vers d'éternelles morts aussitôt oubliées . . .[2]

Then there are forty pages or so which I will skip over. Here and there are lovely, grave, upturned flower-faces in the dull stretches of undergrowth. It is a heath to be crossed. Péguy goes with steady, even pace, setting his quatrains out line by line like a mediæval poet his monotonous *laisses*. Péguy was not unaware of the analogy and he was pleased to put himself under this patronage. But between

[1] Now listen, woman: when the souls of the dead
Come back looking, in each old parish,
After so many battles, and in such anguish,
For their poor bodies' last ignoble shred. . . .

[2] So I salute you, first mortal woman,
You have kissed such numbers of speechless faces . . .

You have wound so many in scanty winding-sheets,
Lying across your knee as in childhood days . . .
. . . Slim boys in such numbers have been taken from you,
Marching to their death, so brave and so alone.

You have laid so many in bonds so constrained,
Never to be unloosed, the only ones so held,
Of all those trudging boys, naked and self-contained.
To death eternal, memory-lost, impelled. . . .

the *trouvères* and Péguy there is this difference, that the *trouvères* had read neither their Sophocles nor their Virgil. Péguy had done so, and what is more, he could imitate them in gathering his strength together when need arose and giving shape to the boundless flood. Turn to page 161. Here a typographical sign appears: a short line is drawn. It is the only sign of its kind throughout the whole of the eight thousand lines. It is there with a definite intention, of course. Péguy evidently had a reason, a very serious reason, for making a break in the majestic flow of words he was unfolding. Thus duly put on the alert, we read:

Heureux ceux qui sont morts pour la terre charnelle,
Mais pourvu que ce soit dans une juste guerre . . .[1]

I need not go on. These lines came to light ten months later, in September, on Péguy's death, and were the true poem of that war, becoming part of the national heritage which it was Péguy's mission to enhance, and from which his contemporaries excluded him so emphatically. Péguy's authority *in secula*, of which he was himself fully aware, was thus inaugurated.

There are eighteen verses, and then another short line: the beginning and end of the all-important passage are clearly marked. The following lines are of great beauty, and are so closely connected with the preceding passage that one wonders that Péguy did not make them part of it. The reason is not far to seek, the passage in question has one clear distinguishing mark, and that is the repeated use of the word *mort*, dead. In the three first verses it occurs twice, in the fourth, fifth and sixth, once only, in the third lines. The ear, grateful for a moment's reprieve, is ready for the return of the toll bell. And *glas*, toll bell, is the right word to use, for here Péguy is not spelling out a litany, he is tolling a knell: I will not say his own, for the page has a far wider scope, but he was one of the multitude whose supreme sacrifice he was celebrating, and he knew it. Péguy was inspired and at the same time perfectly conscious of what was going on.

As soon as these famous lines were written, he got René Johannet to read them. Johannet was at the time writing an extremely penetrating study of Péguy himself, which is still one of the best, and maybe the best, in a quite prolific series. He recited them to him, emphasising the word *juste* in the second line.

Heureux ceux qui sont morts pour la terre charnelle,
Mais pourvu que ce fût dans une juste guerre . . .

He insisted on it, repeating the word: *dans une JUSTE guerre.*

There are many fine things in the following verses, for instance, the admirable theme:

[1] Blessed are those who died for earthy earth,
Provided they fell in a just war. . . .

Mère voyez vos fils qui se sont tant battus.[1]

—and admirable verses on nature and grace already quoted: and there is a lovely cradle-song. We heard it at the *Théâtre Français* rendered by two speakers, and by this means the monotony of Péguy's prosody was obviated and the effect was most striking.

The two themes: *Il allait commencer* . . . (He was to begin) and *Il allait hériter* . . . (he was to inherit) are spoilt by his all too well-known passion for enumeration as such. They cover pages and pages, and are less matter for reading than for exploring like a botanist or a hunter of game. The same may be said of the imprecations hurled at the modern world (two thousand lines). Doctors, scribblers, chamberlains, prefects, porters, barristers (male and female), and dozens of others, are systematically and copiously ticked off. One has no wish to linger at these pages, but here and there, as one hastily flicks a page over, one's eye is caught by a sequence of admirable lines:

Ce n'est pas dans leur tente et leurs lits d'ambulance
Que nous nous coucherons pour notre éternité.
Ce n'est pas dans leur poudre et leur pulvérulence
Que nous retournerons dans notre inanité.

. . . Ce n'est pas dans leur tente et leurs lits d'ambulance
Le jour du dernier jour, que nous serons laissés.
Ce n'est point par leur drogue et dans leur somnolence
Que nous achèverons nos rêves de blessés.[2]

Grown tired of cursing at last, Péguy turned once more to his chosen models and guides, the two Beatrices of his pilgrim's progress:

Et nous serons conduits par une autre houlette.
Et nos bergers seront de bien autres bergères,
Et nous nous délierons d'une autre bandelette,
Et nous serons menés par des mains plus légères.[3]

Two shepherdesses: one, Geneviève, the girl of Paris, who stopped the barbarian in the fifth century by her instant and gentle prayer; the other, Jeanne, the girl of Lorraine, who drove the foreigner away,

[1] Mother, behold your sons who fought so hard.

[2] Not in a tent nor in an ambulance
Shall we be laid for our eternity.
Not in their dust nor their pulverulence
Shall we return to our inanity.

Not in a tent nor in an ambulance
Shall we be left, the day of the last day,
Nor shall their drugs nor shall their somnolence
The wounded dreams of wounded men allay.

[3] And we shall be guided by a different shepherd's crook
And our shepherds shall be quite different shepherdesses.
We shall shake ourselves free of quite different swaddling bands
And we shall be led by lighter hands.

sword in hand. The two girl patrons of France.[1] So this poem is no exception to the rule observed by the *mystères:* it ends, as they do, on French soil. Geneviève and Jeanne are both daughters of Eve. Péguy's poem ends with the commemoration of their diversely glorious deaths:

Et l'une est morte un soir, et le trois de janvier.
Tout un peuple assemblé la regardait mourir.
Le bourgeois, le manant, le pâtre et le bouvier
Pleuraient et se taisaient et la voyaient partir

L'autre est morte un matin et le trente de mai
Dans l'hésitation et la stupeur publiques.
Une forêt d'horreur, de haches et de piques
La tenaient circonscrite en un cercle fermé.

Et l'une est morte ainsi d'une mort solennelle.
Sur ses quatre-vingt-dix ou quatre-vingt-douze ans
Et les durs villageois et les durs paysans,
La regardant vieillir, l'avaient crue éternelle.

Et l'autre est morte ainsi d'une mort solennelle.
Elle n'avait pas passé ses humbles dix-neuf ans
Que de quatre ou cinq mois et sa cendre charnelle
Fut dispersée au vent.[2]

These were Péguy's last lines: as in the eighteen verses of the special passage, the toll bell can be heard. The word *mort* (died, death) occurs in every verse.

•

Tharaud's dismay was not without grounds. *Eve* was a disaster as far as the *Cahiers* were concerned: in six weeks, a hundred subscriptions were withdrawn. Such was the response of the regular readers. Péguy's enemies rallied in great joy. *L'Argent suite*, which made very

[1] Since spring, 1945, the two official patrons are Jeanne d'Arc and Thérèse of Lisieux. (*Tr.*)

[2] One died of an evening, on January the third.
A whole people assembled were there to see her die.
Burghers and louts, the shepherd and neatherd,
Wept and were speechless so to see her lie.

The other died at dawn, the thirtieth of May,
The people were abashed, stricken and wondering;
Horrible weapons, bristling staves made play,
Held her encompassed in a narrow ring.

Of a solemn death so did one die,
And her age was ninety or even ninety-two.
The hardy villagers and peasants too
Had thought her growing old for all eternity.

Of a solemn death so did the other die.
She had not overstepped her nineteen years
More than a score of weeks, and her limbs lie
Where wills the wind that scattered ashes bears.

little stir, was nonetheless carefully read, silently and bitterly scrutinised by those whom it attacked. They had not dared answer it, but the fiasco of *Eve* opened the door to revenge. The pamphleteer had given himself away, he had made himself ridiculous for all to see, and now they could raise a laugh. Péguy was obviously mad: there is no point in answering a madman or bothering about him at all. Eight thousand tum-ti-tum lines to the glory of Eve was nothing but a good joke. I find an echo of this atmosphere in my notes dated January 4th, 1914: 'Words with X. at Mme Duclaux' about that monstrous *Eve* of Péguy's. I will not have it laughed at.'

I had taken a lot upon myself, and in difficult circumstances, for like Tharaud's, my own first reaction was to feel completely at sea. The postman had brought to my door an unknown province, a strange, wild land in which I could not find my bearings. I needed several days' quiet and solitude to explore it and find my way about, and that is never easy in Paris, and most difficult of all round about the New Year. I could do no more than refuse to have it laughed at.

XIV

ULTIMA VERBA

And happily he knows he is going to die.—PÉGUY.

HE STILL HAD eight months of life before him; life, that is the plodding drudgery of the *Cahiers,* as for the past fifteen years, in constant dread of the monthly bills and the daily post with letters from the subscribers, in constant search of cash.

Nous nous sommes lavés d'une telle amertume.[1]

One more half year to run, and six *Cahiers* to publish. The file of the drab battalion deserves our consideration. It consists of a *Villon,* by André Suarès; *L'Exode,* by Delahache; a *Note sur M. Bergson et la philosophie bergsonienne,* by Péguy; *Les Proscrits,* by Maurice Vuillaume; *Notre Pays,* by René Salomé; *Nous,* by François Porché.

André Suarès was not an original member of the *Cahiers* group, he was not a man of groups, rather, in fact, a solitary. He did not appear in the *Cahiers* again till 1920, with *Visite à Port-Royal.* He was never seen at the bookshop Thursdays, nor even in the shop itself: he didn't bring his contribution, Péguy went and called for it, which was very exceptional. But his collaboration was most useful. Romain Rolland withdrew after the end of his *Jean-Christophe,* and left a dangerous gap. The too-ready quarrels had produced other gaps in the ranks. André Suarès, who had an ardent and admiring band of followers at the time (the same, to some extent, as Romain Rolland's) was a great help to the *Cahiers.* His *Villon* is an excellent piece of work. Thanks to Suarès, the poor fifteenth century songster, Péguy's brother in so many respects, took his rightful place in the *Cahiers* of the poor twentieth century songster.[2]

[1] We washed ourselves clean of such bitterness.

[2] It was Johannet who pointed out the likeness in his study of Péguy, so charmingly and with such insight that I want to quote the passage here: 'Péguy is a soul of olden times and there is no one like him. Villon's mother was the same, and one almost regrets that Péguy did not live long ago. He should have been twenty at the Battle of Poitiers, and have followed John II, called the Good, to England; have escaped from Dover on a stormy night and reached toilful, prayerful Flanders. There he would have worked, studied, prayed; and then gone to Paris, as craftsman, traveller and pilgrim, to take his share of the troubles and his scars in the brawls. Chiefly in all the brawls of the Sorbonne quarter. And died young, condemned by the Sorbonne, but leaving us the masterpiece which the French Middle Ages do not provide, a romance of chivalry, adventure and heroism, and mystical heart-yearning, both violent and submissive, to stand side by side with the *Romancero,* the *Canterbury Tales* and the *Divina Comedia.*' This was written in 1913. Note 'he should leave' and the regret implied, which pervades all this piece of imaginative reconstruction. In actual fact,

L'Exode and *Les Proscrits*, by Delahache and Vuillaume, end two of those documentary series which Péguy liked to publish from time to time, both on their own merit and because they brought in straightforward work. In *L'Exode*, the third volume in the Alsatian series, Delahache tells the story of the families who left the province in 1871 in order not to become German. In *Les Proscrits*, the sixth volume in the series on the insurrection in Paris in 1871, Vuillaume told of what became of the commune scattered after their defeat. Péguy had a fellow-feeling for all whom the course of events had set adrift. The poetry of antiquity is full of their trials and adventures. Had their day returned, it would cause Péguy no surprise.

The last were two *Cahiers* by poets, Salomé and Porché, both friends of the early days. I don't remember meeting Salomé at the *Cahiers*. He did not live in Paris. So here he is only a shadow in Péguy's wake. His own verse *Cahier* is itself a reflection and a shadow. Péguy wrote *Notre Patrie*, Salomé, *Notre Pays*, two echoes of the same theme, one virile, the other tender.

The very first lines give one an awkward and almost absurd sense of pastiche:

> *Notre pays est comme un doux berceau*
> *De rameaux verts de moissons et de fruits,*
> *D'arbres géants, de tendres arbrisseaux,*
> *De ceps feuillus. . . .*

Salomé, faithful to his master's manner, starts off on one of those enumerative orgies which we know only too well. One wonders why Péguy printed it, for his terse remark on the subject was well known: 'Don't imitate me; my prose and verse are instruments that belong to me. . . .' Closer inspection does seem to justify Salomé and the place given him in the *Cahiers*. His poetry is not quite authentic, but nearly so, and so near its original source that it has a certain freshness.

There are born imitators who know no better; Salomé is not of these, but rather of the very different race of men whose gift for admiration is almost a vocation. Personal characteristics are effaced and transfigured by those of the object of admiration. Many mediæval painters must have been of this kind, faithfully attentive to an inspiration which carried them beyond themselves. Salomé was like them: his mimicry was straight from the heart, not without feeling and sometimes on the verge of real beauty.

Here is how Salomé deals with pacifists:

> *Qui, pour croupir au fond des eaux pourries,*
> *Vendraient nos feux; nos hameaux, nos villages,*
> *Nos fins coteaux, nos bois et nos prairies,*

---

no regret was necessary, but Péguy's friends found it hard to believe that his immense life's-work, which they saw so emphatically turned down and put out of sight, would ever reach the full light of day it deserved.

. . . Vendraient les cieux où nos âmes s'abreuvent,

. . . Vendraient aussi Ronsard et du Bellay,
L'Ardoise fine et le Petit Liré,
L'eau paresseuse où baignent les palais,

Tout ce qui mène à tout ce que l'on aime.

. . . Vendraient la ferme et l'étable et le puits,
Les fleurs du champ, les pignons de la rue,
Et dans le creux de ce sillon qui fuit

Les nobles os que pousse la charrue.[1]

Many people would take these for Péguy's own and would praise them for qualities which they have indeed. It is the sort of mistake that occurs in museum catalogues; many a lovely specimen has been salvaged by this means. There is still a lot of work to be done on the secondary *Cahiers*.

The last of all is *Nous*, by François Porché. Porché was a *barbiste*, a *cour rose* friend. He had stood by Péguy through thick and thin, and alone had dared to praise the eight thousand lines of *Eve* in the press. His reappearance is to close the series of the *Cahiers*. How neatly everything falls into place.

Porché had not yet become the dramatist and essay writer whom we know to-day. He was the poet of *A chaque jour*, *Au loin peut-être . . .*, *Humus et poussière*, excellent and charming books of verse, idyllic lyrical transcriptions of his youth which he spent in his own province of Angoumois, his own city of Paris, and distant Russia. *Nous* were the French. At Péguy's request, he had gleaned appropriate passages from his published books and gathered a whole set of verses into a sort of poetic exposition of the great city and one particular stretch of country.

[1] Who, so as to wallow in the waters of corruption,
Would sell our hearths; our hamlets, our villages.
Our delicate hillsides, our woods and meadows,

. . . Would sell the skies at which our souls are slaked,

. . . Would sell Ronsard too, and du Bellay too,
The *Delicate slate* and the *Small Liré* (see Du Bellay's famous sonnet)
The dreaming water bathing the feet of palaces,

All that leads us to all we love.

. . . Would sell the farm, the stable and the well,
The meadow flowers, the gabled city streets,
And in the fold of the lengthening furrow,

The plough-upturned time-honoured bones.

Un petit coin de terre est mon seul juge au monde.
Là, pied à pied, les pins combattent avec l'onde
Pour la possession du sable. J'obéis
Au doux charme voilé de ce vague pays,
Bien qu'il m'ennuie un peu parfois comme un poème
Trop sincère, et qui trop ressemble à mon cœur même.[1]

The last is a prose poem of which the style recalls Péguy's, maybe, or still more, Claudel's, but above all, Porché's own. It is sumptuous prose divided into biblical verses: an admirable form much favoured in the 1909-14 days which, like so many other pre-war discoveries, has completely disappeared. The title was *Rêverie derrière les faisceaux*: it was about a troop of men lined up in open country, and bugles sounding.

It was the call to our homes, the age-old call ringing out across the valleys, from hill to hill,
And this call to arms, to the defence of our homes, was turned to song by free and fearless lads; the instinctive call for help when life is threatened became a ringing challenge

The bugles suddenly ceased. Porché goes on:

The flag was only a few paces away, I heard the soft sound of silk stroked by the wind.
It was like something whispered, a loving word which makes the heart turn over.
What else is there to tell? The whole thing was so clear. I could only say, How simple, how simple it all is.

Indeed, how simple love and service are! Salomé and Porché witness to a line of inspiration which it is a delight to re-discover. Those who remember 1914 know there was something missing in the dark pre-war days of 1939, and they regret it bitterly.

Porché's poems came out on July 7th, seven weeks before the war started.

•

This last series of *Cahiers* was as good as any. But let us make no mistake: the *Cahiers* had had their day and their end was near. The uproar over *Eve* and the loss of subscribers was not the only trouble. On many occasions Péguy had managed to put things right by scolding and admonishing his little band and rousing their fighting spirit and sense of unity and purpose. But this time, what was new and irremediable was that Péguy himself had lost heart. The *Cahiers* had fulfilled their function which was to guarantee his own freedom to

[1] My only judge on earth is one small track of land,
Where pines and waves engage to hold the sand,
And neither yields. This featureless dim scene
Compels my love, its taste is so serene,
Though sometimes it annoys for being without art,
Like too-much telling verses, too much like my heart.

write and build up his life's work. That was now achieved. Many plants die after bearing fruit, and the *Cahiers* were of this species: they had borne their fruit, they could afford to die. Or rather, they had to die.

Then, for the first time in his life, Péguy went round looking for outlets. He tried the *Grande Revue*, which his college friend Crouzet ran, the *Nouvelle Revue Française*, and the *Correspondant*. The income from these efforts was too small to live on. He then turned to the idea of applying for an academic award to make his situation secure. He was not concerned with the so-called honour but with the cash value of such an award. The French Academy was naturally closed to him after the insults hurled at Lavisse. But the Goncourt Academy was more approachable. Its members drew six thousand francs a year. At the pre-war cost of living, Péguy could manage on that. He paid a preliminary call on Léon Daudet, and that is as far as he got.

What he wanted was some sort of provisional security. Péguy had lost interest not only in the future of the *Cahiers*, but in any future at all. The future, as such, was not his concern.

The conviction of living at the end of time held him more and more strongly and became an obsession. It is foolish to try to account for this by referring to the continual complaints about his health which he made to all and sundry at this time, in talk or in writing: his stomach was in a state of tension which made digestion and sleep intolerably difficult. It is a condition with which doctors are familiar, of nervous origin, due to some strain outside their scope. Mobilisation cured him and turned him into a thoroughly useful footslogger. The real trouble lay elsewhere. Péguy knew that the pit into which everything would topple, as he put it, was close at hand. He had constant signs and warnings of it. One day, an enthusiastic reader (there were some: public resistance was threaded here and there with gleams of the fame to come) visited the bookshop to tell Péguy of his admiration for *Eve*. He said, 'When a man has written such a work he can die easy.' Péguy rushed off to Mme Favre: 'I've just been told that having written *Eve* I can now die. It's a very serious thing.' To Mme Favre, however, it was just a handsomely turned compliment. 'No,' said Péguy, 'it's a sign, a very serious one.'

War was coming and Péguy longed for it. The entire half-happy consent of which his note to Claude Casimir-Périer, in 1912, is witness, had now turned into ardent expectation. The reasons may be found, but one hesitates to expound them. Did Péguy envisage the war as a means for the country to achieve health? Or being as it was inevitable, did he therefore want it to come straight for him like a flash of lightning? Did it mean for him a freeing from daily drudgery, and the perfect end to his life, as though it should be the act by means of which all the humiliation on the material and moral planes, endured for so long by France, by the young men of France, by himself, should be avenged at last? He knew that the coming trial would be severe, and he referred to it dramatically, violently, brutally, but always with the final vision of a release and a redressal. And also an honour.

Detached from the *Cahiers*, tossed on the storm, he had but one idea in mind, and that was his writing. He had so much to say, he had as much ground to cover in the Christian sphere (Lotte wrote this at his dictation and printed it in the news-sheet of Catholic University teachers) as Goethe covered in the pagan sphere. As the moment rapidly approached when a bullet would shoot through his brain, that brain was like an immense seething yard full of works in process or embryo. Twelve volumes to start with, he announced. First, the *Dialogue de l'histoire et de l'âme charnelle*, at which he had nibbled in spring 1912, which was to expound in a less constrained style the ideas which he had intended to develop into a university thesis in 1906. Alain Fournier and Peslouän had read and greatly admired the first few pages. 'I shall give my Dialogues on history in the *Cahiers*,' he wrote to Lotte in September, 1912.

> I make it live in the person of Clio, the daughter of memory. Poor Clio, she spends all her time looking for traces, and her traces convey nothing to her. . . . The first volume will be called Clio. The second Véronique. Old friend, it is simply wonderful: Clio spends all her time looking for traces, meaningless traces, and a silly little Jewess of no importance at all, young Veronica, takes her handkerchief and the face of Jesus is traced on it for ever. That is simply dumbfounding. She was there just at the right moment. Clio's always behindhand.

The 1906 thesis was thus becoming human, and superhuman. It had become a dialogue, with History taking part in it, and History had now become alive. As a Muse, she bears her womanly name: Clio, daughter of Jupiter, sister of Terpsichore the dancer and Melpomene the Musician.

The manuscript was certainly finished in 1914, for it refers to events that occurred in 1913. The *Note sur M. Bergson* came out on April 21st; it is very short, and must have been started in the second half of March, that is, three months after *Eve* was published. We may assume that the *Dialogue* was completed during those three months.

Dialogue, says Péguy; monologue would be more accurate: Clio is his perfect confidante, she adopts all his ideas. As Jupiter's daughter, she is supposed to inspire historians and guide their work; she leaves the field open, however, for Péguy's assaults and derision. In fact, she really betrays her mission. She is wholly converted to Bergson; this so-called Clio might just as well be called Veronica. What of it: she

Péguy on manœuvres, 1913 (*Collection A. Martin*)

your *Cahiers*. But you can easily picture, and I with you, my child, what you will think on the day of your death.

That is the end of the book.[1]

•

To complete these last months of Péguy's career and bring them to a worthy finish, there was need for a battle to be waged; it did not fail him, and Péguy took up arms at the end of March and went on fighting till the 1st of August.

News came from Rome that Bergson's works would certainly, and without delay, be put on the Index.

It was a very serious matter, and Péguy was concerned from every point of view. His own activities were being observed from Rome, and many ecclesiastics mistrusted him and were the more disturbed in that the younger clergy were beginning to read him. He had strong reasons for thinking that his turn would come after M. Bergson's. Well-informed friends warned him to be prudent. Prudent he had never been. This virtue, theological though it be, had never figured on his law-tables. He considered that it would be foolish of him, as well as mean, to stand by and let M. Bergson receive the blow without a word, and his silence would not exonerate him either. The more able as well as the more courageous course was to take the initiative into his own hands. Post haste, Péguy wrote his *Note sur M. Bergson et la philosophie bergsonienne*, a short *Cahier* of less than a hundred pages which he published at once.

Péguy kept his audience in mind and his pen under control. Anger never got the better of him and he defended his master of philosophy philosophically. Philosophy was the special study which he had taken up at the Ecole Normale, and he had retained his taste for it and use of it. He now expounded that metaphysical pluralism which he so often referred to in passing. He once spoke a few descriptive words which Lotte noted—just six lines of very illuminating ideas in brief: 'What must be seen,' he said, 'is that there is creation, and we don't at all know how it was done. There is the discontinuous and the continuous, and the two united. That makes certainly two creations, possibly three. The great philosophers and the poets discover certain aspects. There is no contradiction between them. They are all right.'

Two creations, possibly three. Péguy, in his thirties, was a great reader of Pascal, and here it is Pascal's disciple speaking, drawing

[1] It is almost certain that the end was written in 1914. Péguy was working on his *Dialogue* in September 1912, we know. Lavisse's jubilee was celebrated in February 1913, and immediately after Péguy drew up the angry retort entitled *L'Argent suite*; and as soon as that was dealt with he set to work on *Eve*. It is evident that it was only after finishing and publishing *Eve* that he took up work on the *Dialogue* again, and wrote all the serenity and gentle irony made possible by the lapse of time with this last page of the *Dialogue*, which shows no sign of stress at all.

attention to the three metaphysical orders from a consideration of which Sorel drew so many applications and viewpoints at the *Cahiers*' Thursdays. It is in flashes and stray gleams that creation is revealed to us. Systematic minds run their systems headlong up blind alleys, because they try to link what we are given separate, and to compose into a whole what we are given as broken pieces. 'In the home, a mended sock is better than one with a hole in it,' said Hegel. 'In philosophy, it is the opposite: darns are no good.' Péguy never came across this metaphysical witticism, he would have enjoyed it; he didn't approve of trying to conceal under laborious darns the incompatibilities which an examination of reality reveals.

There is reason, he wrote, which is not wisdom, and neither of them are logic. And the three together don't make up intelligence. They are three—or four—orders; three—four—kingdoms, and there are many others . . There are *reigns*, there are disciplines. There is faith; there is love; there is art; there is philosophy; there are morals; there is science. And probably others, too.

Thomistic philosophy is a huge piece of patchwork: hence Péguy's declared antipathy. In Bergsonism, on the other hand, Bergson never patches; he is bent on discovering, and his discovery, admittedly only piecemeal, but pursued with unflinching zeal over thirty years, does throw a strong light on that section of reality which he has made his own.

This is a greatly simplified exposition on the theme of Péguy's first short defence, the preface to a more elaborate defence. Time was against him and he forced himself to be brief. In *l'Argent suite* we noticed his new style: the process is a string of short maxims like shooting arrows.

A great philosophy is not a dictation. . . . The greatest of all is not the one with no mistakes in it.

A great philosophy is not the one nothing can be said against; it is the one which says something.

. . . It is not the one with no holes in it; it is the one with amplitude.

A great philosopher is not one without reproach; it is one without fear.

A great philosophy is not one without breaches in the walls; it is one with citadels.

A great philosophy is not finally the one that lies down, and all at once on all positions and every battle-field. It is simply the one which one day fought well there at the corner of the wood:

Heureux ceux qui sont morts pour quatre coins de terre.[1]

•

What an odd quotation: authors do not usually quote themselves. But Péguy cares nothing for that and quotes from his misunderstood

[1] Blessed are those who died for four corners of earth.

Eve. He counts on general incomprehension and hums his funeral hymn under his breath.

In another form of art and a different century, there is a curious analogy to this; it is in Mozart, whose last year of life abounds in signs and presentiments. Take *Don Juan*: where Leporello is humming and Don Juan asks him what he is singing. Leporello answers, 'It is an air from Mozart's *Figaro.*' Mozart, too, was near his death.

There are other curious things of the same kind in the same work. First, this quick, unexplained, unheralded turn of phrase: 'In *convaincre* (convince) there is *vaincre* (conquer), as Hugo used to love to point out to me.' *Used to love* is so astonishingly remote. How is this imaginary meeting to be dated? Can it be that Péguy was conceiving a sort of anticipated dialogue of the dead, and placing himself among the immortals so soon? Secondly, in a passage developing the theme of sin and grace, we come across these words: '*That is what Péguy used to say when he said that by the creation and the freedom of man. . . .*' Never mind the argument, the interesting thing is again the *used to,* attached to the odd intervention of a Péguy named by Péguy. Just Péguy, as one speaks of dead men. Why not say: 'As I said before . . .'—or did he consider himself as no longer belonging to the world of the living . . .?

Time it seems had ceased to exist for him. The end was so near that his mind confused past, present and future.

A note to Lotte is enlightening: 'I am still in this abyss of weariness . . . I feel I am wearing away, and what is so satisfactory about it is that I don't mind.'

•

The *Note sur M. Bergson* is only half a book. Péguy hastened to send what he had done to the printer: he wanted to get it out before the condemnation was issued. His appeal fell on deaf ears. The literary world took no notice of it, it was not interested in philosophy; the philosophers, whether of the university or Catholic, took no notice, because Péguy had no recognised line, and therefore did not count. He was used to this, and his day would come. He went straight ahead with his work and set down that amazingly spirited and most astonishing effort called: '*La note conjointe sur M. Descartes et la philosophie cartésienne*' (additional note on Descartes and the philosophy called after his name). Many days were to pass and much blood was to be shed before it was published, in 1924. There was little public curiosity, clearly, where he was concerned. Even to-day it is not very lively, for there are a number of unpublished pages waiting to appear.

Péguy had referred to Descartes in his *Note sur M. Bergson,* and decided there was more to be said. But the title in this case is merely reminiscent, for the real subject of the *Note sur M. Descartes* is a rapid survey of his own personal work, a rapid indication of what was essential, and then a careful exploring and anticipation of the work never to be written and all that death will prevent him from doing.

A great many people have wondered in the last twenty-five years what Péguy would be writing now, were he still alive. Barrès said, 'He would have been the great poet of the war.' It is not at all so sure. As Péguy was heard to say, 'I speak of war because I have not been in it. When I have, I shall not speak of it any more.' We may believe this to be true. His interventions in public life would have made themselves felt, but what their nature would have been we cannot tell. Again, Péguy gave his warning: 'A voice is missing and no other takes its place.' All this is secondary in any case. What matters is the line of the mysteries, and Péguy himself gladly tells us what we want to know. The *Note sur M. Descartes* (among other oddities, it hardly mentions Descartes at all) contains Péguy's *ultima verba*.

Our days have produced another group of works comparable to this group of Péguy's last works: Nietzsche's *The Case of Wagner*, *The Twilight of the False Gods*, and *Ecce Homo*, written in four months. Both groups reveal the ardour of a mind intent on giving its last sparks, but from what different hearths. Nietzsche knew what awaited him: the madness that was to engulf him already consumed his thought and drove him towards darkness. Péguy, too, knew what awaited him. Not death, we need not print that word which has a meaning only for doctors and in statistics. Péguy knew he was going forward to the most perfect of all fulfilments; to the two most perfect honours, linked in one: the soldier's and the believer's, marching to the supreme sacrifice and attaining glory while on the march.

So once more he sat down to write, for the last time. He was sorry, and sad at having to go so soon, *when he had so much to say, when he felt himself so full of works which will never set out in procession, zebra-lined on paper. Never:* he wrote the word with authority. So be it.

Inside the book, Descartes, 'M. Descartes,' as he calls him, is dealt with in a few pages. Then comes the real matter, Péguy's testament. Once 'M. Descartes' has gone, the atmosphere clears. 'Two friends walking . . . Two friends coming out of the small bookshop . . .' 'We are in the rue de la Sorbonne for the last time, on the well-worn doorstep. The friend is, of course, Benda; Benda, the man who ten years later hit out at Péguy, the great combatant who was no longer able to retort. It is not so surprising: it is a trait familiar to many legends, to show the hero and the traitor together, and a singular attraction of the hero for the traitor. Two friends: 'A secret affinity,' says Péguy, 'brings them together, and if you like, gathers them in from the most secret corners, and preferably the most contrary parties.'

Both were philosophical, both good at parleying. Talk never ran dry, the differences of opinion all helped to keep it flowing. One was a Christian, the other a Jew. The Jew has been vanquished for seventy or ninety centuries, said Péguy, hence his eternal power. And his eternal victory. The Jew has been unhappy ever since Adam and Eve. 'That is the source of his eternal patience, almost a source of happiness.' The Christian is quite a different sort of being: 'Cunning and rebellious, a son of the earth, he lives in a constant state of revolt, in perpetual rebellion . . .' The Christian and the peasant are not apart in Péguy's mind. And the great peasant Christian he has in mind we all know to be himself. Péguy carries on his analysis of the difference between the Jew and the Christian, putting it differently: the Jew, he said, is a man who has always been reading; the Protestant is a man who has been reading since Calvin; the Catholic is a man who has been reading since Ferry.

When I am with M. Benda, I am with a man who has been reading for ever; when I am by myself, I am with a man who has been reading since my mother and me.

So we come to Péguy's point: *My mother and me*: words which jerk him violently into the past; Benda has gone, left high and dry on the boulevard Saint-Germain pavement. He was only brought there to be left there: he does not count, the talk in Paris does not count.

Man turns back to his race and immediately behind his mother and father he sees four more abreast, and immediately after, immediately behind he sees nothing. Why not say so. He plunges among his own people and immediately after, immediately behind he can see nothing. Why not say so, he is proud to plunge into this anonymity. . . .

One of Péguy's great pages. He himself was soon to be absorbed in that innumerable populace assembled for war, whose crowning achievement it was to be absorbed. Now (about May 1914) he was ardently looking back to those he came from, to the faubourg Bourgogne, the permanent and still sufficient source of his inspiration. All the familiar themes assemble for the tremendous last act. The people of France, always in his mind, and the tragedy he had himself witnessed, for in less than forty years the people have disappeared; its customs, which were the very life of its genius, have lapsed. Péguy pondered once more, as he had so often pondered before, on what this tragedy could really mean: were we witnessing *the de-creation of the world*? Péguy insists on this point. The old world grew by steady stages, attentive to its inner promptings: that was how divine creation worked. The modern world has speed instead of steadiness, reading and the distracting daily press instead of inspiration. The result is, *the de-creation of the world*. We have this in three pages, instead of the three hundred had the book ever been written. What would he have said of the talking-machine installed in every house to-day, giving out its travesty of words in place of the old-time silence?

Now we come to Corneille's *Polyeucte*, which he had often mentioned before, but not enough to please him yet. 'Its unique greatness,' he says outright, 'is that Christian greatness triumphs without humiliating the greatness of antiquity.' In Corneille, they are all great and remain great, whether beaten or not, and this sense of the mystery of greatness is the supreme discovery of his genius. 'I see so many fine things in *Polyeucte*,' he wrote, 'and such perfect ones, that I don't know whether everyone sees them all. I should like to grow old enough to be able one day to give myself space to enumerate some of these aspects.' Time and space for that he could not have, and so he hurried on. From *Polyeucte* to Bergson. Bergson's philosophy, too, was an ever-new field for meditation. Bergson conferred youth on whatever he touched: speculations about grace, freedom, hope, 'only come right and only give of their fulness when men have properly explored bergsonian thought.'

Last of all, Jeanne d'Arc. 'I could go on writing about her for twenty years,' he said, and half-disclosed some fragments of the unwritten poem: among them, that prayer for the sins of the city of Paris, which Jeanne prayed before leading the assault in which she was repulsed and wounded at the gate of Saint-Honoré. We almost certainly have the main substance of them in the sonnets entitled *Présentation de Paris à Notre-Dame*. Not to mention the intervention of the eminent Sorbonne men of 1910 (Lanson and Durkheim) turned into inquisitors at Jeanne's trial. The reference is slight; perhaps a mere tag in the course of conversation. The major themes are indicated in the *Note conjointe*, and whoever wishes to meditate on Péguy's unknown Jeanne d'Arc will find what he wants here.

We will pick out two references: first, Jeanne and the King; Jeanne stands for the ideal, the King, for policy. 'She had come to meet a warrior king and found one all of a tremble. She had come to meet a king of grace. She found a paltry negotiator.' The libertarian Péguy would have had full say in this work.

Secondly, Jeanne facing her judges. Jeanne has met with the outstanding misfortune of being mistrusted by her own side, and of having to make her defence against the representatives of the Church whose wonderful child she is. Happy Saint-Louis, who fought only on the boundaries of realms; for Jeanne d'Arc it was not so:

And that is one of the reasons why she was the greatest saint and martyr. Perhaps one should say that she was a saint of the second degree, and a martyr of the second degree. For it is in the heart of Christianity itself that she came across the points where she had to stand out, or to fight, or where honour was in question, or sanctity, or martyrdom. She was like a soldier who fought not only on the boundaries, but whose own hearth and home had become an immense, universal boundary. Happier Saint-Louis only had to cope with infidels.

The allusions to the difficulties of Péguy's own private life are self-evident. The battle on the home-front is his own. 'To go off and fight on the boundaries of a land is fine. But to fight at the heart of one's own home, and to be eaten up with worry in one's own heart, what an involution this is.'

Patience. It was nearly time to go.

•

In June the Reverend Father Baillet died consumptive in the English monastery where his superiors had sent him. His death caused great distress to Tharaud, Lotte, Peslouän and all the Sainte-Barbe crowd. Baillet (not Reverend Father to them, but still Baillet, the endless dreamer, so absently present at the Sainte-Barbe games, walks and studies), was to all of them, believers or unbelievers, a friend and a saint—their own saint. And now they had lost him.

Baillet had kept Péguy constantly in his mind and had returned in contact with him. We have no information as to how Péguy took the news. Maybe this death of a brother seemed to him yet another sign of his own approaching departure. Baillet was no longer there to pray for a change of behaviour, but it didn't matter, for he was about to change worlds.

•

Five weeks after the publication of the *Note sur M. Bergson*, the philosopher's work was condemned from Rome. Péguy wrote and told Lotte at once: 'The placing on the Index of Bergson's three books[1] has brought about a very dangerous situation. Don't mention it at all in your news-sheets.' (June 6th 1914.)

It was indeed dangerous, as Lotte soon discovered. An unknown priest came to see him at Coutances, who asked him very searching questions about Péguy and showed much concern. Lotte defended Péguy most ardently, and gave his surprising visitor the *Mystère de la Charité de Jeanne d'Arc*, the *Mystère du Porche de la deuxième Vertu*, and some other *Cahiers*. The priest departed leaving Lotte full of thought. For once in his life he acted prudently and wrote, not to Péguy himself, though he usually told him everything, but to a sure friend, Riby, to know what to think of this visit. Riby, without hesitation, said it was a warning; Péguy was to be condemned, and to all intents and purposes was already condemned; no doubt he would

[1] *Les Données immédiates de la Conscience, Matière et Mémoire, L'Evolution Créatrice.*

demur, and there would be a scandal; there was concern in high places, and this visit was a sign of it. It was true that Lotte, as editor of the *Bulletin des Professeurs Catholiques de l'Université*, had a certain influence; he had a following of four hundred subscribers, all worthy men, whose opinions deserved consideration; it was important that Lotte should not join Péguy in resisting, thus risking his own fate as well as that of many others. To Riby's mind, the priest was an emissary, and much caution was necessary.

Lotte was horrified. For twenty years Péguy had been his guiding light and rule. We witnessed the simplicity with which he followed him back to the faith.

'I am a Christian,' said Péguy, with tears in his eyes. To which Lotte instinctively replied: 'We are all the same.' Lotte was from Britanny. When he ceased to practise his religion, his soul remained enfolded in its tradition; the faubourg Bourgogne atmosphere was something he and his folk had never known, and his return to the faith had been entire, involving belief and practice. The Church was once more the source from which he daily drew life, pardon and nourishment, Our Mother Holy Church. Lotte trembled to think how Péguy would react under an interdiction. Lotte would never blame him, or even question his motives, but he was not Péguy; though so greatly devoted to him, at this point he would not be able to follow him. He was, as he clearly saw, faced with two absolutes: one, faithfulness to his friend, the other, faithfulness in obedience. He was determined to fail neither of them. A friend was told: 'Rome is concerned about Péguy. The time is coming when I shall no longer be able to protect him, and he must make a definite choice.' Lotte's own choice was made.

Péguy guessed what was going on in Lotte's mind. 'You are the grenadier at the head of the bridge,' he wrote one day. The grenadier was going to give ground, as Péguy surmised. Lotte betrayed his anxiety in two short notes sent one on the heels of the other. Péguy answered:

Old friend, you are one of those I love most dearly. In your last letter there was one word too many, which is that someone could compromise me.

That someone is evidently Bergson.

In this morning's letter there is one word too many, which is that you might let me down.

Here, too, it is all quite clear: Péguy was not going to yield; Bergson was his master and he did not intend to abandon him; everyone knew the sort of man he was and he did not intend to modify his ways. He knew there might be serious consequences. It might mean utter destitution, after so much poverty, for his family. This was, in fact, the most likely outcome of it all. And there was no way out, except the solution of which he was secretly assured and which would free him for ever. So he started to write again, in Bergson's defence.

•

July 1914, and nearly the end of peace. There was no solemn twilight. The country as a whole had no such double-sight as guided Péguy's life. The Serajevo incident aroused interest as such. The country was divided between the somnolence of the masses and the excitement of Paris over the trial of Mme Caillaux. On July 19th came Austria's ultimatum to Serbia. Péguy was still hard at work. The future, the very near future, was suddenly asserting itself, as Péguy well knew but without being disconcerted. When the day came, he would become a soldier. Meanwhile, he was busy writing.

On July 24th he had lunch with Mme Favre who wrote in her diary:

Friday, July 24th.—Péguy and Maurice[1] to lunch on Friday instead of Thursday: we were never so intimately friendly as to-day. We were oblivious of all but the serene joy of our affection. We could hardly bear to separate, Péguy was in amazingly good form. After lunch, Maurice enticed him on from point to point to Paradise; we were held spellbound by the enchantment of his imagination and his verbal felicity. Not a word of the fear of war. It is far from all our minds.

It is far from all our minds, is really sublime. It reminds us of Louis de Gonzague playing rackets and of the Brother who asked him: 'If you were to die to-morrow, what would you do?' 'I should go on playing rackets.' Péguy, Maurice Reclus and Mme Favre were playing rackets on the brink of war.

It all came to a head at last. Péguy wrote to Lotte:

Tuesday, July 28th 1914, 9 *a.m.*—Everything points to its being to-morrow. Try not to get yourself cornered at Belle-Ile.

Next day:

Wednesday, July 29th 1914.—Not to have seen Paris yesterday is never to have seen anything. The city of Sainte-Geneviève is still here.

Péguy did not, however stop working. As a soldier he would fight to the end, as a writer, too. He considered himself offended in the person of Lotte, to whom he dedicated his works: *fidelis fideli,* from the faithful to the faithful. He knew a priest had warned him against his friend, though we do not know how he came to hear of it, for Lotte and Riby, knowing how annoyed he would be, decided to keep it from him. But he never missed much, and had always been good at constructive guesswork. Six weeks had elapsed, which is enough to filter a secret through. However it came about, Péguy was in possession of the facts. A man had gone to Lotte—*the grenadier at*

[1] Maurice Reclus.

the head of the bridge, to undermine his loyalty; a man, a priest had inflicted this hurt on Péguy, and Péguy the fighter was not going to take it lying down. Was it conceivable that his last act as a writer should be chicken-hearted? Certainly not. He would strike with his pen the man through whom he had himself been struck in the heart of his friend.

The plan of the work is very simple: based on straightforward classical comedy. Péguy transposed the Coutances visit. The emissary he imagined coming to see him, Péguy, not plain honest Lotte. At Coutances, the emissary spoke. Here, the tables are turned. It is very hard to give any idea of these pages; they are forthcoming and attractive, very various and profound. A summary impoverishes them to too great a degree: it would be too easy to turn them into a sort of Paul-Louis Courier pamphlet. Not that it would be a falsification, the pamphlet does exist, as such, but rich with undertones which should not be missed at any price.

The emissary says: 'Bergson had to be put on the Index.'[1] Péguy breaks in: 'The Index? I have never discovered what it is. And I know why: it doesn't come in the catechism. I can't help it, what I did not know when I was twelve I shall never know.' (We recognise the twelve-year-old theme.) The priest pursues the subject: 'I will tell you . . .'—'I'd rather you talked about something else.'—'I will explain . . .'—'I warn you I am a bit slow on the uptake.'—'I will make a comparison. Imagine a road.' Péguy pricks up his ears. 'A road,' he says; 'you have found my weak spot; I do so love roads; I have done so much walking.'—'Then you will have noticed that you were passing signposts.'—'Yes; Chartres, 41 kilometres.'—'That's right. Well now, the Index is a set of signposts along a Christian's road. Signposts are useful to travellers.'—'Useful?' Péguy protests. 'Not at all. I've been to Chartres. I saw the signposts; I thought they fitted quite nicely into the official layout of the road, but they were of no use to me at all.'—'I beg your pardon, supposing you required some information . . .'—'If I want information I ask the goodwife sitting on the doorstep; the cartwright, the blacksmith are the people who are useful to the traveller. . . .'

That is only an outline. Here is an actual passage:

—Believe me, Father (and his voice became distant with gravity and melancholy), (involuntarily marking distance and depth), (marking as it were time between), I have been to Chartres myself. Allow me to tell you that what gets one to Chartres is not the milestones nor the signposts.
—Then what is it, my child?
—Father, it is the old wooden cross at the crossroads, moss-eaten and

[1] The inverted commas are to make the passage clear, and are not to be taken to indicate textual quotations here.

age-worn. Sometimes it bears the figure of Christ; then it is what we call a crucifix, Christ fastened on a cross. And sometimes it doesn't, that is all. Sometimes there is an inscription and sometimes it has gone. And sometimes there is none. That is all.

And you don't need an inscription to know what it is.

And when there is one to decipher, it does not tell you anything about distances. Almost as though the cross did not know why it was at this crossroads rather than another. There it stands, somewhere on earth. It just seems to know it is always the same earth.

And the words it bears, generally in Latin, call to mind a different journey altogether.

Péguy had ceased to answer questions and was now speaking out and compelling attention. His improvisation goes on for three more pages. He was improvising the metaphysics of travel and signposts. And then we come to these words:

The Catholic only consults signposts by way of consultation. Protestants . . .

Saturday, August 1st, 1914.

There the sentence is left, unfinished; someone may have opened the door, his wife or a child; or someone said: The mobilisation order is posted at the Town Hall. Péguy wrote the date and put his pen down. It was the end. So much the better. '*To set off and to fight at the frontiers is fine.*'

XV

WAR

Oblationibus nostris, quæsumus,
Domine, placare susceptis; et ad
Te nostras etiam rebelles compelle
propitius voluntates
4th Week in Lent. Secret.

THERE IS ONLY Péguy the soldier and the Christian left. The date for his departure was August 4th, so he had three days more which he could spend at home in the little house at Bourg-la-Reine where they then lived. He did nothing of the sort. 'I must see my friends,' he said to his wife (always the unanswerable *I must* . . .) and he begged her not to take it amiss if he spent his last hours in Paris, and not with her and the children. Mme Péguy agreed, but had a question to ask. She was expecting another child: 'What was she to do? The answer was short: "Bear it in mind."' To the very end Péguy's intention to ask nothing and impose nothing held firm. In all things his practice was to let things ripen and let time show.

Péguy's last hours in Paris should be read in Tharaud's book: such an excellent account is not to be undertaken a second time. These are the chief points. Péguy the untamed militant disappeared; the suspicious, exacting friend disappeared too; we are left with a great-hearted, friendly soul, eager to see those he loved and those he had wounded once more. For the first time in his life, he hired a taxi by the hour. A good many houses were closed for it was holiday time. But a number of his best friends were at home. Charles-Lucas de Peslouän, so dearly loved, whom Péguy had thrown over a few months earlier, welcomed his friend back again. The two men embraced with tears in their eyes. Péguy said goodbye to everyone, the servants, the concierges who were used to seeing him coming and going for many years. One of them, after shaking him by the hand and looking him in the eye, muttered something about his not coming back as she watched him walk away.

From all accounts, the general tone of his remarks was firm and assured, without undue emphasis. Someone uttered the word *victory* in his hearing and he stopped short, knowing it is unwise to tempt destiny with presumptuous words.

He spent his last night at Mme Favre's flat. At six in the morning he went into her room. He had come to talk, for he could not sleep. She noticed his bare feet. 'They need airing,' he said, 'they are going to have a lot to do.' At Mme Favre's he had a visit from the young woman he had so dearly loved, and said goodbye to her. He asked her (she was Jewish) to go to Chartres every year in memory of him, which she promised to do. As he was leaving Mme Favre wanted to give him a basketful of provisions. ‘No,’ he said, ‘my men will feed me. They would be too disappointed not to have me share theirs.’ Then he said his last say to this Republican friend of his, daughter of the 1848 Republican, and said it not without solemnity: ‘Dear friend,—Here I go, a soldier of the Republic in the cause of disarmament and the last of all wars.’ This was his profession of the human hope nurtured with such affection by that mass of the French people among whom he was about to disappear.

To believe and to choose were as natural to him as to deliberate and to doubt are to others.

•

‘A train laden with flowers brought me to Coulommiers on Tuesday,’ he wrote to his family. ‘I was the only officer to lead three thousand Parisians.’ How simple it all was, this new life of his almost childlike. No more problems; one might add, no more fights. Péguy talked of nothing but peace, from now till the end. ‘Live in peace, as we do,’ he wrote to his wife. ‘My Company is one large household.’ To Mme Favre he wrote: ‘My dear, I wish you had some of the great peace which we have here. I am in command of a Company, which means 250 men. At least a third are Parisians, the rest are boys from Seine-et-Marne, from your Crécy and your Voulangis, that is, the two kinds of men you most like.’ *La 19e Cie du 276e d'Infanterie*: Péguy wrote out these figures with obvious delight. There he was, docketed and ticketed, wearing his name on a plate round his arm, like a dog collar, and the old wolf was not at all displeased at the transformation.

The 276th left Coulommiers on August 9th and were taken by railway to Saint-Mihiel. There they stopped and got out; the 276th took to the road and came to the Hauts-de-Meuse country, marching through villages which the war was soon to make famous: Spahn, Thiaucourt, Flirey.

On August 15th, Péguy went into a church to hear Mass. It was his first Mass. As pamphleteer and poet, he did not go; as soldier, he did. He wrote to Maritain's sister: ‘One day, perhaps I will tell you in which church I heard the Mass for the Feast of the Assumption.’ *Perhaps* was prudent: the day never came. Then the regiment was scattered to different billets, and the 19th Company under Péguy was sent to a farm called Sainte-Marie Farm, not far from the Moselle. The Germans were very near. An order was given to reconnoitre their forward positions. Péguy asked for volunteers, and he led seven men off under the trees.

•

We had the good luck to meet one of these men, Alfred Tellier, a yeoman farmer of Yberny, the very village where the fight took place in which Péguy fell, a fortnight later. It was on a field path, and Alfred Tellier was sitting peasant-wise on his cart-horse. On hearing Péguy's name, he stopped his horse and slid to the ground. 'I should think I did know him. He was my chief.'

And he told us all about his patrol.

—We walked through the woods all night long. When we got back, Péguy said: 'You have done enough. This evening, the others shall mount guard. Go and get some rest.' After that, he always wanted to do everything with us, the seven of us.

Here was Péguy once more at the head of a close band of followers, doing everything with them. It had begun at Ste Barbe with the seven there: Tharaud (Jean), Tharaud (Jérôme), Lotte, Riby, Porché, Baillet and Peslouän. Peslouän it was who, forty-five years later, was with me listening to the yeoman's story. It ended with the seven of the 19th Company whom we were then getting to know.

I asked him where the others were.

Alfred Tellier paused a moment, then made a wide, vague gesture with his hand. There are very few survivors among the infantrymen of those first days. All through Péguy's life, as Tharaud wrote, there was the sound of broken glass. Happy last band formed so near fire, sacrificed in fire, and gone before it was breached.

•

On the Moselle front all was quiet. Péguy's three last notes speak of nothing but peace. On the 21st, to Mme Favre:

Billeted in a great rectangular farm in the middle of the woods, we have had no news of the outside world for four days. We live in a sort of great peace.

On the 23rd, to his family:

. . . Immense peace here in a big empty farmhouse. Since Tuesday I have been in command of a section of a hundred and twenty men. We mount guard at small posts throughout the wood. For a week there has been intermittent firing twenty to twenty-five kilometres away. No news.

My dragoon spends his time making manillas.

Love and kisses to all.—Péguy.

To his mother on the same day:

Nothing new, still the same good life. Heavy firing twenty or thirty kilometres away.

Still the good life, still the great peace; Péguy seemed to have stopped thinking about death, his own or any other, his whole concern being that the thing should be properly done. He was already, as he had hoped and written some weeks earlier, caught up and engrossed in that secret joy which he had foreseen and described:

> And with a sort of accomplishment and crowning and plentitude of humility. . . . And even more perhaps, with some inexplicable acquiescence and attainment and plentitude in annihilation.

•

Péguy's battle did not take place in the Hauts-de-Meuse country: the open fields of the Ile-de-France which had witnessed his life were to be the scene of his death too. He was their child, had lived of their air, had breathed no other. He was a man of two cities, Orléans where he was born, Paris where he worked; of two cathedrals, Notre-Dame of Paris and Notre-Dame of Chartres; of two saints, Jeanne, patron of Orléans, Geneviève, patron of Paris; of two plains, Beauce and Brie. One gave him life, the other, burial.

On the evening of August 23rd, Péguy received orders to leave the Sainte-Marie Farm. The whole 276th marched off to an unknown destination, through villages and populations in a state of alarm.

No one knew anything definite, but there was widespread anxiety; there had been some bad battles, people said, and the Germans were advancing. The 276th were taken by train westwards. This transference initiated the manœuvre which in less than three weeks was to turn the fortunes of war. Joffre, beaten in Belgium, was forming fresh armies on his left wing to make a surprise flank attack on the apparently victorious German armies bearing down on Paris.

Péguy was part of this manœuvre. On August 28th, the 276th was deposited somewhere in Picardy where Joffre ordered his first tentative offensive. It was a matter of probing the German lines and if possible finding a weak spot where an attack might succeed. The 276th were engaged, and particularly the 19th Company with Péguy still in command. M. Victor Boudin, in his book called *Campaigning with Charles Péguy*, shows Lt. Péguy's exalted state under his first fire; with clenched teeth and sparkling eyes, he spoke to his men in short, barking tones: '*De l'ordre, hein, de l'ordre!*' The engagement was soon broken off, and in his order of the day, read to the troops the next day, the general mentioned 'the fine comportment' of this company and 'its retreat in perfect order under fire on August 30th.'

Fine comportment and perfect order were what the chief required, or more precisely, were what the men and the chief who held them achieved together. The order of the day mentions no names, and it is better so; Péguy remains in undisturbed possession of the anonymity he had desired.

The order of the day mentions retreat: the 276th were now involved in that tremendous withdrawal which for so many others had begun on the Charleroi plains.

At nightfall after the battle, the march was not yet ended. They marched all night, almost till daybreak. The men had fought and covered the miles without any food. There was some giving in and grumbling. Péguy went from man to man: 'Come on, friends, this is no time to stop; I promise you we shall get there all right. I'm done in and hungry too, but please do what I do!' At 2 a.m. they stopped.

We went to lie down in a barn on some straw: two hundred of us in a place just big enough for a hundred, and even then it meant turning out some refugees who had taken shelter there.

A poor woman with small children, one a babe-in-arms, trailed out of the barn. 'Where are you going?' Péguy asked her.—'These poor boys must rest,' she said.—'No,' he answered. 'I shall not allow you to come out. You won't find anywhere else.' Then he turned to us: '*Allez, mes amis, débrouillez-vous:* Manage as best you can! These poor folk simply must sleep here . . . !' And we managed somehow.

Next morning, after five hours' rest, the men were on the road again. The Germans were on their heels, making for Paris.

On September 1st Péguy wrote his mother a brief note: 'I am well, rather tired, but my body has got back all its old robustness. Ever your loving son.' This is almost certainly his last written word.

On September 2nd, the 276th reached Senlis, where huge depots were on fire: the commissariat was burning its stores of forage so that they should not fall into German hands. The men crossed the smoky town. There was no halt. Orders were to keep on marching. Not far from Senlis the forest begins. The 276th entered it, following the main road to Paris, between the timber-woods of Chantilly and those of Ermenonville. The men were worn out, many could not keep up; at each halt they dropped to the ground and fell asleep. The chiefs had to keep them awake. '19th on foot!' called Péguy.—'There's no 19th left!' came from a chaffing voice—'So long as I'm here, there's a 19th,' Péguy retorted. He set off without looking back, and the men got up and followed him. When they came out of the woods, they read a road-sign which said: Paris, 24 kilometres. A great murmur of voices arose in the ranks, for many of the men were from Brie or Paris and found they were going home, or crossing their own country. In their state of exhaustion they had lost all sense of place and distance.

Those three words: *Paris 24 kilometres*, dispelled the mist from all minds. With sudden, almost brutal force, they felt the call of home stronger even than the call of country. One of Péguy's men died some hours later fighting in his own garden. He fell on the very ground he had dug so shortly before.

Heureaux ceux qui sont morts pour quatre coins de terre,
Mais pourvu que ce soit dans une juste guerre.[1]

[1] Blessed are those who died for four corners of earth.
But it must be in a just war

Péguy was their chief: *of course*, he said once, in circumstances which someone else had taken for mere coincidence.

Paris, 24 kilometres. That meant something would happen soon. If Paris was given up the war was ended. If Paris was to be defended, a great battle was imminent. It was unthinkable that Paris should be given up, and so, as the men realised, this was where the real war began.

At that very crossroads where they read the roadsign, the 276th halted and the companies received orders to billet in the villages. The 19th was sent to Saint-Witz.

•

Saint-Witz is not exactly well known and it is likely that Péguy had never heard of it. It is nonetheless a remarkable place, one of the lovely spots of the Ile-de-France, and as suitable as any to be the scene of Péguy's last hours of life.

Picture a knoll on the edge of the woods to the north of Paris, about six hundred feet up (which is a good height for the district); it commands the whole length and breadth of the Ile-de-France, as Mount Sion commands the Lorraine plain. On clear days, the white crests of the Paris Sacré-Cœur can be seen from the top of it.

We wrote: Ile-de-France. Let us conform to ancient custom and write: France. It is France that lies beneath our eyes. In Picardy, where Péguy had just been given his baptism of fire, they used to say, when they took the road along which he had come: 'I am going into France.' An historian has defined the boundaries of this stretch of land from which it all came: 'They go as far as the slopes of Montmélian to the north-east. They reach a point to the east in the neighbourhood of Meaux.' The slopes of Montmélian are Saint-Witz. The Meaux road is the one where Péguy was to fall, very precisely in France, for France.[1]

The approach to Saint-Witz is surprising. There are some houses under the brow of the hill, a hamlet rather than a village. At the top, visible over the tree-tops, there is a mediæval ruin which some German scouts had reached on August 30th. On the slope itself there is a long ancient wall enclosing some trees, and three chapels, with pointed arch and cross on top, one half-way up, the others near the crest of the hill, two with tombs around them. History had obviously been busy here. Beyond the chapels, on the further slope, sturdy oaks sheltered a spring named the Hermit's Spring. All the signs of a shrine of great antiquity, probably pre-Christian, were here visible: the cult of springs, in Celtic lands, is ageless.

Péguy, as he settled his men, must have talked to the local inhabitants (some, but not all, had fled), and to the priest guardian of

[1] *Ile de France*, by Léandre Vaillat, p. 36.

the pilgrimage, and culled all possible information about the astonishing spot to which the war had brought him. He was told that the Saint-Witz hill was the site of a pilgrimage and a cult of immemorial age; that there had been a monastery between the walls, but it was destroyed during the Revolution; and that a statue of the Virgin, greatly venerated by the pilgrims, had been hidden under the hay in a barn and thus saved from the hammers of impious men, and had then been left, out of gratitude, in this same barn which was consecrated and turned into a chapel. All these details are set out on a notice fastened to the door. Péguy read it word for word.

Then he went in. How simple it all was: the beams of the barn were still there, whitewash was on the walls. We can see it to-day as he saw it then. It was exactly conformable to his type of inspiration. The statue of the Virgin is a charming piece of mediæval workmanship; on the wall, to the left, the instruments of the Passion are naïvely set out: the cross, the lance, hammers and nails. Over them, an explanatory inscription: *These instruments of the Passion were carved in wood by a local shepherd.*

There is no doubt at all that Péguy, that soul so constantly stirred by forebodings and haunted by signs, will have taken this conjunction of events for a sign indeed. A last sign. The Chartres pilgrim was fulfilled: on his behalf the war had taken the shape of an immense pilgrimage with the Virgin at its term, lodged in assuredly her most humble and truly peasant setting in all France, waiting for him to help him through his last trial. Here I see all the ingredients of an unwritten poem by Péguy gathered together by an invisible hand. He picked some flowers and brought them to the consecrated barn, and in the evening, when his men were peacefully at rest, he came back to the chapel for a night of prayer. There is nothing surprising about this, for the chapel was traditionally kept open, night and day. 'We never closed it,' the priest wrote to me.[1] All who slept there that night were to die the next day.[2]

The flowers and the night prayer are incidents recorded in a letter from Claude Casimir-Périer who, as an officer of the 276th, met Péguy on the 4th and heard it from his own mouth. Alfred Tellier, whose talk has been most useful to us, only knew that the officers slept in a chapel. It is quite possible that several went with Péguy and had spent the night there on some bundles of hay they had brought in.

Two or three verses of *Eve* have their place at this point:

[1] Tradition mentions 'a chapel,' without saying which. We are convinced that Péguy, with three to choose among, will have chosen no other than the barn-chapel which occupies the centre and is the very core of the Saint-Witz cult.

[2] Cf. Charles Péguy, *Lettres et Entretiens*, p. 22, note: 'Claude Casimir-Périer, on the evening of September 5th, took over the command of the 19th, of which all the officers had been killed.'

Mère, voici vos fils et leur immense armée
Qu'ils ne soient pas jugés sur leur seule misère.
Que Dieu mette avec eux un peu de cette terre
Qui les a tant perdus et qu'ils ont tant aimée.

. . . Que Dieu mette avec eux dans le juste plateau
Ce qu'ils ont tant aimé, quelques grammes de terre.
Un peu de cette vigne, un peu de ce coteau,
Un peu de ce ravin sauvage et solitaire.

Mère, voyez vos fils qui se sont tant battus.
Vous les voyez couchés parmi les nations.
Que Dieu ménage un peu ces êtres débattus,
Ces cœurs pleins de tristesse et d'hésitation.[1]

The 4th was a day of rest. The regiment regrouped its scattered elements, the men sewed on their buttons and cleaned their equipment. 'My company is a household,' as Péguy wrote a few days earlier, when billeted in Lorraine, at the Sainte-Marie Farm. This was the last household day for many of the 19th company men.

The troops could relax, but not the chiefs. That 4th of September was a day of extreme tension. Galliéni, in command of Paris and its armies, among which the 276th was now included, held that the Germans in driving southwards laid open their flank to the attack which Joffre had been planning for the last ten days. The moment had now come. Joffre, after consultation, decided, that afternoon, that the attack should take place on the 6th, and dictated the order of the day which no Frenchman will ever forget.

Everyone's fate was in the balance, but chiefly that of the men who were getting their breath back to the south of the Senlis forest, and who would be the first to meet the enemy.

The whole regiment in arms heard the order of the day read in a a farmyard near Saint-Witz. That is where Claude Casimir-Périer and Péguy met. 'I spoke to Péguy for the last time in a farmyard at Vémars, near Survilliers,' he wrote. 'If I come through, I shall go there again. He seemed to be aware of his glorious end. Everyone who spoke to him had the same impression.'

[1] Mother, here is the army of those sons of yours.
May they not be judged only by their dearth.
May God put with them a little of that earth
Where they slipped and fell and which they loved of course.

. . . When it comes to weighing, God will include, we hope,
Some fistfuls of the earth they did so dearly love,
Taken from that wild and dreary slope,
Or from the growing vine, or from the hill above.

Mother here are your sons who fought day and night.
See how they lie among the nations.
May God look kindly on their harassed plight,
Hearts full of dismay and hesitations.

On the morning of the 5th, the 276th set out. Captain Guérin was in command of the company. Péguy would have kept it if he had known how to ride. But he did not, and went back to the ranks. It was all in the picture. 'I am an old second-class soldier,' he had written a few days earlier. 'All the additional promotion that has come my way is unnatural to me.'

It was still wonderful weather, summer with a breath of autumn mellowing the air. The 276th left the Valois heights. That was not the day for the battle but merely for drawing up the front which should attack to-morrow. They marched eastward, and the nature of the country changed: the distance grew wider and the ground was covered with beet and stubble. The men of Brie were coming to their own native soil.

At about midday, the regiment halted at a crossroads which many of the men knew by name: 'the Niche crossways,' they said. Ahead were familiar villages, quite close at hand; Villeroy to the right, Yverny to the left. What unexpected turns war has! Men were laughing and joking. 'I know a chap,' said a cheerful voice (Tellier's, the man who showed us round), 'I know a man who will sleep at home!' And indeed (as we have already said), one man slept at home that night, for good and all. But it was not the man who spoke, it was one called Kapoty whom a German ball laid out dead in his garden.

Some of them noticed on a slope ahead of them, towards Monthyon, some soldiers going single file along the edge of a wood. Their dun-coloured uniforms were not French. 'They must be English,' was the general supposition. But a sudden volley broke out and spattered the horizon, and it was all too clear that what lay ahead was new to them and distinctly unattractive. Under orders the men got out their bread and cold meat and had lunch. Smoke was rising here and there in the distance: homesteads, barns or stacks were on fire; and the crackle of invisible battle could be heard.

This is what actually happened: the commander of the IVth German army reserve corps, which was lined up near Monthyon, puzzled by the unexpected activity on his flank, ordered an attack to oblige the French to show their hand.

So on this precise spot of the front, the battle of the Marne was starting eighteen hours ahead of time. That is why the official lists do not show Péguy's name among the dead.

At about two o'clock, the 276th set off again, this time in battle formation. The 19th Company clung on the left to a line of willows that ran across the fields towards the roofs of Villeroy.

Coming on a level with Villeroy (a distance of about fifteen hundred yards: warfaring involves a lot of footslogging), they stopped again.

The 19th Company saw in front of it a sort of hollow, or long bowl of grassland. At the bottom there was a well of rustic design. The surround was made of large stones, coated over and scaly. Above it were two wooden stumps which held the winch. It was Rebecca's well, the well of Samaria, risen from the depth of time in an Ile-de-France meadow. The men bent over the margin and gazed into the water, which was high, very smooth and still. What was it like? 'Excellent, very fresh,' said the local men. Everyone wanted a drink and the bucket was wound up and down, and mugs were filled and emptied. 'Lt. Péguy drank his last drop of water here,' said Tellier.

It was a long halt, lasting perhaps two hours. There was still smoke rising in the distance and the crackle of gunfire. The men dozed or chatted; they knew they were in danger. Péguy was among them. Four village spires framed the horizon ahead of him: Yverny, Monthyon, Neufmoutiers and Villeroy.

At about five o'clock came new marching orders. The men went forward in skirmishing formation, widely spaced across a rough stubble field. Eight hundred yards ahead of them they met a road running parallel to their line and slightly below field level. They huddled up to the bank and wondered what lay beyond. Those who knew the country said the field sloped downwards and on the other side, on higher land, was a wood, and a hollow track along the edge of the wood. Not too good.

•

The time has come to pause for a moment. Only just before firing breaks out and the sequence of events is lost and men are lost, and the memory of the survivors is itself troubled and uncertain.

We may in fact have come fifty yards too far already: it is open to discussion whether they did actually reach the road and the bank. It is one of those cases where it is almost impossible to get the sequence of events right to the last detail. Two witnesses, who did not know one another and did not meet, both saw Péguy's body lying on the ground on the 6th of September, and each of them, quite independently, made a careful note of the exact spot, map in hand: as near as may be to where the y of the name Villeroy comes on the map. That is, to the left of the road, on the Yverny side. Nothing can be more convincing than such concurrent evidence noted at the very time by Claude Casimir-Périer in a letter to his wife, and by the commanding officer Dufestre in his note-book. The letter and the note-book still exist. If they are to be believed, it is clear that the 276th had been fired on before reaching road and bank. But oral tradition differs; M. Alphonse Tellier shows the road and the place where he crouched against the bank; he agrees with M. Victor Boudon's account in mentioning a Staff officer who came galloping along the road, calling to Captain Guérin and conveying to him the order to go forward under fire. 'Forward!' shouted the captain. He leapt forward himself and the rest followed. It was a short sharp run, guns hidden in the woods opposite were on the watch for them and mowed them down. M. Victor Boudon shows Lt. Péguy standing under fire, urging his men on with shouts of 'Fire, for God's sake!' M. Alphonse Tellier is less well informed. He only knows that it was the shelter of a rabbit-warren that saved his life. Of those who fought by Péguy's side, not one survived, it seems. We shall never know more than this.

•

To return to Commanding Officer Dufestre's witness: he had come straight from Morocco with his division and charged with the mission of relieving the decimated 276th, he crossed the fields where the battle had been waged the previous day. Among the root crops he saw blue and red patches at almost regular intervals, and went across to investigate. He found *a whole line of infantrymen of the 276th lying wide apart in skirmishing formation.*

I underline these words, which Commander Dufestre himself underlined in an article published in *Figaro* on November 8th 1932, which I will quote:

There was nothing ghastly about them, even when seen close to, and we examined them carefully. They had fallen the day before, less than twenty-four hours ago, struck down by a hail of bullets, and death had left them as they lay, only making their cheeks fade a little and imparting its own rigidity to their features and limbs. There were no visible wounds. They must have been struck full in the body and the blood had dried up long before, without staining the dark blue of their greatcoats or the red of their trousers.

. . . At the head of the line, the section leader, a lieutenant, had fallen at his post, leading his men to the attack.

I examined him with particular care, minutely and reverently, for my fate might be the same in a few hours' time. These are all reasons for the clarity of my visual impression.

He was a small man, looking almost frail beside his neighbour who was a sort of giant. He lay on his stomach with his left arm bent back over his head. His features, seen side-face, were clear-cut and regular, framed in a stubby beard, blond here and there, but seeming grey on account of the dust, for he was still a young man, thirty-five or forty at the most. The expression on his face was infinitely quiet. He too seemed to be plunged in deep sleep. There was a ring on the third finger of his left hand.

I bent down to read his identity disc: Péguy. He was called Péguy. At the time the name meant precisely nothing to me, for my mind was a thousand leagues away from the *Cahiers de la Quinzaine*, the poet of Jeanne d'Arc, or any other literature whatever. Before going on, I made a mark on the map to show where this unknown comrade of mine had fallen, the first I had met lying on a battlefield. The tail of the y of the name Villeroy gives it almost exactly. I made a brief note of all these details in my official note-book.

So it was that Commander Dufestre, a witness come by chance, with no previous connection, saw the men of the 19th Company lying as they fell, and immediately noted this striking realisation of the lyrical vision which had inspired Charles Péguy some twelve months earlier.

> *Heureux ceux qui sont morts dans les grandes batailles*
> *Couchés dessus le sol à la face de Dieu.*[1]

[1] Blessed are those who died in great battles,
Lying upon the ground in the sight of God.

XVI

ADDENDA

AS THIS BOOK, the fruit of work done three times over now, goes to press, I am all too aware of its insufficiencies. Some chapters already need re-writing or will soon do so. There are neglected features and episodes which found no place in the course of my story. Here are a few of them:

I.—A chapter soon to be re-written: the VIIIth, *Towards belief*. These years of Péguy's life are obscure and witnesses are still lacking. Jacques Maritain's most of all. I am not thinking of the family difficulties in which Jacques Maritain was involved, but of the more important matter of the growth of belief and of the nature of belief. This testimony will come, I am sure. It would be indiscreet of me to ask for it, and I have refrained from doing so. There is no hurry.[1]

II.—A neglected point: I should have laid more stress on Péguy's sedentary habits, remaining as he did all his life the man of two cities, Orléans and Paris; two cathedrals, Notre-Dame de Chartres and Notre-Dame de Paris; two plains, Beauce and Brie, one for birth, the other for death.

This was his beat, and he only overstepped it twice, once to go to Domrémy, the other time to see the plays in the ancient theatre of Orange. He did not go to Domrémy in order to collect local colour for his *mysteries*: there is not a trace of it; it was to breathe the air and tread where Jeanne had trodden. To Orange he went not in search of southern sunshine: there is no gleam of it in all his work; but to renew the profound impression of his twenties when he heard Mournet-Sully in *Œdipus Rex*.

Mme Favre reports that one of Péguy's admirers, on hearing that he had never seen Italy, offered him the trip as a present, for it used to be considered that no education was complete without it. Péguy refused politely. Mme Favre writes with great insight that Péguy would not have wished to disturb the inner landscape by which he lived, in all its greatness and simplicity.

I am told that Courbet, on hearing of a friend's departure for foreign parts, asked with his Franc-Comtois accent: '*Alors, il va dans les Orients? Pourquoi va-t-il dans les Orients? Il n'a donc pas de pays?*' (So he is going East: what does he want to go East for? Hasn't he got a home somewhere?) Péguy heard it from Vuillet and was delighted. He knew what *avoir un pays* meant.

[1] Translator's note: This appeal is answered in Raïssa Maritain's *Adventures in Grace*, ch. 3, pp. 43-80. Longmans Green, London, 1945.

Péguy was all his life the peasant who had never seen the sea. Mme Péguy begged for the children to be allowed to go, but Péguy did not go too.

III.—One episode has been rather scantily treated: I mean the relationship between Péguy and Jaurès. About 1892, Jaurès was giving French socialism a spring-clean: it is through his youthful eloquence that Péguy as an adolescent first knew socialism, and it was on the strength of this magnificent flow of language and images that he came to adopt it himself. In 1898-99, Jaurès often came to the Ecole Normale library and sat down by Herr. Tharaud saw him there and he has given us a striking picture of this endearing creature, with his worn face and shabby clothes, so splendidly keen and generous of speech. A declared dreyfusard, Jaurès had got himself beaten by the Albi electors and was no longer a member of parliament but a sort of hero instead.

'This was his time of true greatness,' wrote Péguy. And elsewhere: 'It is hard to picture the innocent, affectionate, respectful veneration we paid him. . . .' Jaurès accepted it all and welcomed all this youthful expectation centred upon his person. He was playing a dangerous game, as he was to discover in course of time. Perhaps he had some inkling of it even then. 'You,' he said to Péguy, 'have got one serious fault: you get your own idea about people and then expect them to live up to it.' It was perfectly true. Whoever became Péguy's friend found himself from that day on under a constant jealous sort of supervision.

During the first immensely difficult years of the *Cahiers*, Jaurès never failed Péguy once when he appealed to him. Péguy, for his part, never failed to annotate the pages he printed in these circumstances with concise warnings. He was aware that Jaurès, with his amiable temperament but all too vulnerable nature, was being caught in the trend to scientist and marxist dogmatism. We shall never know what he made of his young friend, nor of the warnings. Towards the end of his life, he wrote: 'All the same I have got my own ideas about this so cruelly ambiguous world.' But he never told us what they really were, nor what he really thought of Péguy.

He once made a gesture, one which brought the two men together for a few hours and marked the end of their relationship, which may give us a clue to what was in his mind. In 1904 (they had not met for some time), Jaurès came into the small printing shop at Suresnes where the *Cahiers* were printed and asked for Péguy. He was not there. As soon as he came in, the workmen told him.

It appeared to Péguy that this visit from an older man, and one of the busiest in France, should be returned. He called on Jaurès, wondering why he had asked for him, but without discovering. He found a saddened, disillusioned man, entirely absorbed, perhaps to the point of exhaustion, in the labour of running *l'Humanité*, which he was busy taking over. 'I have to go out,' he said to Péguy. 'Come along with me.' He liked talking and walking together. Péguy could call to mind other walks made memorable by Jaurès' conversation and recitations. Jaurès could let his memory flow, and out would come enchanted streams of poetry from Lamartine, Hugo, Racine, Ronsard, Villon. Péguy had the same gift. It made a lovely game, and they used to cap one another's odes, cantos and exhortations from tragedy. But the day had come when Jaurès had no voice left for Poetry. Near the Champs-Elysées, he called a cab: he was in a hurry. Péguy made a last-minute attempt to solve the riddle, Jaurès might have wanted to talk to him about his paper. He took the bull by the horns and said: 'I can't collaborate, I belong to the *Cahiers*. But I have got some very gifted friends, faithful ones. If you try them, you will not regret it.'—'It's not collaborators I need,' said Jaurès, 'I have got more than enough. What worries me is the question of support.' The cab was there waiting. Jaurès started to climb in. Péguy ends the story thus:

. . . A last handshake. He got in heavily and sat all crumpled up in his cab which went off jerkily. I never saw him again.

So I never knew why suddenly, the day before, after a long interval and with no warning, he came to see me at the printer's. Perhaps at the critical moment, some dim regret, a sort of dull remorse, beset him. At the moment of leaving a land where he had had his moments of happiness and of conscience at rest, at the point of setting out on the marshlands of politics, the swamps and brackish flats, a desire for a last look, a last deep breath of fresh air, a last short trip to the old tracks of true friendship.

It was in November 1905, that Péguy wrote these stern lines. Since then Jaurès had given all his energies to international marxism, and Péguy spared him no longer, only mentioning his name to strike at him, each time with increased fury, till we come to the deadly attack of 1913 quoted earlier: his revenge for the misplaced admiration of yore.

The contrast between the two men is all too clear in those tragic hours in which one of them was killed while the other was making ready to go where he would be killed. Péguy's joy on hearing of the murder of his one-time friend we have already told. It was sheer savage exultation, says a man who witnessed it in the bookshop. It happens that Jaurès mentioned Péguy on the last day of his life. The witness here is M. Léon Bérard, his colleague in the House. He had lent Jaurès Péguy's newly published *Cahier* on Bergson. Jaurès returned it after reading it (he read everything) and made the good-natured remark that came so naturally to him. 'There is no technique,' he said to M. Léon Bérard, giving in one neat phrase a perfectly fair judgment, 'but the philosophy is there.'

There is one more point to be cleared up. Readers who know Péguy's work well will have noticed I made no mention of *Victor-Marie, Comte Hugo*. The reason is that the book was written to put an end to our difference of opinion after my *Apologie pour notre Passé* was published. And it did put an end to it, Péguy not failing to make the most of the occasion. I could not go back over the ground without giving my own commentary a personal tone which I naturally wish to avoid. Hence my omission.

I might perhaps have tackled the subject quite simply. I did not do so and shall not do so. In my first study, published in February-March 1914, I dealt with it in one brief allusion, of which most people missed the bearing, but which Péguy himself certainly took to heart. Here it is:

Péguy the baptised wolf has not ground down his fangs. . . . He goes to war as well he may, wages war wholeheartedly, with all the pamphleteer's disdain of mere justice, and with a harshness that hurts him first and foremost:

Un autre effacera de nos livres de haine
Les traces de chiendent, du grain de senevé,
Mais nul n'effacera de nos livres de peine
La trace d'un Pater *ni celle d'un* Ave.[1]

Continual fighting and termless solitude turn him sour and hate-inclined . . . Péguy has his dour moments; he has candour too.

May he be loved for the one, pitied for the other.

So I wrote while Péguy still lived. Now he is gone, I shall not change a word.

[1] Another will rid our books of hate
Of all the couch grass and sharlock-seed.
But no one will wipe from our work-a-day books
The trace of a *Pater* nor that of an *Ave*.

LIST OF ILLUSTRATIONS

Portrait of Péguy painted by Pierre Laurens *frontispiece*
(Collection Mme Laurens)

Péguy in 1888 *facing page* 14
(Collection A. Martin)

Cover of the first *Cahiers* „ „ 52
(Collection A. Martin)

The book shop, 8, rue de la Sorbonne „ „ 96
(Collection André Bourgeois)

A proof corrected by Péguy „ „ 128
(Collection C.-Th. Quoniam)

Péguy in his book shop „ „ 186
(Photo Dornac, 'Nos Contemporains chez eux,' Collection A. Martin)

Péguy on manœuvres, 1913 „ „ 198
(Collection A. Martin)

Index

Action Française, 105, 119, 121.
Ancel, Jacques, 123.
Andler, Chas., 38, 44, 45, 48, 59, 63, 64, 93n.
Antigone, 23, 24, 25, 26, 35, 57, 91, 140, 166.
Apologie pour Notre Passé (Halévy), 109, 227.
Archambault, Paul, 177.
Arnaud, Michel, 102.
Art Poétique (Claudel), 129.
Aubriot, 58.
Aurore, 55.
Aynard, Joseph, 32.

Bach, Jean Seb., 166.
Badilon, 134.
Baillet, Rev. Fr., 21, 22, 135, 207, 214.
Ballard, 105.
Bardet, M., 14.
Barrès, 14, 45, 60, 104, 105, 108, 122, 123, 145, 146, 204.
Bartet, 23, 25.
Battifol, Abbé, 21, 42, 135, 138, 159.
Beaudouin, Marcel, 21, 42.
Beethoven (Rolland), 66, 73.
Bellais, 43, 44.
Benda, Julien, 65, 73, 167, 171, 172, 173 204.
Bérard, Léon, 226, 227.
Bergson, 25, 29, 65, 71, 93, 121, 155n, 201, 206, 208, 210, 226.
Bernard, 62.
Berth, Edouard, 43, 58, 65, 171, 172.
Biran, Maine de, 96n.
Bloy, Léon, 174, 180.
Blum, Léon, 44, 45, 48, 50, 53, 54, 67.
Boitier, 12.
Boudon, Victor, 215, 221, 222.
Bouglé, 94.
Bourgeois, André, 83, 112, 138, 186.
Bourges, Elémir, 171.
Bourget, 120, 145, 146.
Bourgin, Hubert, 44.
Brémond, Henri, 72.
Briand, Claude, 40.
Briand, Aristide, 119.
Bridault, Eugène, 40.
Bulletin des Professeurs Catholique de L'Université, 208.

Caillaux, Mme, 209.
Campaigning with C. Péguy, 215.
Case of Wagner (Nietzsche), 204.
Casimir-Perier, Claude, 173, 174, 177, 197, 218, 218n, 219, 221.
Catholicisme et Critique (Desjardins), 66.
Challaye, Félicien, 32, 39, 43.
Chevauchez, Théodore, 40.
Claudel, Paul, 28, 72, 121, 122, 124, 125, 126, 127, 128, 129, 130, 131, 133.
Clemenceau, 41.
Colline Inspirée (*La*), 105.
Coltineur Débile (*La*) (Tharaud), 43, 51.
Compte, August, 96.
Corneille, 206.
Corpechot, Lucien, 104.
Correspondant, 197.
Crouzet, 197.
Courbet, 224.

Dalou, 46.
D'Annunzio, Gabriel, 148.
Dante, 178.
Danton, 72.
Daudet, Léon, 171, 197.
Daviot, Emile, 40.
Deherme, 47.
De la Grippe, 55, 57, 58.
De Jean Coste, 57, 67, 68.
Delahache, 193, 194.
De la Raison (Jaurès), 66, 68.
De la Situation Faite à l'Histoire, etc., 84.
Delesalle, 62, 172.
Delcasse, 79.
De Peslouan, 22, 43, 65, 87n, 104, 105, 150, 162, 167, 170n, 176, 198, 207, 212, 214.
De Poncheville, 11.
Déroulède, 45.
Descartes, 204.
Desjardins, Paul, 47, 66, 172.
Dialogue de Clio et de l'Ame Charnelle, 28, 143, 177, 178, 198, 199, 200.
Dingley (Tharaud), 66.

Doumic, René, 146.
Dreyfus, 23, 41ff.
Dreyfus, Robert, 66.
Dufestre, Commander, 222, 223.
Duclaux, Mme, 192.
Dujardin, 61.
Durkheim, 43, 93, 96, 164, 206.

Ecco Homo, 204.
Echo de Paris, 105, 120.
Emperor William, 79.
Essai sur les Données Immédiates de la Conscience, 29.
Essays, 92, 95, 96, 97, 98.
Esterhazy, 41.
Eve, 20, 139, 158, 184, 185, 186, 187, 188, 191, 192, 195, 196, 197, 198, 201n. 203, 218, 219.

Faguet, 146.
Faure, Félix, 45.
Favre, Mme, 68, 162n, 163n, 174, 175, 176, 197, 209, 212, 213, 214, 224.
Fête Arabe (Tharaud), 175.
Fidelis Fideli, 209.
Fournier, Alain, 169, 170n, 174, 177, 198.
France, Anatole, 56, 66, 148.

Galliéni, 219.
Gapone, 87
Gide, André, 102, 103, 123, 172.
Gilbert, Pierre, 110n.
Gobineau (Dreyfus, R.), 66.
Goyau, 144.
Grandes Amitiés (Les), 224n.
Grandes Odes (Claudel), 129, 120, 132.
Grande Revue, 197.
Guéguen, 176.
Guérin, Capt., 220, 221.
Guesde, 48, 49.
Guieysse, 58, 60, 61, 65, 70n.
Guillaumin, Emile, 62.

Halévy, Daniel, 10, 47, 62, 65, 69, 70, 85, 86, 98, 101, 109, 110, 162, 163.
Hamp, Pierre, 66.
Hauriou, 93.
Hegel, 202.
Herr, Lucien, 29, 30, 33, 41, 44, 45, 48, 49, 50, 53, 58, 60, 61, 63, 64, 89, 92, 93, 96, 145, 146, 182, 225.
Histoire Contemporaine (Ancel), 123.
Hommes de Bonne Volonté, 30.
Hugo, Victor, 14.

Ile De France (Vaillat), 217n.
Imitation, 86.
Israel Zangwill, 69, 71.

Jaurès, 20, 23, 41, 44, 48, 61, 66, 68, 70, 88, 89, 225, 226.
Jean-Christophe (Rolland), 66, 72, 73, 74, 75, 76, 77, 123, 167, 172, 193.
Jean Coste (Antonin Lavergne), 53, 54, 67, 140.
Jeanne D'Arc, 12, 14, 25, 26, 33, 34, 147, 164, 191n, 206.
Jeanne D'Arc, 26n, 34, 35, 36, 37, 38, 39, 40, 41, 42, 43, 44, 60, 67, 83, 86, 91, 136, 137, 161, 184.
Joffre, 219.
Johannet, René, 146n, 155n, 176, 189, 193.
Journal Vrai, 28, 31, 59, 60.
Justice (Sully Prudhomme), 175.

Krakowski, 176.

Labeyrie, Emile, 47.
La Cité Harmonieuse, 43.
La Jeune Fille Violaine (Claudel), 130.
La Colline Inspirée, 105.
L'Affaire Crainquebille (Anatole France), 66.
Lagardelle, 43, 58.
Lanson, 27, 28, 164, 184, 206.
La Présentation de la Beauce, 168, 169, 170n, 177.
A *Notre-Dame de Chartres L'Argent*, 9, 180, 181, 182, 184.
L'Argent Suite, 182, 184, 191, 200, 201n, 202.
Laudet, Fernand, 147, 148, 149, 177n.
Laurens, Pierre, 175, 199.
Lavergne, Antonin, 53, 67.
Lavisse, 145, 146, 147, 149, 150, 182, 197, 200, 201n.
Lazare, Bernard, 67, 111, 112, 172.
L'Echange (Claudel), 129.
Le Grix (François), 146, 147.
Leo XIII, 48.
Le Propre de l'Espérance, 178.
Les Données Immédiates de la Conscience, 207n.
Les Fins et les Aspirations sont les Mêmes (Biran), 96n.
Les Proscrits (Vuillaume) 193, 194.
Lettres et Entretiens (C. Péguy), 218n.
L'Evolution Créatrice, 207n.
Lévy-Bruhl, 29, 93n.
L'Exode (Delahache), 193, 194.
L'Humanité (Jaurès), 226.
Litalien, 43.
L'Occident, 129.
Lorrain, 144.
L'Otage (Claudel), 130, 131, 132, 133.
Lotte, 18, 21, 22, 43, 98, 118, 120, 134, 136, 138, 150, 158, 167, 170n, 176, 186, 198, 201, 203, 207, 208, 209, 210, 214.

Loups, Les (Rolland), 51, 72.
L'Urne, 162.

Maire, Gilbert, 67n.
Malebranque, 62.
Mallarmé, 124.
Marcel, Pierre, 68.
Marée Fraîche (Pierre Hamp), 66.
Maritain, Jacques, 68, 134, 135, 174, 213, 224.
Maritain, Raïssa, 224n.
Mathiez, 28.
Matière et Mémoire, 29, 207n.
Maurras, Charles, 72, 104 105, 106, 107, 108, 120, 121, 122, 123.
Mauss, 93n.
May, Mme Dick, 60.
Mémoire sur l'Enseignment Primaire et ce qu'il devrait être (Naudy), 179.
Millerand, 119.
Mithouard, André, 129.
Moreau, 61.
Mounet-Sully, 23, 25, 224.
Mystère de la Charité de Jeanne D'Arc, 39, 83, 98, 99, 100, 101, 102, 104, 105, 119, 121, 129, 139, 140, 141, 142, 158, 161n, 185n, 207.
Mystère de la Porche de la Deuxième Vertu, 119, 121, 151, 152, 153, 154, 155, 156, 157, 158, 159, 161, 166, 178, 207,
Mystère du Porche de l'Espérance, 180, 185n.
Mystère des Saints-Innocents, 86, 121, 158, 164, 165, 166, 167.

Naudy, 16, 17, 179.
Nietzsche, 204.
Noel, 17, 19, 29.
Notre Cher Péguy (Tharaud), 110n.
Note Conjointe, 121, 206.
Note Conjointe sur M. Descartes et la Philosophie Cartésienne, 203.
Note sur M. Bergson et la Philosophie Bergsonienne, 193, 198, 201, 207.
Nourry, 62.
Nous (François Porché), 193, 195, 196.
Nouvelle Revue Française, 129, 132, 175, 197.

Œdipus Rex, 23, 24, 89, 90, 166, 224.
Ollivier, Emile, 146.
Ordination (Benda), 171

Pages Libres, 53n, 60, 61, 62, 69.
Paradise, 178, 179, 184, 185n.
Partage de Midi (Claudel), 130.
Pascal, 26, 55, 57, 66, 67, 69, 101, 201.
Payen, 138.
Péguy (grandmother), 9, 11.
Péguy (mother), 9, 10, 11, 12, 86, 133, 134, 214, 216.
Péguy (wife), 21, 42, 43, 51, 86, 138, 212, 225.
Péguy, Marcel, 140.
Péguy, Pierre, 167.
Perrot, 32, 42, 43.
Peslouän de, Chas. Lucas, 22, 43, 87n, 104, 105, 134, 150, 162, 167, 170n, 176, 198, 207, 212, 214.
Petite République, 55, 61.
Picquart, 41.
Plon, 84.
Poincaré, Raymond, 181, 182.
Poisson, 51.
Polyeucte (Corneille), 206.
Poncheville de, 11.
Porchet, 21, 87, 88, 102, 103, 193, 194, 195, 196, 214.
Présentation de Paris à Notre-Dame, 206.
Prévost, Marcel, 183.
Proust, Marcel, 123.
Proudhon, 58, 61.
Prudhomme, Joseph, 147.
Prudentius, 164.
Psichari, Ernest, 174, 175.

Quatorze Juillet, 72.
Quelques, Nouveau Maîtres, 185n.

Reclus, Elisée, 114.
Reclus, Maurice, 68, 162n, 209.
Reinach, Joseph, 108.
Reinach, Saloman, 149.
Renan, 65, 70, 71, 97, 124.
Revue Blanche, 48.
Revue Critique, 63.
Revue des Deux Mondes, 175.
Revue Hebdomadaire, 146, 147, 148.
Revue Universelle, 61.
Rhythme du Progrès, Le, 96n.
Riby, 43, 207, 208, 209, 214.
Rivière, Jacques, 129.
Rocheblave, 17, 19.
Roget, General, 45.
Roi Dagobert, 161.
Rolland, Romain, 29, 30, 51, 66, 123, 124, 145, 175, 193.
Roque, Mario, 44.
Route de Saclay, Le, 87n.
Roy, Henry, 19, 43.

Saint Catherine, 86.
Saint-Claude, Ponnard de, 62.
Salomé (René), 193, 194, 196.
Scéailles, Gabriel, 181.
Scheler, Max, 136.
Scheurer-Kestner, 41.
Seignobos, 43, 183.
Société Nouvelle de Libraire et d'Edition, 44, 48, 49, 50, 53, 59, 60.
Société Socialiste, 92.

Sorel, George, 58, 61, 62, 63, 64, 65, 71, 121, 135, 147, 171, 172, 177n, 202.
Souvenirs (Mme Favre), 67.
Spire, André, 53n.
Suarès, André, 193.
Suppliants, Les (Porché), 24, 88, 89, 90, 91, 92.
Suppliants Parallèles, Les, 90, 91, 92.
Symiand, 44, 45, 50.

Taine, 70, 71.
Tapisserie de St. Geneviève, 175, 177, 184.
Tapisserie de Notre-Dame, 177, 184.
Tellier, Alphonse, 214, 218, 220, 221, 222.
Tête D'Or (Claudel), 125, 126.
Tharaud, J-J. and Jerome, 16n, 19, 21, 33, 39, 43, 44, 50, 51, 55, 60, 61, 62, 66, 105, 110n, 135, 170n, 186, 191, 192, 207, 212, 214, 225.
Thérèse of Lisieux, 191n.
Thierry, Albert, 101, 185n.
Thomas Aquinas, St., 121, 134.
Tolstoi, 30, 74.
Triomphe de la République, 46, 47, 58.
Twilight of the False Gods, 204.

Un Episode (Halévy), 69.
Un Nouveau Théologien (Laudet), 147, 148, 149, 151, 158, 161.

Vaillat, Léandre, 217n.
Valéry, Paul, 123.
Variot, Jean, 98, 113, 171.
Victor-Marie, Comte Hugo, 227.
Vie de Nietzsche, 85.
Viélé-Griffin, Francis, 114.
Vigny, 27.
Villon, Suarès, 193.
Visite à Port-Royal, 193.
Vuillaume, Maurice, 193, 194, 199, 224.

Weber, Louis, 96n.
William, Emperor, 79.